Kuxlejal Politics

Kuxlejal Politics

MARIANA MORA

Indigenous Autonomy, Race, and Decolonizing Research in Zapatista Communities

University of Texas Press
Austin

♾ The paper used in this book meets the minimum requirements of
ANSI/NISO Z39.48-1992 (R1997) (Permanence of Paper).

Library of Congress Cataloging-in-Publication Data

Names: Mora Bayo, Mariana, author.
Title: Kuxlejal politics : indigenous autonomy, race, and decolonizing
research in Zapatista communities / Mariana Mora.
Description: First edition. | Austin : University of Texas Press, 2017. |
Includes bibliographical references and index.
Identifiers: LCCN 2017017819 | ISBN 978-1-4773-1446-3 (cloth : alk. paper) |
ISBN 978-1-4773-1447-0 (pbk. : alk. paper) | ISBN 978-1-4773-1448-7
(library e-book) | ISBN 978-1-4773-1449-4 (nonlibrary e-book)
Subjects: LCSH: Indians of Mexico—Mexico—Chiapas—Government
relations. | Indians of Mexico—Mexico—Chiapas—Social conditions. |
Social movements—Mexico—Chiapas—History. | Chiapas (Mexico)—
History—Peasant Uprising, 1994– | Indians of Mexico—Political
activity—Mexico—Chiapas—History. | Peasants—Political activity—
Mexico—Chiapas—History. | Representative government and
representation—Mexico—History. | Chiapas (Mexico)—Politics
and government—20th century. | Chiapas (Mexico)—Politics and
government—21st century.
Classification: LCC F1256 .M718 2017 | DDC 972/.75—dc23
LC record available at https://lccn.loc.gov/2017017819
doi:10.7560/314463

To the future generations of Zapatista community members, in honor of the paths their parents and grandparents have walked

and

to Luis Felipe and our son, Camilo, whose presence is the horizon on which these pages are written

Contents

Acknowledgments

I often find the task of writing to be such a lonely endeavor that I prefer taking my computer to cafés so as to offset the isolation. Writing this book, however, proved contrary to my general experience, for page upon page surfaced through an acute awareness of events lived alongside those with whom I have enjoyed close collaborations over the years, including the numerous (too numerous to count) conversations, exchanges, and debates held with friends and colleagues over the span of two decades. This book reflects a point of convergence of those utopian conspiracies that, I am certain, will continue to bear fruit in unexpected ways. For this confidence, especially in such times of global darkness, I am eternally grateful to all of you.

First and foremost, *jokolawal* to the Tseltal and Tojolabal Zapatista communities of Caracol IV, particularly in the municipalities of Diecisiete de Noviembre and Miguel Hidalgo, as well as communities in Caracol III, in the municipality of Francisco Gómez. María, Roselia and Marcelo, Mercedes and Pablo, Tomás and Gabriela, Mateo, Saúl, Juan Miguel, Abraham, Eliseo, Miguel, Don Antonio, Don Rafael, Vicky and Eliseo, Lucia and Roberto, Rosa, Eudalia, Mario, Doña Julia, Otelina, Ofelia, Raymundo, and others, all brilliant human beings whose deep sense of humanity shapes their intellectual wisdom — I thank you for being teachers of life in more ways than I can possibly describe.

The town of San Cristóbal de las Casas offered me the opportunity to participate in Mexico's electrifying historical moment of the late 1990s and early 2000s. My engagement in political endeavors alongside individuals from all parts of the country, as well as in Barcelona, the Bay Area of California, and other locations on the world map provided me with critical insights that in many ways inform what I offer in these pages. Thank you especially to my dear friends Paco, Timo and Luz, Hilary, Ana, Gabriela, Claudia, Marcela, Olly, Rocío, Afra, Ximena, Rosaluz, Ramor, Antonio, David, Marco, Siscu, Ana, Laura, and Joan. Thanks as well to the members of the University of California, Berkeley, Comité Emiliano Zapata: María Elena Martínez Torres, Peter Rosset, Arnoldo Garcia, Pinti Jaramillo, Diego Vasquez, and MaryAnn Tenuto. I am deeply grateful for the mentorship of Mercedes Olivera, Jorge Santiago Santiago, Don Andrés Aubry (deceased), and Angélica Inda (deceased); their commitment to intergenerational dialogue helped me learn to tread carefully through volatile terrain while maintaining a solid ethical base as a horizon.

I first began reflecting on what would later unfold in these pages as I was pursuing my master's degree in Latin American studies at Stanford University. I thank Terry Karl and Rento Rosaldo for their guidance during that time and Jia Ching Chen for assuring me that I had something to say and was able to say it. In the Department of Anthropology at the University of Texas at Austin, where I was a doctoral student, my dissertation advisor, Charlie Hale, along with my committee members, Shannon Speed, Aída Hernández, Joao Vargas, María Elena Martínez Torres, and Richard Flores, set a course of study that combined meticulous rigor with a solid engagement in struggles for social justice. My scholarly work has similarly been deeply imprinted at UT Austin by the opportunity to think alongside such brilliant scholars and generous human beings as Mohan Ambikaipaker, Pablo González, Christopher Loperena, Courtney Morris, Viviane Newdick, Marc Perry, Theresa Velázquez, Jennifer Goett, Jaime Alves, Halide Velioglu, Can Aciksoz, Peggy Brunache, Gilberto Rosas, Korinta Maldonado, Keisha-Khan Perry, Celeste Henery, Fernanda Soto, Alan Gómez, Nick Copeland, Angela Stuesse, and Melissa Forbis. I hold deep in my heart the loving support of Briana Mohan and her parents, Jim and Ora Shay, who offered me a second home in which to finish writing my dissertation.

Over the years, I have had the privilege of participating in academic spaces committed to collaboration, joint projects, and collective forums. I feel blessed to have taken part in multiple initiatives at my home institution, the Centro de Investigaciones y Estudios Superiores en Antropología Social, alongside Aída Hernández, Teresa Sierra, Rachel Sieder, Carolina Robledo, Dolores Figueroa, Alejandra Aquino, Lina Rosa Berrios, and Natalia de Marinis. Thank you to my dear friends in the Red de Feminismos Descoloniales: Sylvia Marcos, Márgara Millán, Raquel Gutiérrez, Guiomar Rovira, Aída Hernández, Verónica López, Oscar González, Mariana Favela, Gisela Espinosa, and Meztli Yoalli Rodríguez; to the Red Integra, under the coordination of Olivia Gall; and to the Decolonial Summer School in Barcelona, particularly its scholars Ramón Grosfoguel, Roberto Hernández,

Nelson Maldonado-Torres, Ruth Gilmore, Linda Alcoff, and Kwame Nimako, along with the scholars of the Feminist Decolonial Spring School, Karina Ochoa, Aura Cumes, Ochy Curiel, and Carmen Cariño.

As this book entered its final stages, I participated in the Red Acción Investigación Anti-Racista (RAIAR). Though our discussions centered on grappling with expressions of resistance under what appears to be a new global racial project unfolding as part of neofascist tendencies, the words and wisdom expressed by members of the network led me to ask new critical questions about the particular historical context of the events covered by this book. I am grateful for the clarification of ideas that emerged during group discussions with Irma Alicia Velásquez, Juliet Hooker, Pamela Callas, Leith Mullings, Tianna Paschel, Charlie Hale, Carlos Rosero, Eduardo Restrepo, Héctor Nahualpan, Eliana Antonio, Luciane Rocha, Jurema Werneck, Cecilia Salazar, and Rigoberto Choy. My participation in the RAIAR took place thanks to the Colectivo para Eliminar el Racismo en México, to which I belong along with colleagues such as Mónica Moreno Figueroa, Judith Bautista, Gisela Carlo, Fortino Dominguez, Bruno Baronnet, and Emiko Saldivar.

A dissertation research fellowship from the Wenner-Gren Foundation for Anthropological Fieldwork helped fund the fieldwork for this book, and a Ford Foundation Diversity Fellowship permitted me the time to formulate and articulate its initial arguments. Thank you to Fionn Petch, who helped me with the difficult task of translating five chapters of the book from the original Spanish version; to the two anonymous reviewers for their valuable feedback, detailed comments, and suggestions; to Casey Kittrell, acquisitions editor at the University of Texas Press, for believing in this project, and to Gloria Thomas for her meticulous editing. I also thank Edgars Martínez for revisions to the map of the Zapatista territory in Chiapas and Juana Horas for designing the graphic of the Zapatista autonomous governing bodies of Diecisiete de Noviembre as part of Caracol IV.

A profound thank you to my parents, Miguel and Nuria Mora, and to my sister, Andrea, and her family, Matt, Maya, and Kai, for their patience during those family vacations that I spent writing. I value deeply your unwavering support. Thanks as well to Monsterrat, Xavier and Rafi, Jordi, and Elvira (deceased) for showing never-ending enthusiasm for my projects and for reminding me how present endeavors connect to the legacies from my grandparents.

Finally, my boundless gratitude to Luis Felipe and Camilo, my family, who provide me with the beautiful, loving, and constant challenge of grounding in our everyday lives those utopias about which I write.

Some of the following material was previously published in somewhat different forms. I thank the respective publishers for their permission to reproduce those excerpts.

A version of chapter 2 appeared as "Producción de conocimientos en el terreno de la autonomía: La investigación como tema de debate político," in *Luchas "muy otras": Zapatismo y autonomía en las comunidades indígenas de Chiapas*, edited by Bruno Baronnet, Richard Stahler-Sholk, and myself (Mexico City: Universidad Autónoma Metropolitana, 2011).

Excerpts of chapter 5 were published in "Repensando la política y la descolonización en minúscula," in *Más allá del feminismo, caminos para andar*, edited by Márgara Millán (Mexico City: Red de feminismos descoloniales y Pez en el Árbol, 2013).

Earlier versions of content from chapter 6 appeared in both "La politización de la justicia zapatista frente a los efectos de la guerra de baja intensidad en Chiapas," in *Justicias indígenas y estado: Violencias contemporáneas*, edited by María Teresa Sierra, Rachel Sieder, and Rosalva Aída Hernández Castillo (Mexico City: CIESAS, FLACSO, 2013); and "The Politics of Justice: Zapatista Autonomy at the Margins of the Neoliberal Mexican State," special issue, *Latin American and Caribbean Ethnic Studies* 10 (1), available online at http://www.tandfonline.com/doi/full/10.1080/17442 222.2015.1034439.

Unless otherwise noted, all translations of excerpts from published Spanish works, unpublished writings by Zapatista support bases, and historical documents are my own, and I conducted the interviews for this book in Spanish and translated the responses into English.

Introduction

On December 21, 2012, the date the Mayan calendar marked the beginning of the era of the sixth sun, a new *b'akt'un* (historical cycle), tens of thousands of Tseltal, Tsotsil, Tojolabal, and Ch'ol indigenous civilian supporters of the Zapatista rebel army marched in silence through the streets of the colonial town of San Cristóbal de las Casas, Chiapas, Mexico. Despite the lack of visibility resulting from thick fog and light rain, despite the ski masks obscuring individual identities, it was possible to decipher the different generations forming the contingency. Many of those marching were youth, born and raised after the January 1, 1994, declaration of war against the Mexican state by the rebel army, the Ejército Zapatista de Liberación Nacional (EZLN, Zapatista National Liberation Army), named for the early twentieth-century peasant leader Emiliano Zapata. Others represented a generation of political cadres who took leading roles at the time of the uprising and in subsequent years, when their communities engaged in the dynamic exercise of autonomy and self-determination. And still others represented an older generation, many of whom worked in *fincas* (estates) and whose parents had previously lived as indentured servants. The march of the sixth sun marked one of the rebel movement's largest public gatherings in a decade.

Shortly after dawn that day in 2012, at least twenty-nine contingents from the five Zapatista regions, referred to as *caracoles*, arrived in vari-

1

ous forms of transportation from the valleys of the Lacandon Jungle, the highlands, and the northern region of the state of Chiapas. They descended from pickup trucks, cargo vehicles, and old school buses at the outskirts of town, and then they marched together through the same streets that the EZLN had occupied almost two decades earlier during the uprising. In a thin line, the marchers wove through the urban grid to the main plaza, where they circumvented the local municipal administrative building. The entire event until that point occurred in absolute silence, with only the light pounding of many pairs of feet on the cobble streets making any sound.

In contrast to the public demonstrations in which I actively participated in San Cristóbal over the years, on this occasion I observed the march through live streaming on the Internet from a small town near the city of Oaxaca. The independent media source broadcasting the event included a sidebar window where one could write comments and questions, many of which centered on guessing what was to occur. What will the Zapatistas do when they finally stop marching? Where will they stop? When will they break their silence? Who will speak? Will it be Subcomandante Insurgente Marcos, the *mestizo* political military authority of the EZLN, delegated by the indigenous Comandancia General (General Command) as the rebel army's spokesperson from 1994 to 2014, or one of the indigenous Mayan EZLN commanders who form the Comité Clandestino Revolucionario Indígena (Clandestine Indigenous Revolutionary Committee)? The majority of opinions expressed by others who, like me, were virtually observing the event showed that they assumed that the tension of silence would break at a culminating moment with a message condensed into a communiqué read aloud by one of the commanders or autonomous Zapatista government authorities.

The computer screen demonstrated the contrary. Those marching walked onto a raised platform behind the municipal administrative building. Each and every Zapatista followed the slant upward, lifted his or her arms into the air, and, rather than stopping, walked back down so as to continue ahead. There was no pause, much less a culminating point, no area of concentration, not one act of speaking. The political action that day was the act of walking itself, its meaning posited in the movement, its politics converted into a poetics of silence stretching beyond metaphors, a silence encompassing the possibilities of the possible, what Josefina Saldaña Portillo once described as a silence whose content, as part of Zapatismo, "is the condition of possibility for differentiation and fullness" (2003, 193).

A short time later, I ran into Mauricio, a Tseltal man in his late fifties with a sharp gaze and a talent for translating into words life's apparent complexities.[1] A decade earlier he had acted as a member of the Zapatista autonomous government in the rebel municipality Diecisiete de Noviembre, which was named for the date the EZLN was founded, November 17, 1983. The three years he spent on the autonomous council of Diecisiete de Noviembre overlapped with my years of fieldwork, a coincidence that provided me the opportunity of working closely with him. As a figure of authority, Mauricio was expected to coordinate political-administrative matters, including overseeing autonomous education and health projects, ensuring the implementation of decisions regarding Zapatista land reform, and taking part in conflict resolutions within the autonomous justice system, all in a context framed by militarized manifestations of state counterinsurgency tactics. During that time, it drew my attention that the intensity of activities under his and other council members' responsibility, rather than removing them from community life, grounded and fused the Zapatista government into the mundane activities shaping a Tseltal peasant existence. Government obligations were interspersed with the tending of his cornfields, coffee plants, and cattle and his participation in community commitments, such as meetings of the agricultural collectives as well as spiritual ceremonies held to ensure a healthy rainy season and corn harvest. His capacity to convey the ideas of an innate philosopher through his interpretation of such mundane affairs is something I particularly admire, so I found myself gravitating toward him for guidance on numerous occasions over the years. The same impulse led me to ask him about the significance of the march. I was curious as to why there was not one moment of political discourse within the mobilization. Mauricio responded: "To us, speaking is done by walking. And speaking, which is also our walking, can be done in silence. Our word isn't just done by a few, it is in all of us, all the communities, not just the authorities. That is what autonomy is, and that is how we propose to move history."[2]

This book is about the everyday politics of Zapatista indigenous autonomy that emerges from and thrives on the constant acts of speaking through walking. Such quotidian movements suggest the inseparability of the political from the act itself. The everyday politics of Zapatista indigenous autonomy simultaneously interacts with the state through what Pablo González (2011) terms a politics of refusal and enacts multilayered forms of engagement internal to the rebel autonomous project, including dialogue with vast webs of national and international political actors

(Rovira 2009). From this double-pronged politics emerge particular Tseltal and Tojolabal cultural practices — concentrated in three central realms, knowledge production, ways of being, and the exercise of power — that partially unravel the colonial legacies of a racialized and gendered neoliberal Mexican state.[3]

I develop this argument through an ethnography of the autonomous municipality where Mauricio lives, Diecisiete de Noviembre, the geographic borders of which roughly coincide with those of the official government municipality of Altamirano, located between the highlands and the Lacandon Jungle regions of Chiapas. The overlapping jurisdictions and competing social programs of the autonomous Zapatista municipality Diecisiete de Noviembre and the official municipality Altamirano form part of a highly contested terrain that includes non-Zapatista-aligned indigenous communities, *mestizo* citizens, and politically divergent peasant organizations. It is a region I first came to know in 1996, shortly after completing my undergraduate degree at the University of California, Berkeley, where I was a member of a solidarity organization, the Comité Emiliano Zapata, along with other students, professors, and community activists from the Bay Area committed to supporting the Zapatista struggle. At the time, the EZLN was briefly immersed in the first round of the San Andrés peace negotiations with the Ernesto Zedillo administration (1994–2000), which was on indigenous rights and culture.[4] On February 16, 1996, both parties signed the San Andrés Accords, a document recognizing indigenous rights and culture, particularly the right to self-determination and autonomy, that then served as a basis for enacting constitutional reforms.

The San Andrés dialogues forged dynamic conditions for creative political endeavors at the margins of the state. Shortly thereafter, the Zapatista support bases, or community members who actively support the political-military structure of the EZLN but are not part of the rebel army's military ranks, organized self-governing bodies and administrative units to implement collective decisions and initiated their own education, justice, agrarian, and health-care projects as part of their autonomous municipalities. Sympathizers of the movement also mobilized in support of these initiatives, myself included. Among activities designed to strengthen women's participation in the incipient project of autonomy, between 1997 and 2000, I, along with my friend and colleague Hilary Klein, supported and trained women participating in agricultural and store collectives in Diecisiete de Noviembre and two other autonomous municipalities using the popular-education methodologies of Paulo Freire. We worked in these popular-education workshops in what we considered to be an ethically grounded accompanying role shaped and directed by community dynamics and regional Zapatista decisions. At the same time, we engaged in intense discussions, both with members of Zapatista communities and with other nonindigenous and indigenous activists, on ways to effectively participate in a politics of solidarity across racialized and gendered differences. Such participation is an ethical commitment that shapes much of the methodological underpinnings and theoretical reflection of my scholarly endeavors. After years of solidarity work, I entered graduate school, later returning to the same region as part of doctoral fieldwork with the Anthropology Department at the University of Texas at Austin, research that serves as the foundation for this book. Though Klein's and my earlier projects undoubtedly inform my analysis of the daily practices of autonomy, this book is based primarily on interviews, observations, and informal conversations I conducted between 2005 and 2008.

Moving beyond Epistemological Blind Spots with Decolonizing Research

Particular forms of Mexican state formation under neoliberal economic policies and governing logics shaped the Zapatista project of autonomy and generated a set of conflicting conditions that I sought to analyze during fieldwork. By 2005, Mexico had undergone a little more than two decades of neoliberal reforms.[5] For example, Mauricio would point to when the Carlos Salinas de Gortari administration (1988–1994) directed privatizations and budget cuts in the agricultural sector. His family, along with most in the region, grow coffee, which at the time they sold to the national marketing board, Inmecafé. In 1988, the federal government eliminated the fixed pricing of coffee and concomitant subsidies for growers at the same time that a crash in the world market for their product created economic havoc in the Lacandon Jungle. While Mauricio and other members of his *ejido* (communal landholding), Lázaro Cárdenas, had for decades solicited extensions of their land, in 1992, changes to Article 27 of the Mexican Constitution sealed shut such possibilities, opening the door to the privatization of the *ejidos*. Both state decisions directly influenced many to join the clandestine ranks of the EZLN.

With the turn of the century came a second wave of reforms, no longer strictly privileging privatization but rather emphasizing more efficient forms of governance. Mexico brimmed with social unrest, primarily by way of mobilization of indigenous organizations alongside the Zapatistas. The country was still attempting to recover from the dramatic 1994 crash of the Mexican peso. Vicente Fox, of the right-of-center National Action Party, represented a superficial transition to electoral democracy after almost seventy years of rule by the Institutional Revolutionary Party. The Fox administration could not politically afford to eliminate social policies entirely; it needed to maintain neoliberal efficiency in public social spending while curbing further social mobilizing. In line with tendencies documented throughout the continent (Schild 2013), Mexican leaders reconfigured social policies as highly focused antipoverty and improved social-capital programs, where the targeted population was encouraged to participate in co-responsibility and co-investment initiatives.

Mexico entered this second wave of neoliberal reforms at the same time that the EZLN implemented de facto indigenous autonomy, a collective enterprise that Zapatista civilian members in Diecisiete de Noviembre repeatedly explained with statements such as, "Hacer las cosas nosotros mismos, con nuestros propios recursos y nuestras propias ideas porque no necesitamos nada del gobierno" (Autonomy means to do things ourselves, with our own resources and our own ideas, because we don't need anything from the government). In concrete practice, such a conceptual definition of autonomy translates into a rejection of all government programs—incuding agricultural incentives, state-funded teachers, and public health services—while creating parallel institutions that replace and usurp those of the state. Despite the fact that the question appears counterintuitive, I wondered whether a position of independence from state institutions could spur the withdrawal of state programs and facilitate more diffuse logics of governance, hence facilitating the very neoliberal conditions the Zapatista movement was struggling against.

This overarching question included an additional dimension. Zapatista community members affirmed their commitment to do things themselves based on their own ideas and with their own resources at the same time that the Mexican state recognized limited juridical frameworks that made such steps a legal possibility. In Mexico, as in other parts of Latin America, states implemented neoliberal reforms while indigenous and Afro-Mexican organizations pushed for the legal recognition of collective rights. As part of the first wave of neoliberal policy changes, in 1992 the Mexican Congress simultaneously amended Article 4 of the constitution to recognize the pluricultural makeup of the Mexican state and Article 27 to open the door to the privatization of *ejidos*. In 2001, during the influx of the second wave of new neoliberal policies, Congress approved the alteration of Article 2 to recognize indigenous people's cultural rights; although the new policy outlined a very watered-down version of collective rights, they were cultural rights nonetheless (Gómez 2004). In this sense, the recognition of indigenous rights could sit quite comfortably with neoliberal structural reforms (Hale 2002). The question arises, then, are there potential points of convergence between the official recognition of indigenous rights as part of neoliberal governance and the daily practices of Zapatista autonomy?

Responses to these inquiries have concrete implications for historically contingent strategies of social transformation. Yet during the years I spent actively participating in solidarity projects in Zapatista communities, these questions rarely came up in conversations or discussions. There was the assumption among many sympathizers of the EZLN that autonomy was by its very essence radical in its unsettling of state projects. As the years unfolded, I noticed that for many of these solidarity groups, autonomy slowly became an unquestioned dogma that dissolved critical lines of inquiry. In the Zapatista communities, I observed, rather than a blind conviction, a collective self-assurance as Tseltal and Tojolabal men and women proposed and carried forth initiatives, even when there was a deep uncertainty as to where their proposals would lead. At the same time, many men and women with whom I spoke situated current projects of autonomy in long-term trajectories of struggle. In this sense, Zapatista municipalities were neither the starting nor the ending point for social transformation. Such attitudes led me to ponder whether there were aspects of the claims to autonomy that I was not considering.

Here emerges a third central line of questioning: What role does a politically committed researcher have when she elaborates questions that initially appear absent from discussions taking place within a social movement itself? How should she pose these critical questions so that they come not from a place of absolute certainty but along dialogical lines of productive critique? In what ways do these questions become associated with fields of power when the researcher supports a struggle promulgated by Tseltal, Tsotsil, Tojolabal, and Ch'ol Mayan communities yet is herself from a middle-class Mexico City background and was raised in the United States? What methodologies and ethical commitments are required to effectively listen to responses that perhaps overflow the initial sets of questions? I recognize that such statements may appear out of place where, despite widely accepted critiques of positivism and objectivity, explicit political positioning continues to occur silently in written formats as the concern that it may affect disciplinary rigor continues to permeate scholarly decisions (Estrada Saavedra 2007).

I write this book from within a genealogy of socially committed research in Latin America (Aubry 2011; Cumes 2009; Fals Borda 2008; Hernández Castillo 2006; Leyva 2015; Olivera Bustamante 2015; Sieder 2017) and the United States (Hale 2008; Gordon 1991; Vargas Costa 2008; Gilmore 2007; Stephen 2013; Speed 2006) that transforms such silences into a series of critical questions designed to support collective political actions for social transformation. In fact, I highlight the ways in which a politics of method (Naples 2003) expanded my initial research questions so as to render visible aspects previously unconsidered. In using the term "politics of method," Naples refers to making explicit the ways in which the epistemological and methodological choices made during social science research, rather than being neutrally positioned, represent political choices that have concrete implications (14). In this sense I suggest that politically engaged research has the potential to shift the ethnographic gaze and shed light on epistemological blind spots (Castillejo Cuellar 2009, 59), adding new dimensions to original framing lines of interrogation, dimensions that in turn unlock new critical questions. This is particularly relevant when research is situated within alliances that cut across gender, racial, and class differences, where a common political project generates cohesion yet diverse situated knowledges (Haraway 1991) filter the multiple ways in which we grasp sociopolitical realities and truths.

I found it possible to shift my ethnographic focus in large part because I opened the methodology of my research to the scrutiny of and alteration by Zapatista community members in Diecisiete de Noviembre and because I had a long-term working relationship with these communities. As I detail at length in chapter 6, I was granted permission to conduct research in Zapatista communities after a series of back-and-forth dialogues with autonomous authorities over the course of a year, during which time they requested on several occasions that I reformulate my proposal because they believed the objectives remained unclear or the methodology proposed was insufficient. At the end of 2004, representatives from all the municipalities in Caracol IV convened in their assembly at the *caracol* center in Morelia, where they accepted my proposal, yet conditioned various aspects of the research, including that I could not conduct interviews in the communities until each community assembly (in which everyone in the village participates) had discussed the proposal and accepted or suggested changes to the methods. In the twelve villages where I eventually engaged in fieldwork, each assembly opted for gender-divided group interviews. In these spaces, Tseltal and Tojolabal men and women placed great emphasis on historical processes of long duration, specifically the over one hundred–year presence of the agricultural estates, to explain the relevance of their autonomous municipalities. In fact, their narratives of suffering and trauma on the estates magnified the meanings attached to neoliberal reforms, rendering visible their particular racialized effects, aspects I had not underscored sufficiently in my initial formulation of the research questions.

Racialized Effects of Color-Blind Neoliberalism

Official EZLN discourse highlights the fact that the decision to declare war on the Mexican government in 1994 was the direct result of the implementation of the North American Free Trade Agreement (NAFTA). The EZLN *comandancia* declared during the first days of the uprising that NAFTA meant death to indigenous people (EZLN 1994c). Yet community members like Mauricio not only referenced specific neoliberal policies, particularly the elimination of coffee subsidies and the end to land reform, but repeatedly offered descriptions of lived experience on the agricultural *fincas* to explain their reasons for actively supporting a political-military organization. These estates, owned primarily by local *mestizos* who made up a select network of landowning families in Chiapas, largely existed from the end of the nineteenth century until the 1970s, while some persisted until the uprising. Though in the interviews originally proposed, I had included questions on the history of the region, including the role of the estates, I assumed that the responses would offer important contextual information to help me understand the heart of my fieldwork, the current neoliberal moment. However, community members displaced and relocated what I assumed to be the central focus, returning time and time again to reference personal and family narratives of suffering, trauma, oppression, and exploitation on the *fincas*. Their insistence forced me to shift my gaze toward how Zapatista support bases interpreted such experiences and how they established connections between this collective past and their current struggles through indigenous autonomy.

I eventually came to understand that Zapatista autonomy as a form of struggle against neoliberal conditions could not be fully understood in its local manifestations unless read in light of intergenerational life experiences on the *fincas* and unless the estates were viewed as racialized and gendered economic enterprises. Leaving these experiences out of the framing analysis generates fundamental blind spots that render invisible local forms of racialization. By "racialization," I mean social processes that place onto bodies, populations, and cultures constructed biological differences, created categories linked to hegemonic processes of domination that maintain certain stability across historical or spatial frames (Barot and Bird 2001; Campos García 2012; Das 2007; Goldberg 2002; Omi and Winant 1994). Such mechanisms are activated through a series of ambiguous processes that hinge upon both biologically and culturally defined forms of alterity though are not subsumed under either.

Mayan Kakchiquel scholar Aura Cumes (2014) argues that domestic service and the *mozo* (indentured servant on an estate) operate as institutions of servitude constitutive of the (neo)colonial social ordering of indigenous lives in Guatemala specifically and Latin America more generally. These institutions of servitude surpass strictly economic forms of control as they expand to encompass the domination of life itself; indigenous lives are placed at the service of the Spaniards, *criollos*, and *ladinos*, ensuring the social reproduction of those sectors of society in positions of racialized economic privilege.[6] These institutions generate economic niches and naturalized tropes of racialized inferiorization whereby indigenous men and women are constructed as only suited for manual labor and as subjects to be given orders. Both these institutions of servitude not only shape current forms of global and internal colonial conditions (González Casanova 2005) but condense particular forms of colonial power-knowledge (Quijano 2000) that circulate under certain historical contexts.

I draw from Cumes's argument to suggest that neoliberal forms of governance in Chiapas, rather than being counterbalanced by limited indigenous-rights reforms, reproduce racialized social hierarchies that were condensed in the estates as cultural economic enterprises. The demise of most of the estates in Chiapas during the 1970s, with the remaining properties confiscated by the EZLN and indigenous peasant organizations after 1994, failed to dismantle these discourses and practices. Rather, particular tropes were rearticulated through racialized building blocks (Bonilla-Silva 2010) onto apparently color-neutral neoliberal policies, fueling continued forms of domination and inferiorization of indigenous peoples. Here it is important to note that although I am focusing on local production in Chiapas, the estates were part of globalized political economic forces and discourses of alterity. Hence, while I discuss racialization as historically and spatially contingent, it exists in tension with globalized racial relations of ruling (Smith 1987).

After the 2001 constitutional reforms on indigenous rights and culture, state institutions spurred a series of cultural-rights policies, such as intercultural education programs (Baronnet 2010), plurilegal forms of conflict resolution (Sierra 2013), and the juridical recognition of municipal elections through *usos y costumbres* (customs and traditions) (Aragón 2013; Martínez 2013). While these multicultural reforms fueled state making during the Vicente Fox (2000–2006) and Felipe Calderón (2006–2012) federal administrations, as well as during the Chiapas state administrations of Pablo Salazar (2000–2006) and Juan Sabines (2006–2012), they articulated to deceptively color-blind or racially neutral policies that have remained at the center of Mexican state formation. When I began fieldwork, the Fox administration was heavily investing in the push for transparency and accountability as part of greater citizen participation resulting from the end of the seven-decade rule of the Institutional Revolutionary Party. The apparent move toward democracy centered almost exclusively on the electoral realm and was largely limited to political party politics. In terms of the social-development policies implemented at the time, they privileged a focus on alleviation of extreme poverty, particularly the program Oportunidades (Opportunities). At the time, Oportunidades transferred cash to female heads of household who agreed to ensure that their children attended school, their family members visited health clinics, and they themselves maintained adequate levels of household hygiene, among other behaviors that marked alterations in cultural habits. In terms of the programs targeting peasant communities, these centered on reconfiguring land tenure largely through the Programa de Certificación de Derechos Ejidales y Titulación de Solares Urbanos (PROCEDE, Program for the Certification of Ejido and Urban Land Ownership Titles). PROCEDE in essence established procedures to grant *ejidatarios* (recognized members of communal landholdings) individual parcels and land titles as part of the implementation of the 1992 reforms to Article 27 of the Mexican Constitution.

In this book, I focus on these national priorities, which, in contrast to cultural-rights policies that specifically target indigenous communities, either appear universal in scope or address class-based forms of economic marginalization, making little reference to indigenous, much less Afro-

⌐ focus on cultural-rights

Mexican, communities, except when described as part of the category "vulnerable groups."[7] While these policies do not appear racialized, nor do they even appear to account for cultural differences, this does not mean they do not have racialized effects that fuel social hierarchies. In fact, it is toward the effects of these policies that I suggest we need to turn our gaze in order to understand particular forms of racialization as linked to Mexican neoliberal state formation.[8]

Indigeneity and Racialization

Before I lay out the ways that color-blind state formation reproduces racialized hierarchies, it is first necessary to explain why I focus on race rather than on the dominant category of ethnicity, which is typically used in Latin America to analyze indigeneity. Ethnicity since the late 1930s has been the privileged social category used to explain alterity in Mexico, a category fueled by the work of anthropologists and often linked to *mestizaje*[9] state-making projects. Despite the differences in their specific professional trajectories, the founding fathers of anthropology in Mexico, such as Manuel Gamio, Ricardo Poza, Aguirre Beltrán, and Juan Comas, shared a rejection of scientific racism, opting instead to promote cultural forms of progress. For example, the physical anthropologist Juan Comas dedicated an important part of his career to unraveling scientific racism by demonstrating that no racially defined population bears any biological distinction that makes it superior or inferior to others (Gómez Izquierdo 2000). Comas sought to disprove the existence of superior and inferior races or levels of intelligence based on superficial biological attributes such as the shape of the eyes or nose or the size of the head (Comas 1945). He insisted that alterity is cultural in form and therefore argued for social forms of progress by way of education, corrected expressions of spirituality, and the adoption of modern ideas, such as scientific medicine in place of traditional medicine (Gómez Izquierdo 2000).

The underlying logic of such thinkers unfolds in the following manner: If race as a category emphasizes the biological differences of human populations, and if biological differences justify scientific racism, then an emphasis on cultural differences, such as language, dress, ritual, and traditional practices, markers that tend to fall under the social category of ethnicity, effectively erodes justifications for racism. If differences are cultural, these anthropologists argued, then indigenous communities could be "culturally improved," and mixture as well as advancement are possible.

It is through this explicative line that the overrepresentation of ethnicity as a social category of alterity became the norm in Mexico, as in other parts of Latin America.

While critical Mexican anthropology during the 1960s and 1970s generated important fissures in the discipline's direct fueling of state policies and enterprises, advocating instead for endeavors committed to popular movements and supporting the political actions of indigenous communities and organizations, it by and large left untouched the use of ethnicity as a category of alterity. Critical anthropologists such as Mercedes Olivera Bustamante and Rodolfo Stavenhagen centered power and domination as a central axis of inquiry so as to analyze the ways in which cultural differences are situated within political and economic forms of inequality and exploitation (Olivera Bustamante 1970; Stavenhagen 1965). Despite the unquestionable contributions of these critical anthropologists to understandings of domination in Mexico, their largely uncritical use of the category of ethnicity continued to limit understandings of how racism and racialization shape socioeconomic hierarchies.[10]

More recent scholarship in the United States and Latin America identifies how constructions of race are embedded with cultural overtones, as well as how culture is biologized through naturalized markers (Gotkowitz 2011; Hale 2006a; Holt 2000; Lewis 2006; Rosas 2012; Wade 2011). When cultural traits, such as respect for land and nature, are read as inherent to particular indigenous peoples, those cultural traits are biologized and hence racialized. Similarly, when physical markers, such as what some sectors of society label more "indigenous phenotypes," are assumed to account for particular forms of behavior, such as being "subservient" or "ignorant," there is an explicative linkage between biology and culture. The resulting analytical windows locate the ambiguous use of alterity ~~..............~~ ~~...... ....~~ ~~..~~ ~~their many slippages.~~ Rather than clean-cut separations, research points to a messiness expressed in colloquial speech, in urban centers (Moreno Figueroa 2012) as well as in rural areas, including in the Zapatista communities of Diecisiete de Noviembre.

In fact, throughout my research for this book, I heard Zapatista community members speaking of alterity in non-uniform ways. In everyday talk, those interviewed sometimes pointed to differences between indigenous people and *kaxlanes*, the Mayan term used to identify nonindigenous people as "those from the outside" or "outsiders," based on economic forms of oppression. Eudalia, a woman from the community Diez de Abril, for example, explained, "The *kaxlanes* are those who have good pants and shoes, nice hats, while the indigenous are poor, we walk in bare feet, and have our stomachs filled, not with food, but with bugs." At other times, men and women interviewed referred to bloodlines and phenotype to both distinguish and draw similarities between "those from the outside" and themselves. Aurelio, from Zapata, explained that "those who have indigenous blood are indigenous. The others are from outside. Though the *kaxlanes* say they are not indigenous, that is where their roots lie. Look at their faces and their skin." And on still other occasions, community members referenced innate forms of cultural inferiority. Many spoke of tensions between Tseltales and Tojolabales that existed prior to the uprising, with the former using derogatory terms such as "Tojolabalero" to refer to the latter and labeling in absolute terms the laziness and backwardness of their Mayan neighbors.

Though diverse and even contradictory, what these meanings share is an emphasis on what varying forms of inferiorization *do*, that is, both biological and cultural markers justify profound material and symbolic manifestations of inequality that are not only naturalized but internalized. Taking these ambiguous narratives as a base, I aim in this book to contribute to the body of literature on racialization in Latin America that shifts the gaze from trying to locate what racism *is*, whether it is culturally or biologically activated, or a combination of both, to trying to determine what it *does* (Gotkowitz 2011). This emphasis on the effects of racism is relevant given that it forces us to listen to the particular ways that Zapatista community members identify expressions of racism and processes of racialization. In everyday talk as well as in official Zapatista discourses, rarely is the term "racism" used, and when it is referenced, it is often through the apparently less politically charged word "discrimination."[11] However, just because the term is largely discursively absent does not mean that community members are not pointing to racism as socially constructed notions of inferiority that have very real material impacts in their lives. One hears about these effects when they are described through narratives of dispossession, through stories of how *kaxlanes* systematically negate indigenous people's access to their land; one sees them in the exacerbated levels of poverty in the regions where indigenous people live, in the consistent denial of knowledge produced by community members, and in the daily treatment by local *mestizos* and *kaxlan* government representatives of local indigenous populations as if they were animals, part of the local scenery, or simply people born to work and obey. The summation of these daily acts points to the effects of racism as varying forms of dehumanization, as daily practices that essentially accuse Tseltales and Tojolabales of possessing a devalued humanity in relation to a *kaxlan* or a *mestizo* or a *ladino*.[12]

Zapatista community members I interviewed tended to concentrate on narratives of dehumanization when referencing collective intergenerational experiences on the estates.[13] Even when discussing current neoliberal conditions, Tseltal and Tojolabal men and women would return to social memories on the *fincas* to explain what would be at risk if autonomy were not exercised. As Vicario, from the community of San Pedro Guerrero, explained,

> What the *priistas* [local term used to refer to any community members not aligned with the Zapatistas, though not necessarily aligned with the Institutional Revolutionary Party, the PRI] don't understand is if we don't work the land, if we don't defend our land, if we don't struggle against the bad government, then the times of the *mozo* can return. That is why our autonomy as indigenous people is so important.

Though Vicario speaks metaphorically of the return to the time of the *mozos*, he condenses in the figure of the indentured servant conditions of inferiority that he goes on to identify in current-day interactions with state institutions, in the threat posed by individual land titling, in the private investment that potentially transforms indigenous people's territory into natural resources to be exploited, and in the continued silencing of indigenous people as part of dominant forms of political participation. "They treat us as if we were *mozos*, when the bad government doesn't listen to us as indigenous people but tries to give us orders and when they say that as indigenous people we no longer have rights to communal lands," continued Vicario.

I argue that the figure of the *mozo* serves to establish continuities between past and current forms of exploitation, as well as to render visible the fixed locations of indigenous people and *kaxlanes*. From the *testimonios* offered by Zapatista community members, such as Vicario, emerge particular racialized and gendered tropes that continue to shape ostensibly racially neutral or color-blind neoliberal policies. Throughout this book I focus on three racialized tropes that, while concentrated and exemplified through narratives of life on the estates, rearticulate and reconfigure neoliberal forces.

The first trope is the infantilization that is associated with indigenous people and their communities, equating indigeneity to childlike innocence, to an innate vulnerability, and to populations in perpetual need of assistance.[14] This infantilization establishes dominance in the terms of engagement with the Mexican state through relationships of tutelage, where the logics behind central public policies, as well as the attitudes by those who implement them, tend to hinge upon establishing forms of protection for those labeled indigenous. State institutions and officials act as "guardians" for those who cannot fend for themselves. While such a trope appears in contradiction to neoliberal state priorities that emphasize self-entrepreneurship and co-responsibility, I illustrate that the underlying logics of neoliberal antipoverty programs such as Oportunidades establish a direct corollary to the ways estate owners treated their *mozos*, as children to be disciplined who were dependent on owners for their well-being and who failed to possess the adequate cultural habits to fend for themselves. In fact, this relationship of tutelage is such a powerful trope that the Tseltal language provides a term referring to an authority who can be a government official, an estate owner, or both: *ajvalil*, which translates as "master-governor."

The second trope activates the social niche of the *mozo*, the peon or servant, as the naturalized location of indigenous people, who are labeled as those born to work and to obey, in contrast to the *kaxlan*, *mestizo*, or *ladino*, who is born to govern and to give orders. The role of the peon becomes fixed onto indigenous bodies read as innately designed to serve others, to be at the service of the productive capacities of others' lives. Indigeneity as equated to a peonage status contrasts with notions of progress associated with those people who can more effectively turn natural resources, particularly land, into accumulative wealth. I trace the continuities of this trope through shifts in land tenure and citizenship projects from the end of the nineteenth century into the neoliberal era marked by the Article 27 constitutional reforms. At the same time, this trope overlaps with the one described above in that dynamics founded on paternalistic relations presuppose that those infantilized are only apt to receive orders and need to be continually disciplined to obey.

The third trope activates representations of indigenous bodies as inherently deficient and thus in constant need of cultural and biological improvement. In contrast to representations of the glorious Mayan civilization of the past, current Mayan peoples are described as bearers of cultural degeneracy, a deficiency that operates in a contradictory manner. In some cases, the trope appears to reproduce European-derived eugenics ideologies that label those deemed inferior as a genetically inadequate stock that requires bodily separation from others so as to avoid contamination. In other moments, the trope activates a positive eugenics, what Nancy Leys Stepan refers to as "constructive miscegenation" (1996, 147), that is, a selective use of corrective and correcting cultural practices that foster the whitening effects of *mestizaje* ideologies.

In the following chapters, I point to the ways that these three tropes operated as overlapping racialized disciplinary mechanisms that continued to circulate through the apparently color-blind neoliberal policies during the Fox and Calderón administrations. I analyze the land-tenure program PROCEDE as a state policy that under Fox and Calderón promoted the transformation of communal lands into individual, privately held parcels. I illustrate how the program continues to shape particular racialized geographies, as linked to global economies, that resituate indigenous peasants as those who halt the productive potential of natural resources as well as those only suited to work for the well-being of others. This reinscription of indigenous people as born only to work operates not just in their rural regions of origin but progressively more so as they migrate to urban centers as day laborers, including in tourist zones. I also focus on the social-development program Oportunidades as a poverty-reduction program that reactivates "constructivist miscegenation" as characteristic of *mestizaje* so as to advocate for the improvement of the cultural capital of families identified as living in conditions of extreme poverty. In addition, I situate the Zapatista cultural politics of *mandar obedeciendo* (governing while obeying) as that which seeks to unravel the naturalized location of indigenous peoples as born to obey the orders of the *ladinos* or *kaxlanes* in a historical moment when the nonindigenous elite in Mexico continue to decide and define the terms of political participation.

Through an analysis of these programs and political concepts, I argue that these racialized and gendered tropes operate not as residual elements of past historical phases or modes of production but as active, constitutive forces of neoliberal forms of government. Zapatista indigenous autonomy is the sum of multifaceted cultural political actions attempting to dismantle the resiliency of these tropes linked to Mexican state formation. It is against these continued forms of racialized inferiorization that the Zapatista municipalities engage in uneven, ambiguous daily practices that affirm collective "life-existence" through what I describe as *kuxlejal* politics.

Kuxlejal Politics, the Power to Be, and Zapatista Autonomy

FROM MY POINT OF VIEW, AUTONOMY MEANS KNOWING AND DOING. IT MEANS HAVING CONFIDENCE IN OUR HEARTS THAT, EVEN IF WE DON'T KNOW HOW TO DO SOMETHING, WE ARE GOING TO LEARN FROM ONE ANOTHER. BASED ON THIS NEW KNOWLEDGE, WE WILL CONSTRUCT THINGS. I BELIEVE THAT IN AUTONOMY THESE ARE THE STEPS TO BE TAKEN AND THAT IS WHY WE FEEL WE ARE WORTH SOMETHING, WHY WE HAVE VALUE. WE KNOW WE ARE VALUABLE BECAUSE WE CAN DO AND LEARN THINGS ON THE BASIS OF OUR KNOWLEDGE, EVEN WHEN WE DON'T YET KNOW THE PATH AHEAD.

JAIME, SAN PEDRO GUERRERO, DIECISIETE DE NOVIEMBRE

Throughout my years of solidarity and fieldwork activity in Diecisiete de Noviembre, I heard a comment repeated time and time again by support bases: "Autonomy is for life, it is about the possibility of a new life." This apparently simple enunciation is deceptively straightforward. On first reading, one could identify in it religious references, specifically the liberation theology of the Catholic Church, as promulgated by the Diocese of San Cristóbal de las Casas during the forty years that Samuel Ruiz García served as bishop (1960–2000). In this case, "a new life" would refer to the commitment of God's children to work for justice for the poor and disenfranchised on this mundane terrain, where a new life can be forged. One could also read in the explanation revolutionary figures of decades past calling for the forging of a "new man," the aspirational term of Ernesto "Che" Guevara. Certainly both figure as influential reference points in the political genealogies influencing Zapatista communities. I suggest, however, that we must locate an additional layer, introduced through what Aimé Césaire calls colonialism's pseudohumanism: "And that is the great thing I hold against [pseudohumanism]: that for too long it has diminished the rights of man, that its concept of those rights has been—and still is—narrow and fragmentary, incomplete and biased and, all things considered, sordidly racist" (2000, 37). Associating autonomy with the struggle for a new life, as read through Césaire's anticolonial and antiracist argument, reveals a particular Tseltal and Tojolabal theoretical political praxis.

When I asked Mauricio what the Tseltal word for "life" is, he explained that its rough equivalent is *kuxlejal*, "life-existence." *Kuxlejal* as a term is but a mere point of anchor granted meaning when used as part of the term for the concept of expressing living as a collective, *stalel jkuxlejal-tik*, a way of being in the world as a people, and as part of the term for a daily aspiration to live in a dignified manner, *lekil kuxlejal*.[15] The horizon of struggle for *lekil kuxlejal*, with its Tojolabal equivalent, *sak'aniltik*, as a good way of living refers not only to an individual being but to that being in relation to a communal connection to the earth, to the natural and supernatural world that envelops as well as nurtures social beings and is thus constantly honored.[16] Without land, without the ability to plant and harvest sufficient food, without the constant remembering of ancestors in connection to the future and as part of revering the earth, the elements that provide sustenant meaning to life dissipate.

When Zapatista community members associate the political practices of autonomy with creating a new life, they refer to *lekil kuxlejal*, to a life politics understood as involving these interconnected realms. Autonomy as the foundation of life politics thus is expressed in gathering fallen branches for firewood, in harvesting corn in the fields, in praying for abundant water—not too much, nor too little, just what is necessary for the corn and beans to flourish in the fields, in collecting edible leaves in the forest or picking vegetables in the backyard gardens, in taking care of the children and the elderly, in sharing memories of past events so as to produce knowledge effecting changes in the present. It is the sum of activities in such arenas that allows for the dignified reproduction of life, not only as a physical presence but as a series of cultural processes that allow for the perpetuation of *kuxlejal* in its collective form and as a collective force.

In this light, Tseltal scholar Juan López Intzín speaks of *lekil kuxlejal* as a basis for transforming a sense of humanity based on a social life of plenitude, dignity, and justice as part of another world mediated not by power but by the power to be, or what he terms "el poder sentirsaber-sentirpensar" (the power or ability to feel-know and to feel-think) (2013, 78). Recall that the Spanish *poder* translates both as "power" and as "the ability to do or to be." When the act of living affirms the power to be rather than power over something or somebody, then living becomes a political act in itself in that it ensures the sociocultural and biological continuation of life. In fact, the lived horizon of *lekil kuxlejal* is so central to autonomy that the mural that adorns the offices of the *junta de buen gobierno* (good government council) in Caracol IV states, above a painted rainbow, "Smali yel lequil cuxlejal" (Seeking a dignified life).

In this book, I trace *kuxlejal* politics through the different spheres of autonomy, beginning with community members' relationship to land as part of a constructed sense of territory. When Zapatista community members settled land previously controlled by *mestizo* estate owners, they defined in their revolutionary agrarian reform its collective use and prohibited its distribution for individual benefit (EZLN 1993a). A sense of belonging to the land as well as to the community emerges through working the soil, planting corn kernels and beans for next year's harvest, and asking the earth's permission to plant; it also emerges in the weekly activities of Diecisiete de Noviembre's agricultural production collectives and in the act of reaping that which is sown through one agricultural cycle as a way of ensuring repetition. Working the land grants individuals the right to participate politically in the Zapatista communities. It is the reproduction of concrete actions that fuels the politicized life of the collective in its relationship to the earth.

While Zapatista agrarian reform generates the necessary conditions for autonomy through *kuxlejal* politics, I suggest that the politicization of life condenses in spheres typically relegated to the margins of the Zapatista autonomy project, specifically in the women's production collectives, vegetable gardens, bread ovens, village stores, fruit orchards, and spaces where they raise chickens or rabbits. It is in these intergenerational spaces where women engage in critical reflection on their lives as Tseltal and Tojolabal peasant women in relation to their family members, to the men in the community, and to the state. At the same time, they participate in collective activities typically defined as everyday household tasks, yet they situate them in collectivized areas of the village; family activities are thus transformed into group work that brings together the women of the community as a whole. The merging of economic activities with collective self-reflection entangles production with learning, pedagogy with politics. I argue that the women's production collectives synthesize *kuxlejal* politics such that daily life becomes inseparable from the political, while imbricating materiality in a collective sense of belonging and self-making. Activities in the women's collectives focus on the dignified provision of care for each others' lives as work that seeks to ensure the well-being of the collective. In this sense, autonomy is situated in the communal drive to define the terms for the reproduction of social and biological life.

Such expressions of *kuxlejal* politics condense in the women's production collectives, and they diffuse into the spheres where decisions are implemented in the autonomous municipality—in the assemblies, in the various autonomous commissions, in the male agricultural production collectives—the sum of which engenders the cultural politics of *mandar obedeciendo*, governing while obeying. To govern while obeying implies that community members in positions of authority respond to a particular Tseltal and Tojolabal political ethic that complies with the needs communicated by divine powers and the earth, as well as those who inhabit it. These sets of cultural practices render inseparable political action and the collective actor. Here I highlight that one of the effects of the autonomy project of Zapatismo includes the extension of a collective identity beyond the community and into interregional alliances with other indigenous people (Rus 2012). Similarly, *mandar obedeciendo*, as a collective sense of purpose, opens the possibility of *ser y hacer gobierno*, to be and to make a collective authority, to govern by learning to govern, as that which spurs knowledge production grounded in embodied learning, as Jaime from San Pedro Guerrero explains in the opening epigraph of this section. In this sense, *kuxlejal* politics surfaces from actions linking power to knowledge, where autonomy directs the production of new *saberes* (knowledges) toward a series of cultural practices seeking to unravel gendered and racialized forms of domination.

The relationship between knowledge and power in Diecisiete de Noviembre includes the scrutinized role of academic research. In this book, I critically analyze the ways that my research was subjected to the processes of autonomy, including being restricted by collective decisions on what methods made most sense to community members. By a large majority, they privilege intergenerational group interviews, which shifted the focus of what is ordinarily considered "data." Rather than interviews' serving to gather preexisting knowledge, that which is simply lying there waiting to be picked, community members emphasized that knowledge is produced within the space of research itself, thus bringing together points of convergence between Paulo Freire's (1970) legacy of popular education and Orlando Fals Borda's (1986) participatory action research. Our group interviews merged politics with the pedagogical, wherein autonomy allows the possibility of generating knowledge that permits community members to walk beyond the limits set by current conditions. In this case, the emphasis placed on method does not just refer to a series of techniques but links practices to broader epistemological frameworks and to notions of the political. At the same time, the interviews established points of convergence with research projects elsewhere, such as with the Coordinadora Regional Indígena del Cauca (Cauca Regional Indigenous Committee) in Colombia, where the joint production of knowledge figures prominently in practices of self-determination (Lozano Suárez 2017; Rappaport 2005).

Kuxlejal politics, as understood through these combined elements, both dialogues with Michel Foucault's notion of "biopower" and engages in a different set of premises. In *Society Must Be Defended*, Foucault defines biopower as the power of the sovereign in "making live and letting die" through the activation of a series of knowledges, techniques, and technologies that extract life forces so as to "tak[e] control of life and the biological processes of man-as-species and of ensuring that they are not disciplined, but regularized" (2003, 246–247). States take care of the physical and intellectual capacities of those populations considered worthy, while creating the conditions that let the remainder die. Sovereign power is reflected through the dividing line separating those whose lives are deemed valuable from those whose lives are deemed expendable. Michael Hardt and Antonio Negri (2004), on their part, seek to establish a distinction between life power that fuels the sovereign entity, what they, too, refer to as "biopower," and life power that generates subaltern collective politics, what they name "biopolitical production." Though both of Hardt and Negri's terms refer to the political terrain as inseparable from biological and social life, their "biopower" refers to processes that continually bolster the forces of sovereign power in ways that parallel Foucault's definition. Biopower, under post-Fordist economic conditions, links to current capitalist logics that seek to regulate all spheres of life rather than just those, such as assembly lines, that previously defined the worker. By contrast, biopolitical production feeds collective actions enacted by political agents without limiting them to those of a sovereign entity. According to the authors, "biopolitical production" refers to the constitutive life power that operates in antagonism to, and seeks to transform, world capitalist logics.

Kuxlejal politics differs from biopower in that rather than fueling sovereign power, it directs autonomous practices toward the sovereign's destruction (Reyes and Kaufman 2011). It seeks to disintegrate sovereign power's capacity to separate those whose lives matter from those labeled disposable through a collective affirmation of that which sustains collective life. At the same time, while similar to biopolitical production in that its effects move away from sovereign power, life politics in the Tseltal and Tojolabal communities in Diecisiete de Noviembre insists upon unsettling the gendered and racialized underpinnings of capitalist logics by affirming the collectives' grounded relationship to the natural, to a life-sustaining present, in its connection to a past with its future possibilities.

At the same time, *kuxlejal* politics explicitly references particular legacies of resistance as emerging from between the dehumanizing gendered and racialized forms of exploitation of indigenous people. *Kuxlejal* cultural practices walk through resistance as a politics inseparable from life itself and from specific actions granting meaning to life, as the march of December 21, 2012, illustrates. Rather than defining the political as the culminating point of an event, such as the final speech at a mobilization or the moment when community life condenses into a series of public political participations, such as in an assembly, this expression of life politics emerges through the constant, albeit low-decibel, registers of biocollective actions.

In this book, I point to *kuxlejal* politics as a part of Zapatista autonomy that negates imposed racialized techniques and technologies that dehumanize life, including the paternalistic and racist government social-assistance programs, the vertical power relations reproduced by the *mestizo ajvalil* (master-governor), at a local level, and the inertia toward reconcentration of collective land into individual titles. When the foundational stone of political action emerges in rejection of that which negates a collective's humanity, the subsequent act affirms a call to humanness (Maldonado-Torres 2008; Winter 2003) as that which references not only the individual but a collective of bodies in relation to nature and to a constructed sense of territory. In this sense, *kuxlejal* politics steps away from claims that politics is confined to daily life or to the personal. Rather, for indigenous Zapatista community members, as for many Afrodescendant and indigenous organized peoples throughout the continent, the very act of living as part of a dignified commitment to the reproduction of social life directly confronts the dehumanizing conditions of racialized colonial states of being.

Thematic Organization

This book is structured in the following manner. The first chapter provides a brief overview of the Zapatista struggle leading up to the time the research for this book was conducted, including the unfolding of the autonomy project in Diecisiete de Noviembre. Chapter 2 critically examines the anthropological research for this book as seeking to unravel particular colonial legacies of the field of anthropology. It focuses on the methodological critiques as well as the contributions provided by Zapatista community members as potentially fueling a decolonizing praxis. Chapter 3 considers the history of the estate economy as a racialized cultural enterprise consolidated during the late nineteeth and early twentieth centuries. It argues that the main political organizational spaces that influenced Zapatistas prior to the founding of the autonomous municipalities actively sought to dismantle the power of the estates as well as contribute to the local alternatives created by indigenous communities.

Chapter 4 focuses on Zapatista agrarian reform as a series of actions that spurred autonomy in the region of Diecisiete de Noviembre and that sought to challenge state-led agricultural and land policies. Regaining access to land and carrying out its collective redistribution were the first major achievements of the EZLN uprising and became an essential point of departure. The chapter explores the ways in which Zapatista agrarian reform altered life in the local communities, primarily through decisions on how the land would be collectively worked and administered, as well as how members of the communities would later engage with the increasing reality of migration.

Chapter 5 brings to the forefront the cultural practices associated with women's production collectives as spaces that constitute some of the most profound reconceptualizations of the political within the project of Zapatista autonomy. It focuses on the cultural practices in the collectives as setting the terms through which social and biological life are reproduced. It then relates these Zapatista women's political contributions both to state regulating techniques located in the cash-transfer antipoverty program Oportunidades and to fragmentation of the capacities of social reproduction brought on by low-intensity warfare mechanisms.

The sixth and final chapter focuses on the cultural practices associated with figures of authority in the autonomous municipality. It traces different spheres in which decisions are carried out, in particular, on the practice of governing by obeying as engendering particular power dynamics between the governed and the governing. The chapter argues that rather than having practices reduced to the community, municipal, or *caracol* assembly, what could be understood as a Zapatista public sphere, the decision-making practices associated with governing by obeying are distributed throughout mundane activities, generating a politicization of daily life that offsets the racialized figure of the *ajvalil*.

And what is the purpose of all these pages? This question was posed by a Zapatista authority during a 2008 meeting I attended with representatives of the autonomous councils and the health and education commissions from the municipalities in Caracoles I (centered in La Realidad), III (in La Garrucha), and V (in Roberto Barrios). The authors of a book that would be published three years later, *Luchas "muy otras": Zapatismo y autonomía en las comunidades indígenas de Chiapas* (Baronnet, Mora, and Stahler-Sholk 2011), met with these Zapatista government authorities, along with the advisors to that book project, the sociologist Pablo González Casanova, the anthropologist Mercedes Olivera Bustamante, and the pedagogist Elsie Rockwell, to discuss the draft versions of each of the chapters. The meeting was the first time the initial arguments of a future publication on Zapatista autonomy were discussed with the very political actors whose actions were being written about. Following in the steps of the historian, philosopher, and social activist Andrés Aubry, a key political figure in Chiapas (who died tragically in 2007), those who met during the first days of January 2008 elaborated political and professional projects under the conviction that analysis, critical reflection, and research necessarily accompany processes of social transformation.

We began the meeting discussing what purposes research serves, in what ways it can strengthen the processes one studies, and what questions one needs to ask to identify the risks, contradictions, and tensions that potentially direct research toward contrary ends. Arturo, a member of the autonomous government of Ricardo Flores Magón, in Caracol III, asked a question that directed us immediately to the heart of the mat ... "Find these chapters, articles, or theses, are they just to make pretty books, to get a job, and to archive in a library or in some school, or is it to *do* things? And what things can we do with them?"

To encourage us to reflect, Rockwell reminded everyone that knowledge exists not in books, not even in individuals, but rather between individuals, between texts and individuals, in what people share and create among themselves. The critical question posed by Arturo, as well as Rockwell's response, resonates with the objectives of this book, as it groups together numerous reflections on the thousands of actions, conversations, and debates generated throughout almost two decades with female and male Zapatista indigenous support bases, along with colleagues involved in political projects who share similar commitments for social justice. By illustrating these interactions, I attempt with this book to illuminate processes of transformation set in motion, thus continuing the movement of speaking while walking, with the hope that each shifting step allows us to act from within new political imaginaries of liberation.

purpose

A Brief Overview of the First Years

ONE of the Zapatista Autonomous Municipalities (1996–2003)

The mural that marks the entrance to the political-cal administrative center of Caracol IV in Morelia bears the image of Emiliano Zapata, the peasant leader of the 1910 Mexican Revolution, surrounded by the phrase "Center for cultural and social events for indigenous and nonindigenous people with dreams of freedom, justice, and democracy" (see fig. 1.1). This symbol of the agrarian demands of peasants and other indigenous people appears to sustain the small building made of cement blocks and wooden boards, to which a metal gate is attached. The wire fence around it serves "to keep the horses out and stop them from trampling the vegetables the *compañeras* plant," a group of men once explained to me apologetically. Behind the entrance, a series of wooden buildings dot a grassy field. This *caracol* center, which also served for a few years as the administrative center of the municipality of Diecisiete de Noviembre,[1] is located between two mountains, at the beginning of the Tzaconejá River valley, in a natural amphitheater guarded by hundreds of pine trees that observe the goings-on from the slopes above.

The first time I visited Caracol IV, then still an *aguascalientes*, was in July 1996 as a participant in the Encuentro Intercontinental por la Humanidad y contra el Neoliberalismo (Intercontinental Meeting for Humanity and against Neoliberalism), which brought together more than six thousand people from over forty countries to discuss the social struggles against the impacts of neoliberal economic policies. The *encuentro* prefig-

27

Figure 1.1. Entrance to the Caracol IV administrative center in Morelia, 2006; photo by author

ured what would emerge in the World Social Forums of Porto Alegre at the start of the new millennium and would become part of the political imaginary of social movements that coalesced around the Arab Spring in the Middle East, the Indignados of Spain, and the Occupy Wall Street movement in New York. During this meeting, the Aguascalientes IV center in Morelia, along with the four other *aguascalientes* centers—located in the Zapatista communities of La Realidad, Oventic, La Garrucha, and Roberto Barrios—served as a venue for discussions on the struggles of indigenous people as well as the social, economic, and political impacts of neoliberalism, the topic in Morelia being neoliberal culture and its opposing cultural struggles.

More than a thousand people from many different parts of the world, along with their tents, hammocks, camping gear, and audiovisual recording equipment, shared the *aguascalientes* center with an even greater number of EZLN civilian support bases, who, as hosts, prepared the food, served coffee, organized cultural activities, and approached, sometimes timidly, the "internationals" with questions and comments. I attended the *encuentro* as a member of the solidarity committee from the University of California, Berkeley, the Comité Emiliano Zapata. During the three days of the gathering, we participated in countless exchanges, discussions, debates, and reflection sessions with Chileans, Brazilians, Japanese, Guatemalans, Catalans, and Basques, with other *mestizo* and indigenous Mexicans from Mexico City, Oaxaca, and Guerrero, as well as with the Tseltal,

Tojolabal, and Tsotsil support bases, the inhabitants of the commu.
that had organized themselves into the autonomous municipalities 1
resented at this *aguascalientes*. Zapatista authorities, including repre
sentatives of the Clandestine Revolutionary Indigenous Committee and
Comandante Zebedeo, listened attentively, took notes, and surveyed the
scene from the vantage point offered by their seats on stage. The ambience
was one of euphoria, a liminal moment in which a group of individuals imbued each other with the scope of the possible.

When I came back several months later to live in San Cristóbal and to
participate in solidarity projects in nearby Diecisiete de Noviembre, the
contrast between the effervescent energy of the *encuentro* and the daily
rhythm at the *aguascalientes* was striking. On the day I returned to the
center, the wind highlighted the silence of the venue, moving warm air
among the still-new buildings that housed the incipient projects of Zapatista indigenous autonomy. The apparent tranquility of that day, however, was deceiving. Two or three times a week during my time there, I
would see hundreds of representatives of the Zapatista communities fill
the *aguascalientes* compound as they participated in municipal assemblies
to decide how to implement the different spheres of autonomy, including
land-reform, education, and health projects. The venue would also host
workshops on human rights, health, and education organized by members
of nongovernmental organizations (NGOs) from San Cristóbal. I would
soon find that the gatherings were saturated with volatile tensions, the result of the suspension of peace talks with the federal government and the
constant rumors of possible military incursions. The sound of helicopters
and light aircraft morning, noon, and night fractured the silence.

This military surveillance, along with the political impasse with the
Ernesto Zedillo administration (1994–2000), increased the urgency of
generating alternative social proposals in Zapatista territory. For this
reason, the indigenous autonomous municipalities were formalized that
year. The international *encuentro* served as the presentation of this political project to global social-justice movements, with the collective construction of the *aguascalientes* buildings, symbols of future projects, and
the community assemblies, meetings, and workshops as the first fruits
of their struggle. However, the seeds of the project had been planted two
years earlier.

Zapatista Municipalities as Rebellion and Indigenous-Rights Claims

In light of Mexican Army incursions into EZLN territory, Subcomandante Insurgente Marcos announced in a December 19, 1994, communiqué the existence of thirty rebel municipalities, including Diecisiete de Noviembre, as part of a political and military strategy to achieve geographic control of their territory:

> Troops from the Zapatista National Liberation Army (EZLN), 75th and 25th Infantry Divisions, broke the [Mexican] military circle . . . and with support from the civilian population, took up position in the following [official] municipalities of the state of Chiapas: Chanal, Oxchuc, Huixtán, Comitán de Domínguez, Altamirano, Ocosingo. . . . The civilian populations of these municipalities set about designating new authorities and declaring new municipalities and rebel territories in this zone. (EZLN 1994b)

Little more than a year later, at the San Andrés peace talks with the federal government, the EZLN added the terms "autonomous" and "indigenous" to "rebel territories." After the signing of the San Andrés Accords, on indigenous rights and culture, on February 16, 1996, the autonomous municipalities began to implement their stipulations, independently of whether the accords would actually lead to substantive constitutional reforms and concrete public policies (see Hernández Navarro and Vera 1998). Two strategies intermingled from the outset: the rebel strategy of maintaining political-military territorial control and the civilian strategy of putting in place processes aimed at generating organized democratic practices.[2] Over the following two decades, the two logics at times converged or came into conflict, as there is an inherent contradiction between a vertical, authoritarian military structure and one that aims to foster participatory democratic practices.[3] At the same time, the combination generates an enduring relationship between rebelliousness and autonomy: "Autonomy and resistance are part of the same struggle; one cannot exist without the other. For this reason we expect nothing of the government. . . . We do not accept their projects nor the crumbs from their table. Instead we resolve things ourselves," explained Marisa, from the community of Zapata, during a conversation with me in 2005.

Resistance here is summarized, on the one hand, by a series of actions that reject the presence of government institutions and official social programs—government-backed teachers, agricultural subsidies, housing-construction projects—and, on the other hand, by the creation of indigenous technical and administrative commissions that design and execute alternative social projects. Both aspects manifest themselves in varying forms, depending on shifts in the political juncture and on the power dynamics among the different sectors of the local population, between women and men, between generations, and between Tseltales and Tojolabales. Political conditions established by state and federal governments, the relationship to indigenous peasant organizations, and economic factors further influence local dynamics. In this sense, the Zapatista autonomous municipalities are located in a highly politicized terrain where unequal and contradictory processes continually operate.

At the same time, each Zapatista region exercises its cultural practices differently, rendering it impossible to make generalizations. For example, while the highland region lacked significant amounts of land to redistribute during the armed uprising, in the valleys of the official municipalities of Ocosingo, Altamirano, and Las Margaritas the very basis for what is understood as autonomy has been, precisely, the redistribution of the lands that were previously managed largely by *mestizo* estate owners. In fact, as I will discuss in detail in chapter 4, the origin of the autonomous municipality of Diecisiete de Noviembre lies in the Zapatista agrarian reform.

In the first days of January 1994, estate owners who still owned large tracts of land in the valley of the Tzaconejá River were forced to abandon their ranches. Most were far from their properties at that moment, celebrating the new year with their families. Such was the case of Constantino Kanter, whose estates would subsequently be divided into four Zapatista communities. In an interview Kanter confessed that he had never anticipated the scale of the movement that had been brewing until it erupted on January 1, nor did he imagine the political actions his former workers were capable of carrying forth (Avendaño 2005). After taking over his and other estate owners' lands, the support bases left fallow the "recovered" fields until the beginning of 1996, when, after the first round of the San Andrés peace negotiations, they along with other families established new Zapatista settlements. The invitation was extended, with varying results, to non-Zapatista organizations and individuals from the region, regardless of whether they were indigenous or *mestizo*, under the condition that they accept the Zapatista organizational makeup and activities.

That spring, whole families packed up their belongings to descend into the valley and build their houses on the fertile land on both sides of the

Tzaconejá River. In an interview, Graciela, from Siete de Enero, described how the women had to improvise temporary housing using materials such as tarpaulins and set up the kitchen as a simple campfire:

> In the first months we had nothing but a pot and a saucepan. One day it rained so hard it almost swept us into the river! Everything and everyone got stuck in the mud. . . . I was happy in my heart because it is very good land, but we were very afraid. It wasn't all to my liking. We thought the soldiers would come.

The land under Zapatista control is communally controlled, although the support bases lack any official titles. Besides subsistence-based agriculture, the community members organized into work groups to collectively cultivate maize, beans, and coffee, as well as to care for livestock. The earnings are shared among the families and used as communal funds to respond to community needs and to finance political mobilizations, such as marches to San Cristóbal and even to Mexico City. This material base acts as the foundation of autonomy, which cannot simply be reduced to a question of land redistribution; rather, it is part of the demonstration of territorial control through the implementation of mechanisms of self-government. In this convergence the logics of the armed uprising intermingle with the demands for the right to autonomy for indigenous peoples. At the same time, negotiations with the federal government spurred the reinterpretation of local experiences by Zapatista support bases so as to inject particular meanings into the term "autonomy." As Teodoro explained during an interview in the community Siete de Enero,

> At first, we didn't have a very good idea of what "autonomy" meant, it was an unusual word. But we soon realized that although we had new land, it wasn't enough. We had to figure out how we were going to work the land, how to coordinate activities on the land, how to take collective decisions. That's when we realized that what we were doing was autonomy.

The Tzotz Choj Region

From the outset, the municipality of Diecisiete de Noviembre was conceived as part of a larger Zapatista territory, named Tzotz Choj, that covers an extensive area that would later form part of Caracol IV, including parts of the official municipalities of Altamirano, Ocosingo, Chanal, Oxchuc, Huixtán, and Comitán.[4] Initially, the Zapatista Tzotz Choj authorities proposed that its autonomous municipalities would work in conjunction with members of the "local autonomous parliaments" of each community.[5] The "locals," in turn, formed part of the community representation at the level of the municipality, known as "regional parliaments," who met to coordinate administrative tasks, identify communities' socioeconomic needs, and ensure the implementation of the different autonomous projects. The initial organizational makeup would later become the basis for the future autonomous governing bodies, including the autonomous councils and later the *juntas de buen gobierno*.

In 1996 the assembly of community and municipal representatives in the Tzotz Choj region created autonomous commissions as political administrative units overseeing the implementation of the various spheres of autonomy at both the municipal and (at the time) Tzotz Choj regional levels. These included the following commissions: land and territory, works and services, agricultural production, honor and justice, appropriate technology, education, and health. For a brief period of time, there existed two other commissions, the women's commission and the commission of the elders; the former promoted women's participation in the autonomous project, while the latter grouped together elders who played the role of moral authorities during conflict resolutions and decision making over delicate affairs. The administrative commissions implement social and economic programs that operate parallel to the official government institutions, which continue to operate in non-Zapatista communities and households in the same region. Over time, priorities in the Tzotz Choj region more generally, and Diecisiete de Noviembre specifically, expanded and changed. For example, the women's commission and the commission of elders existed only from 1997 to 1998, after which time the former was dissolved when Zapatista authorities decided to focus on women's participation throughout all the commissions rather than concentrate their political activities in a single commission.

The resulting decrease in political participation by elders and women meant that between 1999 and 2003, the administrative responsibilities and project implementation were carried out above all by groups of Tseltal men between twenty and forty years of age.[6] The participation of the elders was limited to presiding at community affairs, such as ceremonial events in the municipality or community, and at youth gatherings. Over the same period, the women's leadership in the municipality converged in the collectives producing crops, bread, and handicrafts and in the workshops on medicinal plants and education. The previously mentioned factors—the relation between the political-military structure and the civil government, the reduced involvement by women in leadership and political roles, the tensions that sometimes surfaced between Tseltales and Tojolabales, and the changing role of the elders—all figure in the power dynamics and frictions that arose in the first decade of the autonomous municipality.

At the same time, shifting political factions in the official municipality also impacted the development of the autonomous municipality. During the first years of autonomy, dynamics between Diecisiete de Noviembre and the official municipal government of Altamirano were marked by the election of Rogelio Sántiz Méndez as municipal president. Sántiz was a Tseltal man from the *ejido* Venustiano Carranza who officially belonged to the left-of-center Party of the Democratic Revolution but sympathized with "the organization," a term colloquially used to refer to the EZLN. During Sántiz's term in office (1996–1998), the municipal government channeled resources to and provided logistical support for the autonomous municipality (Van der Haar 2004). This is the sole instance of coordination on this scale in the autonomous areas, brief as it was, although at a much lower scale, communication (but not coordination) exists, as I describe in chapter 6. Such points of political convergence quickly changed, however, during the following municipal and state elections, in 1998. The electoral period coincided with the indefinite suspension of the peace talks between the EZLN and the federal government. The elected governor, Roberto Albores Guillén, of the Institutional Revolutionary Party, began his administration by implementing a series of repressive measures, including promoting the creation of paramilitary groups, especially in the Los Altos region and in the north of the state (CDHFBC 1998b).

Repression by the Security Forces

The year 1998 is engraved in the local memory of Chiapas due to its high tally of violent incidents of state repression. The government-trained paramilitary group Mascara Roja (Red Mask) brutally assassinated forty-five Tsotsiles from the organization las Abejas (the Bees), mostly women and children, in the community of Acteal three days before Christmas 1997.[7] Acteal was the first in a series of repressive actions against the Zapatista movement in the highlands and the Lacandon Jungle valleys of the state the following year. In a context of impunity, fear, and collective trauma, members of the armed forces entered Zapatista indigenous communities across the region. In the first three months of 1998, over one hundred military incursions were recorded in the same number of Zapatista communities (Ramírez Cuevas 1998). In only two days, between January 3 and January 5, police and soldiers attempted to enter the communities of Morelia, Diez de Abril, La Florida, Nueva Esperanza, San Miguel Chiptic, and San Pedro Guerrero in the municipality of Diecisiete de Noviembre. Members of the armed forces and police repeated their operations in the Ocosingo valley and in the highlands.

These dates are engraved in the popular imagination thanks to a photograph, taken by Pedro Valtierra in the displaced persons' camp at X'oyep, of a Tsotsil woman shoving a soldier with all her strength. The expression on the face of the armed man is one of incredulity. Similar actions by women confronting the armed forces were repeated throughout Zapatista territory. Tseltal, Tsotsil, and Tojolabal women, often accompanied by their children, blocked access to their communities with their own bodies, a few piles of stones, and some sticks. In Diecisiete de Noviembre more than a hundred women blocked the road into the *ejido* Morelia, throwing stones at an equally large group of soldiers.[8] Amalia, a forty-year-old woman who lives in Morelia, recalled how the women joined forces to defend the village:

> We got organized, though we had nothing but sticks. We weren't afraid because we were really angry. . . . We organized ourselves well. There was nothing to be afraid of. The bell rang, and out we went, running. We waited all night for two or three days. If it hadn't been for us, the soldiers would be here. We didn't even have time to do the laundry.

The violent actions of the army in 1998 took the conflict between the Zapatistas and the Mexican state to a level of tension not seen since the armed uprising in 1994. Until June of 1998, the police and the armed forces systematically invaded dozens of communities with the aim of dismantling the autonomous communities and sowing fear among the population. Governor Roberto Albores Guillén labeled the autonomous municipalities a threat to the consolidation of local state power (Leyva and Burguete 2007). State violence caused the deaths of at least eight Zapatista support bases, the detention of hundreds of individuals accused of usurping authority due to their participation in the autonomous government, the destruction of hundreds of homes, and the expulsion of 120 international human rights observers (CDHFBC 1998a, 5).

Instead of simply reacting to state tactics, the EZLN focused on expanding its support networks and setting up dialogue with diverse social actors. At the time, the federal government promoted constitutional reforms on indigenous rights and culture in line with the various initiatives put forward by the National Action Party and the Institutional Revolutionary Party rather than focusing on the bill, based on the content of the San Andrés Accords, proposed by the Commission for Peace and Reconciliation (Cocopa). The bill was the sole initiative approved by the EZLN and by the majority of indigenous organizations across the country. In this context, the rebel army exerted pressure on the Zedillo administration by convoking a national referendum. Almost 5,000 Zapatista support bases traveled to most of the country's 2,500 municipalities to converse with interested people on the significance of constitutional reforms on indigenous rights and culture. Almost 30,000 individuals organized 20,000 ballot boxes that received nearly three million votes—a figure slightly higher than the number who voted on a government Banking Fund for the Protection of Savings (Fobaproa) initiative in 1995. It was one of the few countrywide plebiscites held during the 1990s and the first decade of the 2000s.[9]

In 2001, the Zapatistas organized a national march as a final attempt to persuade the federal government to approve the Cocopa bill. The March the Color of the Earth toured the country with Subcomandante Insurgente Marcos and the EZLN *comandantes* at its head until reaching the Zócalo, the central plaza in Mexico City, which was packed with sympathizers (CIZ 2001). A few weeks later, EZLN commanders wearing ski masks walked onto the podium of the National Congress. Of the half dozen speeches made by the Zapatista commanders and by members of the National Indigenous Congress, the most notable was the much-quoted speech by Comandante Esther:

This is why we want the law on Indigenous Rights and Culture to be approved. It is of the greatest importance for us, the indigenous women of Mexico. It will enable us to be recognized and respected as the women and indigenous people that we are. By this we mean that we want our ways of dressing, speaking, governing, organizing, praying, and healing to be recognized, together with our manner of working in collectives, of respecting the earth and understanding life, which is the nature we are all part of. This law takes into account our rights as women and means that no one can prevent us from participating or deny the dignity and integrity of our work, in equality with men. (Comandante Esther 2001, 347)

Esther's public speeches crystallized the demands of organized indigenous women in Mexico at the time (Rovira 2001). Rather than just focusing on the constitutional reforms, Esther proposed decolonization in the everyday, a radical recognition of gendered difference that simultaneously demands political and economic restructuring.

The moment of greatest political openness by the EZLN turned out to be that of the greatest deafness on the part of the members of Congress. As I watched the event on the Senate television channel, I was struck by how the congressional chamber was only half-filled, with those few senators and representatives in attendance yawning or looking bored. Their participation was limited to questions that demonstrated little knowledge of indigenous demands for recognition, such as, "Does self-determination mean that autonomy for the indigenous peoples will cause them to split the country and establish a new state?" "Do indigenous rights harm human rights?" and "Do traditional customs harm the rights of indigenous women?" (Gómez 2004, 179). At the same time, such questions were underpinned by a racist logic according to which indigenous communities are treated as "people of customs," outside of modernity and the liberal state, in contrast with the "people of reason," who are governed by laws and the rationality inherent in institutions.

A few months later, Congress unanimously approved a mutilated law that replaced the Cocopa bill. Its content fails to acknowledge the two key demands of the indigenous people of Mexico: the right to the use and enjoyment of natural resources and the rights to self-determination and autonomy. Four months after that, the Supreme Court dismissed the 331 complaints presented by indigenous municipalities against the new law. President Vicente Fox argued that Mexico was a full-fledged democracy and that the concentration of power in the hands of the executive branch was a thing of the past: for th... ...not to exercise his veto power. The decisions of all three government branches, then, essentially closed the possibility of juridically transforming indigenous people's relationship to the state. It is in this context that the autonomous municipalities in Zapatista areas acquired greater political significance, as they became the geographic spaces where indigenous rights were being exercised on the ground regardless of Mexican juridical frameworks.

Two years later, in 2003, the EZLN celebrated a decade since the uprising—not on January 1, 2004, ten years after the rebels' declaration of war, but rather on August 6 of the previous year, the date of both the 1994 National Democratic Convention and the 1973 founding of the Fuerzas

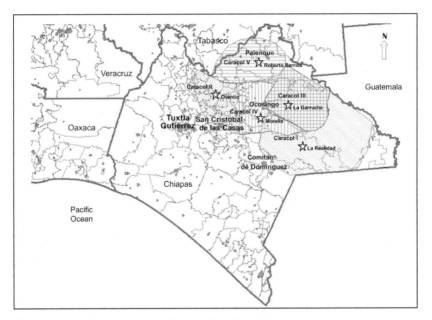

Figure 1.2. Zapatista territory in Chiapas, divided into five *caracoles*

de Liberación Nacional (National Liberation Forces), the political-military organization that gave rise to the rebel army. In Oventic the EZLN announced that the five Zapatista *aguascalientes*, regions created by the EZLN in January 1996, would be changed to *caracoles* and that five corresponding *juntas de buen gobierno* would be instituted as coordinating bodies for the multiple autonomous councils in the five Zapatista areas. In a seven-part communiqué issued just prior to the celebrations, Subcomandante Insurgente Marcos launched a severe critique of the NGOs and support groups that over the years had supported the autonomy projects (EZLN 2003). He acknowledged that a new phase for the autonomous municipalities inevitably implied a new and different relationship with "external" actors, which required moving from the paternalistic attitudes rooted in notions of charity and handouts to a focus on processes of mutual learning and multidirectional solidarity. He pointed out that the exchanges of different forms of knowledge would be an essential step to achieve this. It is in response to this challenge, in the context of a new phase of social transformation in the autonomous municipalities, that the research presented in this book unfolds.

The Production of Knowledge
on the Terrain of Autonomy

TWO

Research as a Topic of Political Debate

During our first meeting in Diecisiete de Noviembre, in 2005, Juan Miguel and Santiago, members of the municipality's autonomous council, explained that they had discussed my research proposal at the previous month's meeting of the municipal assembly, which includes representatives from the thirty-five communities in the autonomous municipality as well as autonomous council and commission members. The assembly delegated the two men the task of communicating to me the decision on whether permission was granted. Juan Miguel and Santiago, both in their late twenties, are part of a generation of Zapatista community members who were in their adolescence when the uprising took place, young adults who at the time looked to the political cadres of the region for guidance. In fact, for both of them, their *cargo*, or political responsibility, as council members was their first "important" position within the autonomous municipal structure. For that reason, during moments of my research, they were as doubtful as I was about how to proceed. On this occasion, however, Santiago carried an air of self-assurance as we spoke. We met on a Monday morning in the council office, a wooden building with three desks, a typewriter, and half a dozen folding chairs. The *bastones de mando* (literally, "staffs of authority"), which the elders handed over to the council as a symbol of their three years of service to the communities, hung on the wall behind the two men. Santiago's words determined the path along which three years of my fieldwork would go:

Three months ago, the *caracol* assembly [made up of members of the autonomous council and members of all the commissions from all seven municipalities that at the time formed Caracol IV] decided that you will be allowed
to do your research here in Diecisiete de Noviembre. During the [municipal]
assembly, we read and discussed your proposal. You will travel to twelve
communities in the municipality, some are *ejidos* and others are new settlements, just as you requested. There you will carry out the interviews you proposed. However, each community will decide how it wants to participate in
your project. That was the decision of the [municipal] assembly. You will remain in contact with us so that we can monitor your progress. When you have
visited two or three communities, you will turn in a report with copies of the
interviews so we can all analyze them. The final text will be presented to the
junta [*junta de buen gobierno*] and to all of the assembly representatives [in
the *caracol*]. That is the agreement.

Through his words, I quickly understood that my objectives for this
research would undergo substantial changes and that the process would
be partially defined by those on whose participation it depended. In con-
firming my acceptance of the decision, I replied that because of my political commitments, I wanted this to be a collaborative endeavor and therefore understood that the proposed modifications to the project formed a
necessary part of the interactions. The meeting left me reflecting on the
fact that if the political project of Zapatista indigenous autonomy implied
transforming relationships with the state, as well as among diverse indigenous and nonindigenous social actors, then the research process itself
would necessarily have to become one of my objects of analysis.

In July 2003, Subcomandante Marcos published a series of communiqués entitled "Chiapas: La treceava estela" (Chiapas: The thirteenth
wake) (EZLN 2003) that announced the formal closure of the five *aguascalientes*—Aguascalientes I, centered in La Realidad; II, in Oventic; III, in
La Garrucha; IV, in Morelia; and V, in Roberto Barrios—and their transformation into *caracoles*, along with the creation of five *juntas de buen gobierno*. He argued that, among other reasons, the *aguascalientes* had begun
to symbolize a dynamic of "handouts and pity" rather than respect toward
the communities, as had originally been the Zapatistas' intention in creating them:

In the Aguascalientes broken computers pile up alongside out-of-date medi-
cines and extravagant clothes that are useless, even for theater productions.

... Not only this, but there is a more sophisticated form of charity, consisting broadly speaking of others deciding what the communities need and imposing not only predetermined projects, but also how and when these should be implemented. (EZLN 2003)

By changing the term from *aguascalientes* to *caracol*, as part of the reorganization of political activities within the Zapatista regions, the EZLN and its civilian support bases sought to radically transform relationships with NGOs, social organizations, and all other political actors external to the communities, including academics.

In this new phase of autonomy, Marcos's communiqué explicitly stated that Zapatista members would welcome research as long as it was put to the service of the people and "provided benefits to the communities" (EZLN 2003). That is, the EZLN political-military leadership established an expectation that research projects should be part of subversive counter-hegemonic endeavors seeking to reverse the production of knowledge and practices that keep indigenous peoples in subservient positions. This decision reflected in essence a challenge: how to conceptualize research under parameters that, in contrast to the legacy of positivism and the myth of a universal neutrality, determine new, socially committed and ethical concerns. Such a question in no way entails abandoning critical introspection. In fact, the creation of the *caracoles* and the explanation presented in the above-mentioned communiqué imply processes of explicit critical and constructive collective reflection. How to maintain political commitments while maintaining a sharp gaze nevertheless proved a challenge throughout my fieldwork. With this declaration, the EZLN made it evident that a fundamental aspect of their autonomous project exists at the level of knowledge production. If autonomy attempts to transform social relations between indigenous people and the state, as well as between indigenous Afro-Mexican people and *mestizos*, and if an inherent relationship exists between knowledge and power, then research itself becomes a disputed arena of possible social transformation and political critique.

In this chapter, I situate the fieldwork I conducted in Diecisiete de Noviembre as an object of analysis and reflect critically on the epistemological frameworks that guided the endeavor. Throughout the development and application of this study, my main reference points were feminist methodological proposals designed by self-declared Third World women of color in the United States, notably Chandra Mohanty, Julia Sudbury, and Kamala Visweswaran, alongside Latin American participatory action research methods, particularly by the Chiapas researchers Andrés Aubry, Jan Rus, Mercedes Olivera Bustamante, and Aída Hernández Castillo. From the genealogy of participatory action research, I borrowed the principles that situate research as part of the dialectics of action and reflection directed toward transforming relations of social inequality (Fals Borda 1986). To this legacy I added the contributions of a sector of feminist scholars that emphasize that research itself embodies micro-power relations reflected and encapsulated within the broader processes we claim to transform; thus the research process becomes an intrinsic component of social-justice praxis (Naples 2003).

This chapter illustrates how both bodies of knowledge situate academic research as a dialogue immersed in unequal relationships of power, alliances, and resistances. I argue that what I refer to as a decolonizing feminist framework revealed the ways the Zapatista support bases—both at the community and at the municipal level—subjected my fieldwork to the same processes of autonomy and transformed it into a topic of political debate. As a result of such discussions, those men and women who participated in the research offered a series of political critiques, while at the same time they offered a series of methods for collective knowledge production that trace an alternative roadmap for potential decolonizing research methodologies.

A (De)colonizing Gaze from the Southeast

> THE POWERFUL ARE ALWAYS LESS CURIOUS THAN THE POWERLESS BECAUSE THEY THINK THEY HAVE ALL THE ANSWERS. *AND THEY DO.* BUT NOT TO THE QUESTIONS THAT THE POWERLESS ARE ASKING.
>
> CORINNE KUMAR, "SOUTH WIND: TOWARDS A NEW POLITICAL IMAGINARY"

The arguments of this chapter emerge from the tensions and contradictions arising throughout the fieldwork process and suggest paths required to continue to push forward new proposals for socially committed research. When I use the phrase "socially committed research," I refer to a range of methodological proposals linked to epistemological frameworks, including investigations that render explicit the political standpoints of those engaged in the research rather than keeping them concealed behind a supposedly objective neutrality (Baronnet, Mora, and Stahler-Sholk 2011). Similarly, the term encapsulates the development of collaborative methods that scholars have referred to as "co-labor projects"—based on the word "collaborative"—in reference to the skills and interests of the researchers and "research subjects" who enter into a series of dialogues over the course of the study (Leyva, Speed, and Burguete Cal y Mayor 2008, 66).

In this chapter, I place the methods of participatory action research—which first emerged in the 1970s, inspired by the ideas on pedagogy of Paulo Freire (Fals Borda 1986)—together with feminist methodologies. At the same time, I situate my own research in relation to recent decolonizing research proposals aimed at reversing the effects and legacies of colonial power-knowledge and the ethnic, racial, and gender hierarchies it gave rise to in the production and circulation of subaltern knowledge (Hale 2006a; Rivera Cusicanqui 2010; Cumes 2009; Lemus Jiménez 2013; López Intzín 2013). My work reprises aspects of these different trajectories as part of broader decolonial struggles. Drawing from the genealogies of committed research, I ask, in what ways can academic research render visible subaltern practices and knowledge without reproducing neocolonial relations?

Though researchers, academics, and NGO workers reflect on similar questions, in this case I draw our attention to the critiques through which Tseltal, Tojolabal, Tsotsil, and Ch'ol indigenous communities in Chiapas decide on the implementation of academic research in their regions and the conditions they set for it if it is approved. Debates on autonomy and self-determination, both as part of Zapatismo and prior to the uprising, have had a concrete impact on whether and how members of indigenous communities accept research in their villages. In setting the conditions for research, they have forced scientists to reconsider their methods and to critically reflect upon the ethical and political implications of their studies. Perhaps the most notorious example in Chiapas is that of the International Cooperative Biodiversity Group. In 2001, an organization of traditional healers and midwives accused researchers from the Colegio de la Frontera Sur, from the University of Georgia, and from the biotechnology company Molecular Nature Limited, based in Wales, of having extracted, recorded, and systematized medical knowledge for profit without the consent of the local population (Alarcón Lavín 2010). The subsequent legal proceedings led to the development of guidelines drawn up by traditional-medicine organizations. As a result, follow-up research of the project was canceled. Cases such as this make scientific research in Chiapas a key subject of political debate in indigenous and peasant organizations, including Zapatista communities (Chiapas-based anthropologist Ronald Nigh, interview by author, August 2006).

These types of discussions have brought about innovative proposals to approach aspects of the scientific method from alternative perspectives and knowledge bases. For example, the phase of the Zapatista movement that began in 2005 known as la Otra Campaña (the Other Campaign) centered part of its attention on the construction of alternative forms of knowledge and other ways of doing research/being social scientists. Adopting the argument of the sociologist Boaventura de Sousa Santos that global justice cannot exist without cognitive justice (Santos 2009a), the Zapatistas invited groups of intellectuals to participate in political gatherings and discussions, such as those held in Guadalajara in March 2006, in the Zapatista *caracol* center of Oventic in January 2007, and at the colloquiums held every year at the Centro Indígena de Capacitación Integral (Indigenous Center for Integrated Training) in San Cristóbal de las Casas, with the aim of debating the ways in which the social struggle of subjugated groups is linked to other forms of understanding and acting in the world. Similarly, debates across political and academic platforms in Chiapas question the historical role of social science research in Mexico, particularly by the discipline of anthropology. Indeed, perhaps no state has been studied as much by anthropologists as Chiapas. I pause briefly to describe the discipline's legacy so as to contextualize current debates.

The discipline arrived to the southeast of Mexico with the nation-state project at the beginning of the twentieth century fueled by the ideologies of modernism and *mestizaje*. Anthropologists' main task at the time was to compile and categorize information on communities that represented the opposite pole: indigenous peoples. During the 1940s, government representatives, such as Gónzalo Aguirre Beltrán, decided that anthropological knowledge could be placed at the service and interests of the Mexican state. Thus was born the field of applied anthropology, in which the state was the primary promoter of social transformation, while anthropological knowledge played a key role in the design of assimilationist and integrationist policies. The critical anthropologist Mercedes Olivera Bustamante described the arrival of the discipline to the region in the following manner: "To Chiapas arrived the anthropology of change and as the promoter of change. The discipline was born with the sin of racism and discrimination, clothed in nationalism" (interview by author, January 2007).

Knowledge developed by US anthropologists who conducted research in Chiapas at the end of the 1930s and during the 1940s originally fueled the anthropology of the Instituto Nacional Indigenista (INI, National Indigenist Institute). Anthropologists from Harvard University and the University of Chicago, such as Evon Vogt and Sol Tax, developed studies of closed corporate communities as part of their investigations on the Chiapas highlands (Vogt 1973; Tax 1947), which represented indigenous peoples as survivors of a pre-Columbian past, as people suspended in time and space, separated from national political economic relations and from *mestizo* culture. This type of research served to apply technical solutions to national problems: the "problem," in essence, was the continued presence of indigenous peoples and what was seen as their backwardness; the "solution" became to "modernize the indigenous population by modernizing their cultures" (Rus 1977, 3).

During the 1960s, Aguirre Beltrán coined the term "regions of refuge" to describe social relations in the "backward regions," where the majority of indigenous communities are located. However, the logic of applied anthropology failed to undergo substantial changes, and methods continued to operate in line with the interests of state policies through the INI's Tseltal-Tsotsil Coordinating Center, founded in 1951 in San Cristóbal under the direction of Aguirre Beltrán himself. The objective of the center was to reduce inequalities in indigenous communities by introducing capitalist relations so as to fragment their supposed isolation and their feudalistic socioeconomic models. Thus, applied anthropology continued to function as a form of social engineering at the service of government institutions, heavily influenced by the ideology of development originating in the United States, which promulgates the concept that the social "disorder" of poor countries results from the gap between the delayed "modernization" of traditional cultural patterns and the development of social and political institutions (Escobar 2007).

During the late 1960s, Mexican critical anthropology emerged in response to the indigenist policies of Aguirre Beltrán and the functionalism of US anthropology. In Chiapas, its presence coincided with efforts to reject new plans for economic integration promoted by presidents Luis Echeverría (1970–1976) and José López Portillo (1976–1982) as well as an increase in state repression against students and political dissidents (Hernández Castillo 2002). At the time, anthropologist Jan Rus published a document whose arguments signal the following fundamental paradox in the INI model: "If the Chiapas Highlands is one of the most studied regions in Mexico, with anthropological data utilized by the INI to develop and implement its policies, then why have these policies failed, and why is the indigenous population, rather than seeing improvements in their standard of living, suffering greater and greater conditions of social exclusion?" (Rus 1977, 3).

A series of independent initiatives supported by the Catholic Church under Bishop Samuel Ruiz García emerged in the 1970s with the objective of creating new social alternatives, including the Instituto de Asesoría Antropológica para la Región Maya (INAREMAC, Anthropological Advisory Institute for the Mayan Region), created in 1974.[1] Andrés Aubry, who founded INAREMAC, and Jan Rus, who worked with Aubry in the institute, both argued that the concepts "closed corporate community" and "regions of refuge" prevented a critical analysis of the structural relations that generate social inequality (see Aubry 1984, 1985; Rus 1977). With methods inspired by Paulo Freire's theories of historical materialism and popular education, the work of INAREMAC offered alternatives to the INI model. INAREMAC used the principles of participatory action research to raise local awareness and fuse local and academic knowledge through the implementation of literacy workshops and the systematization of agricultural and traditional community medicinal knowledge (Aubry 1985). Throughout its history, INAREMAC played an important role in dismantling classical anthropological studies of the "closed corporate community" and demonstrated how political-economic forces, rather than external to indigenous cultural practices, are ingrained in the production of what is deemed indigenous culture.

In the 1980s and 1990s, feminist anthropologists such as Mercedes Olivera Bustamante and Aída Hernández Castillo participated in diverse action-research projects aimed at empowering marginalized women in situations of oppression in Chiapas. Drawing on a Marxist legacy, in which the role of the intellectual consisted of raising the consciousness of oppressed women, both anthropologists developed action-research projects with Guatemalan refugees and economically disenfranchised women in San Cristóbal. Subsequent critical reflections by both scholars suggest that their projects reproduced a Eurocentric Marxist perspective in which a gender analysis emerges from a Western vantage point, one that is largely incapable of effectively addressing cultural differences (Hernández Castillo 2006). Olivera highlights an example of the type of action research organized by the Centro de Información y Análisis para la Mujer Centroaméricana (Information and Analysis Center for the Central American Woman) with Guatemalan refugees designed to "raise consciousness" and develop their leadership capacities. In the 1980s, when female participants assumed leadership roles, they questioned both the paternalistic attitudes and the feminist perspectives of the researchers. As Olivera states, "There were very violent confrontations that affected us at a personal level and forced us to reflect on our internalized Eurocentrism and racism. These experiences forced us to transform our feminist political agenda and rethink how collaborative research is developed" (interview by author, August 2006).

The aim of this brief historical overview is to emphasize that in Chiapas, beginning in the 1970s, groups of social scientists situated their anthropological research alongside broader actions for social change, through methods based on dialogical encounters with diverse subaltern actors, no longer through state institutions, as had been the case of those anthropologists associated with the INI. In the case of INAREMAC, its researchers defined such dialogues as being between "popular knowledge and institutionalized academic knowledge" (Aubry 1984, 2). Subsequently, in specifically feminist spaces in San Cristóbal and with Guatemalan refugees, researchers have defined their endeavors as dialogues between women who understand patriarchal domination and women who have yet to name and label their experiences of oppression (Hernández Castillo 2006).

Research Proposed as a Dialogue Immersed in Frictions and Transformations

The research that underpins the reflections set out in this chapter was situated within the contributions, efforts, challenges, and critical reflections detailed above. To such a legacy, I add what I refer to as decolonizing feminist research, that is, a committed research produced through its tensions and contradictions, and through recognition that the production of knowledge shifts how all participating actors understand themselves within broader racialized fields of power, as a necessary precursor to the unsettling of (neo)colonial ties. Under this lens, research acts as a dialogue incorporating solidarity and critical self-reflection through a politics of commitment (Mohanty 2003) to transform the concept of "fieldwork" to that of "homework." Rather than understanding the field as a place "out there" where one travels to for temporary periods of time, the notion of "homework" establishes social and political relations in such a way that researchers do not extract information to then process it in another location but rather maintain commitments with actors and their social movements and therefore experience the consequences of their actions (Gordon 1991).

My framework draws on three fundamental tools emerging from diverse currents of Third World and decolonial feminist thought. First, there is the understanding that research is a dialogue between unstable and changing fields of power that continually question yet reproduce unequal relations (Behar 1993; Géliga Vargas and Canabal 2013; Hernández Castillo 2015). In this case, the term "dialogue" is not to be confused with a search for universal reference points, but rather seeks to work from within the tensions and particularities that emerge. A common political project is constructed by emphasizing the universal on the basis of the particular.[2] Second, there is the invitation to incorporate critical self-reflection as a necessary part of any research project, without reproducing a colonial gaze, through which listening to, translating, and narrating the story of a woman labeled as socially inferior serves to maintain social hierarchies (Eber 2012; Hurtado 1996; Sieder 2017). Third, constant reflection on one's position allows one to identify moments of identification and "disidentification" (Visweswaran 1994). In every interview there exist moments when one identifies or fails to identify with the other person, where one individual either sees his or herself reflected in shared experiences or responds to these as alien processes. All research in this sense contains both moments of conflict and moments of mutual understanding that reflect the articulation of different expressions of power. Engaging with these contradictions and tensions enables us to understand how the constant interactions between research subjects and researchers continually question, confront, reproduce, and potentially transform power relations implicit in fieldwork (Hale 2008). Rather than erasing differences in the space of an interview or in an ethnographic encounter, decolonizing feminist research attempts to work on the basis of the contradictions in order to transform divisive borders and thus confront the microdynamics of power, which reflect broader structural problems of social inequality.

Here lies a fundamental difference between decolonizing feminist research proposals and the vein of anthropological thought referred to as "cultural critique." When, at the end of the 1970s, the discipline of anthropology, primarily in the United States, entered into a crisis of representation, various theoretical currents began to question representations of "the other" and signaled ways in which the history of the discipline reproduced colonial epistemologies. Anthropologists were forced to seriously analyze their methods of conducting activities within the discipline (Asad 1973; Denzin 2002). Two important currents emerged from this crisis. There emerged, on the one hand, as Shannon Speed (2008) notes, a focus on textual deconstruction and cultural critique, and on the other, the development of collaborative proposals. This latter current pursues an activist anthropology (Hale 2008) that has its roots in the anthropology of liberation. In this vein, anthropologists propose to accept responsibility for the impact of their research and to decolonize the relationships between researchers and their "subjects of study" (Gordon 1991; Tuhiwai Smith 1999).

My research is framed by the second of these options, given that an activist proposal highlights that the production of knowledge emerges through concrete actions. For that reason, the effects of an investigation cannot be reduced to a textual level, or to a single outcome, such as a book or an article. The research itself becomes an object of analysis, not only in the preparation of the questions posed but in the mutual exchanges generated throughout the entire process; the potential for reconfiguring social relations resides in the spaces where research decisions are made and their stipulations enacted: in the discussions in the community assembly, during an exchange or a subtle (or not-so-subtle) criticism expressed in the course of an interview, and in responses to a fieldwork progress report submitted to local authorities.

As an integral aspect of this research, the women and men who form the support bases of the autonomous Zapatista municipality Diecisiete de Noviembre contributed their own analysis and critique of knowledge production, both of which point to the possibility of engendering new decolonizing grammars. In the following sections, I detail three key elements. The first highlights the ways in which the knowledge produced through research forms part of political debates in the community assemblies and other spaces of decision making within the autonomous municipality. The second and third highlight the main critiques that surfaced during these debates. During the group interviews, participants critiqued the division of labor existing between oral and written essays; and as part of the evaluation and analysis of the interviews conducted, autonomous council members questioned dominant representations of indigenous political actors. I now direct my attention to the first of these.

Democratizing Knowledge Production

The first town named by the municipal assembly to participate in my field-work was Siete de Enero, one of the thirty new population centers founded in 1996 on land appropriated by the EZLN after the January 1, 1994, up-rising. The more than forty families who populated the village were for the most part young couples whose parents had participated actively in peasant organizations such as the Asociación Rural de Interés Colectivo (Rural Association of Collective Interest) and later as support bases or in the ranks of the EZLN.

"They rang the bell. Let's go, the assembly is about to start," said Gra-ciela, a representative of the autonomous government. She briefly grabbed my hand to lead me out of the house and show me the path that wove around the soccer field marking the center of the village, ending at the rustic wood-plank building where the meeting was to be held. A mural adorned the walls with images of those whom the inhabitants of Dieci-siete de Noviembre refer to as the three martyrs, three elders brutally tortured and murdered by the Mexican Army on January 7, 1994, whose memory is constantly evoked when people say the name of the town.

The community members slowly trickled into the building. First the women entered and sat on the wooden planks of the first row, next to the small cement stage. The men remained standing outside, talking in small groups of three or four. Some simply leaned against the wall to rest for a few moments before initiating yet another activity in their already busy day. Only when the meeting began did they head toward the rear or sides of the room.

While waiting for the community assembly to begin, I asked Juan Miguel, of the autonomous council, whether he had already explained to those present why I was there. He responded curtly that I needed to ex-plain everything myself and then retreated to his seat, thus playing the role of the observer. I quickly learned that as he had been responsible for presenting my proposal to the municipal assembly, his political jurisdic-tion did not extend to this community space. To intervene in this proceed-ing would have been considered disrespectful.

The assembly started. A man stood up to announce my presence and then indicated that it was my turn to speak. I explained the reasons why I wanted to conduct research in Diecisiete de Noviembre and detailed the process that had brought me to Siete de Enero. I had originally presented a proposal to the council to study the practices of autonomy under neoliberalism, and now I was visiting all the communities chosen to form part of the study. I presented my plan to conduct interviews about the last century of regional history and to gather residents' reflections on the current political project. My explanation ended with a question: How would you like this study to be carried out here?

The response came in the form of a long discussion in Tseltal, which excluded me since I do not speak the language and only partially understand conversations. The women grouped together on one side of the building, the men on the other, as I remained in silence. Questions later surfaced through a translation in Spanish, and someone took advantage of the opportunity to scold me for my lack of Tseltal. The translator relayed the questions to me: "Who are we going to pick [to participate in the interviews]? What will the format of the interviews be? Will video cameras be used? What purpose will the study serve? Will it be for internal or external information, or for both? And what if we don't remember something?" Without waiting for my response, others answered certain questions and made additional comments: "It is a good idea to relate our history among ourselves. That way we can teach each other. It will be a good thing for the children to hear the stories. We have lived through many things."

After a discussion lasting two hours, the assembly finally decided to conduct gender-separate group interviews with the participation of individuals who had undergone different experiences in the region and could share diverse reflections on the process of autonomy for an external audience. Video cameras and other recording equipment were not to be used, for security purposes. Then a woman stated, "The autonomous council representatives gave us copies of the questions, but we want you to make more, for everyone. We want to study them before you return. By next Tuesday we will start work."

And so we began.

The active participation on the part of the support bases in Diecisiete de Noviembre transformed my research into a political debate about knowledge production on the disputed terrain of autonomy. To my original proposal that the fieldwork contribute to understanding the ways in which the political practices of autonomy interact with certain neoliberal logics, participants added their own questions and concerns, including the ones expressed in Siete de Enero. They placed emphasis on the importance of the social circulation of local history, particularly lived experiences on the estates, as a basis for critical reflections on the current political moment. In fact, the sharing of social memories became a primary tool that the participating Zapatista members used to subvert dominant representations of their social struggle and the role that different actors have played in these constructions. At the same time, those interviewed decentered my role as the compiler of information, as I will detail in the following sections.

I presented the proposal to do fieldwork in Caracol IV in 2004, a little more than a year after the founding of the *juntas de buen gobierno*. At the time, the autonomous council was still defining how to exercise its functions and had yet to clearly decide how to proceed and evaluate the proposals received to conduct research or interviews in the region. Autonomy was an incipient endeavor on an unclear terrain that Juan Miguel and Santiago experienced firsthand. For that reason, they generally tended to discuss issues that I raised between themselves, as well as with other community members, in order to define a plan of action. Perhaps in part because of this, the decision to accept the study took over six months. Initially, I proposed that the questions be defined collectively and that men and women from the community participate in the data collection. Autonomous authorities rejected both proposals under the argument that the fieldwork was my responsibility and thus soliciting the help of "local assistants" was unnecessary. Members of the autonomous council argued that even though I had proposed a collaborative process, the final products would be my doctoral degree and a book, and for that reason, the sole responsibility for completing the project was mine.

However, it is important to highlight that their response did not reflect a passive stance with regard to research, as if the presence of academics was tolerated as long as it helped maintain the presence of solidarity actors who could advocate on their behalf in the case of state repression. In contrast, every aspect of the research process, including the interview questions, the format, and the timeline, was discussed collectively in virtually all the participating communities. Though I was absent from the original debates in which Zapatista authorities reviewed my proposal, members of the autonomous council later explained that the *caracol* assembly initially approved the research project. They then determined that the study would be conducted in Diecisiete de Noviembre and that the municipal assembly would decide the methods to be deployed, the sites for data collection, and the mechanisms to be used to ensure that the local authorities stayed informed of my work as well as of any additional logistical matters.

In our first meeting, Juan Miguel, Santiago, and the other members

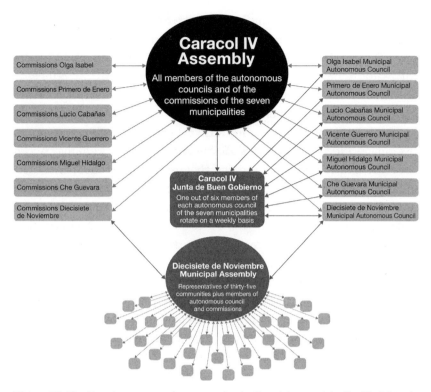

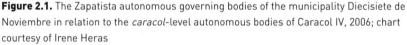

Figure 2.1. The Zapatista autonomous governing bodies of the municipality Diecisiete de Noviembre in relation to the *caracol*-level autonomous bodies of Caracol IV, 2006; chart courtesy of Irene Heras

of the autonomous council explained that each of the communities had received copies of the interview questions, as was later confirmed by the women of Siete de Enero during the community assembly described above. I divided the questions into three main themes: the history of the region since the Mexican Revolution in 1910; the activities of the peasant organizations prior to the uprising; and reflections on the Zapatista autonomy project, including the practices of the council, as well as the honor and justice, the education, and the agricultural production commissions, among others. The inhabitants of the communities, the council members explained, would analyze the questions and then define the interview format, whether individual or collective narration, mixed groups, or men and women interviewed separately. In addition, the council asked that I periodically submit progress reports and that I transcribe copies of the interviews so that they could review the material produced.

During this same meeting, the council asked about my motivations and intentions with the study. I explained what I set out in the introduction to this book, that I considered it fundamental to understand how autonomy relates to the neoliberal state as well as the political imaginaries that emerge through the daily practices of autonomy. My intention was to tease out the counternarratives and the production of counterhistories in order to situate the daily practices of Zapatista autonomy as part of broader reflections on social struggles in the present day. I then redirected the same question to the council members, asking them what they hoped to see me accomplish. They responded that for the Zapatista communities, history and its documentation played a central role, particularly with a new generation of young people in Chiapas and in Mexico born and raised after the uprising whom they were interested in involving in key political reflections. For that reason, the research made sense to them.

The conversations that I detail illustrate the ways in which this anthropological fieldwork project was subjected to the very same practices of autonomy I proposed to observe in Diecisiete de Noviembre, including discussions in the offices of the *junta*, assemblies, interviews, and evaluation meetings. It was not until 2003 that the Zapatistas opened their territory to research in an explicit, systematized, and organized manner. The members of the autonomous municipalities had previously granted journalists and academics permission for interviews as well as for specific research, but for the most part they had withheld information on what was unfolding in their regions. The rebel army was particularly mistrustful of information collected on the movement in light of an abundance of cases in different regions of the world linking academic research to counterinsurgency strategies (Price 2000). Reducing access to information became a way to exert control over knowledge produced about the movement.

In the early years, from 1996 to 2003, the autonomous municipalities unfolded largely in silence. However, by the tenth anniversary of the uprising, a shift in strategy occurred. Through its communiqués, the EZLN announced the creation of the *caracoles* and the *juntas* as part of a new phase that culminated in the Other Campaign (EZLN 2003, 2005a, 2005b). The rebel army then accepted the production of knowledge and public documents on the processes underway in Zapatista autonomous communities, but not before establishing new mechanisms of control over information, including questioning and confronting positivist and apparently neutral research methods that counteract the production of knowledge as linked to social transformation. For that reason, rather than closing off or concealing information about Zapatista autonomous political practices, actions that they believed could lead to isolation, the support bases chose to reestablish the terms through which knowledge about their struggle was generated.

Similarly, the active participation of the support bases in defining the terms for my research signaled the importance attached to the production of knowledge on autonomy, as part of the process itself. How information is gathered, what is done with it, and how it is discussed form indispensable elements of any struggle for social change. Zapatista women and men, through their questions, active interest, and the time they dedicated to reflect upon, discuss, and make decisions about this fieldwork, highlighted that knowledge forms a fundamental aspect of the power relationships they confront. The sharply directed questions that arose during the assembly in Siete de Enero provide only one example among many.

Rather than rejecting or censoring the study, the Zapatista support bases incorporated it into the very practices of autonomy and subjected it to their decision-making bodies. This active participation by the support bases underscored the importance placed on the circulation, production, and use of knowledge, hence endowing the term "democracy" with new meanings linking power to knowledge. At the same time, this permitted two fundamental critiques to emerge from the fieldwork, both of which serve to advance critical reflections on the possibilities and limits of decolonizing feminist research.

Power between the Written and the Oral

Halfway along the dirt road that extends to the end of the Tzaconejá River valley, the Zapatista support bases founded a new Tojolabal population center. Ocho de Marzo. In October ̲ ̲ ̲ ̲ ̲, I stayed in the community as stipulated in the agreement on my fieldwork.

One day before the interviews were set to start, community members met in the late afternoon, after finishing their respective tasks in the cornfields and in their homes, to prepare their responses. First the women met briefly with the men to ensure that each group had the questions jotted down in their notebooks. They then headed in two separate groups to the building they colloquially refer to as the "big house," a term used in communities to refer to the residential buildings of previous estate owners, in this case the residence of Pepe Castellanos. The building now serves as the autonomous primary school. While the men and women discussed their responses for what would later be our group interviews, I remained a respectful distance away, as I was not invited to be part of this exercise.

Groups of men and women discussed the questions from the late afternoon until after nightfall. The men opted to separate into groups according to their age and lived experience. They divided the questions by theme and decided who would offer verbal responses the following day. The women chose a different method. They formed a circle with wooden stools and had one of them read the questions to the rest of the group. The questions revolved around their experiences during specific moments of regional history, particularly when community members worked for the estate owners as indentured servants, during their subsequent participation in peasant organizations, and in other political spaces that existed prior to the EZLN's founding, as well as questions about the current daily implementation of the project of Zapatista indigenous autonomy.

Each woman shared her responses by standing in front of the rest and narrating, not only her own experiences but also the memories of her mother or grandmother. From where I observed their interactions, I could make out a particular tone of voice typically associated with the delivery of *testimonio* to a public audience. The other women, as they listened to the stories, would then interject words that I took to be adding to or correcting historical details. Sometimes the questions generated many simultaneous responses, creating confusion as to which woman gave which answer. In a corner, Dolores, a twenty-five-year-old Tojolabal woman, took notes, as she had been delegated to record the collective voices.

The next day, the women met in the church, and they again delegated Dolores the role of translator and initial spokeswoman for the now group interview. She opened the session by flipping to the pages in her notebook where the reflections from the day before were written (see fig. 3) and in a loud, self-assured voice read in Spanish,

> In our childhood we lived on an *ejido*, but our lives with our families were very sad. The great problem that we suffered in those times was illness, but also a lack of food. . . . We, as indigenous people and as women, thought that we were not worth anything, and we didn't know if we had rights. We organized against injustices as indigenous people in order to create a better life for our children.

After a brief first reading that extended only a few paragraphs more, Hilda, the women's coordinator for Ocho de Marzo, invited the partici-

Figure 2.2. Notebook with written testimony used in group interviews, Ocho de Marzo, Diecisiete de Noviembre, 2005; photo by author

pants to continue their conversation from the day before. Mixing Tojolabal with Spanish, which partially excluded my participation, she encouraged other women to speak about their lives prior to the presence of the EZLN in the region. One of the elders stood up and directed her gaze at the rest as she related,

> I was born here, where this village now stands. Here my dear father worked. When I was a child, the wife of the landowner would yell for me to come to the house and work. I had to strip the corn stocks of their grain, make tortillas, and toast coffee in the big house. Since I was my father's daughter, it was all obligatory. I didn't come home until seven o'clock at night. If the coffee turned out yellow, they would beat us with sticks. The wife of Don Pepe was very mean, that is why to this day I don't like to sit outside the big house. That life was nothing but pure suffering.

Thirty-two women participated, almost all the women in the community. Most were younger than thirty and had lived all their adult lives after the uprising. Only six or seven were over forty. Each woman also brought all her children between the ages of three and eight years to the interview, and they constantly interrupted it by running into their mothers' arms in tears or giving a spontaneous performance that made us all laugh.

The rest of what was shared resonated with what the elder had communicated. "Pain," "sadness," "suffering," "rape," "physical violence," and "fear" were the words the women used to emphasize what they or their mothers had lived on the estates. Sometimes the women interrupted each other, or conversations arose that Dolores only partially translated. When the interview fell into a silence broken only by the children's laughter, she would attempt to encourage the participation of the rest, who responded by lowering their eyes to avoid contact or by turning their faces in another direction. Finally, a twenty-year-old woman summoned the courage to speak: "I get very angry because it is so sad. It makes me furious when I hear these stories of what life was like before. It makes me want to continue struggling. I don't want the ranchers to come back or for those days to return."

Another young woman continued this thought:

> If we hadn't organized ourselves, I think we would still be indentured servants. Those that stop struggling have forgotten how the *kaxlanes* and the ranchers treated our mothers. But listening to these stories motivates me to continue working in the collectives and to participate politically, because it is to ensure that the past doesn't return.

After listening to the words of these two young women, I was interested in encouraging others to speak as well. I found myself drawing on the popular-education methods I had used in workshops years before, when I had worked in solidarity projects, to generate reflections that linked "the time of the *mozos*" with the present. I took up the comments of the few young women who had spoken in order to offer my impressions of the important role of remembering history. I explained that by listening to them I understood that people do not embark on a struggle out of nowhere, but rather they first reflect on their experiences, and those of their community, and then they decide to struggle. I offered my own political reflections so as to ask how they as women began to participate in their communities. Throughout my intervention, I must admit, I questioned the extent to which I was inserting myself into the conversation or directing the women's answers toward a specific type of response.

Despite my attempts, the interview continued with the same dynamic. A few women offered statements in Tojolabal, and these were subsequently commented upon by only a few. The discussions would be interrupted when Dolores decided to translate and I would take notes. I gave up my efforts for a dynamic discussion and opted to conclude the conversation by asking how they felt and what they thought about the interview. Finally a few women who had not uttered a single word explained their silence. As one of them said, "I apologize for not speaking, but I didn't know how the organization [the EZLN] began or what the region was like before. I was very little. I thank the *compañeras* for sharing their stories of before so that other women like me could learn."

A similar scenario unfolded in approximately half the communities where I conducted interviews. The women and men would meet to prepare their participation, a process that excluded my presence. After analyzing and responding to the questions, each group would produce a summary of their conversation to serve as a starting point for the interview and only then would the conversation unfold.[3] Initially, I thought the preparatory exercise served as a way to exert control over the narration of history, so as to create a homogeneous and consensual version of specific regional events, and undoubtedly this was one of the aims. But when I considered not the groups' intentions—something difficult to decipher—but the effects of the decisions taken by the participating women and men, this surfaced as only a minor element. What I find particularly significant are two aspects: the production of a written text in contrast to the exclusive presentation of oral testimony and the emphasis placed on lived experiences, including those sustained through silence.

The description of the interview in Ocho de Marzo reflects how the space not only was one intended for "gathering" data but was simultaneously used by the support bases to generate collective political reflections on specific critical events, with an emphasis on the time of the estates. The process of discussing the questions, of remembering lived experiences during a preparatory meeting and writing out a collective document, to be read aloud later, illustrates the emphasis placed on the collective circulation of specific memories of struggle across generations as part of an open invitation to endow them with political significance. The silence of some younger women revealed that despite their not uttering a word, they were able to use the interview space as one both to learn from the histories of other women and to appropriate such narratives for themselves. This demonstrates a decentralization of the objectives I originally presented for the research in my role as the "data collector," because the female participants, too, assumed specific roles.

Dolores and others offered their stories through the genre of *testimonio*, as the telling of a truth often negated or silenced by other actors in positions of domination. This type of intervention in the procedure was a common cultural practice throughout the interviews, particularly by women. Acknowledging that an oral *testimonio* is not only a partial interpretation of history but also a public performance makes it possible to pay particular attention to the actions through which individuals share memories and lived experiences (Stephen 2013). A significant number of the female interviewees took advantage of the barrier created by language and directed their *testimonios* not toward me but to the other participants. At the same time, the comments and reflections that personal histories evoked generated conversations that excluded me until Dolores made the decision to share what was discussed, with different degrees of partiality, by way of the translation. Both spaces of discussion, the preparatory meeting as well as the interview, filtered my participation, thus forcing me to be attentive to the process itself.

While the oral statements generated critical collective reflections that ran parallel to the aim of "data collection," the written text transmitted critiques of orthodox research methods. In a more traditional interview format, the oral narrator offers the data that will subsequently be systematized, classified, and interpreted by the researcher. The mental process culminates in a material product, such as a public document. The difference between the oral and written forms of expression is that the latter is subject to a capitalist neocolonial logic. The "primary material," that is, the spoken word, acquires surplus value from the point of extraction until it is processed through the course of transforming it into a published document that contains classified data interpreted through particular forms of legitimated analysis. The final product is situated in sharp contrast to the ephemeral value often granted to oral narratives.

When the Zapatista support bases—as in the case of the women in Ocho de Marzo—arrived at the interview with a written text, the product of a collective oral effort, and offered it as a starting point for discussion, they critiqued the unequal power relations associated with this division of labor and unsettled them. Given that in all the communities where I conducted interviews, the orally shared experiences surpassed the limited content of the written document, it would appear that the text the women read at the beginning of the sessions served to guide the initial interview conversation rather than to construct a uniform version of history. The women who spoke in Ocho de Marzo, for example, orally added a wide range of complexities and contradictions to the highly condensed written text. However, the presence of a paper document notably modified the dynamics of the interview, as it served as a physical presence of the first interpretation of their regional history. The women established the dynamic and pace of the interview, forcing me to adapt to their framework. In this sense, both phases of the interview, their preparation alongside the formal space for data collection, put into question the power relationships that mark the gendered and racialized division of labor between she who writes and she who orally offers information, between the actor who narrates and the one who records speech in a written manner, between the individual who describes and the one who interprets the depiction.

Feminist academics point to the relevance not only of recording history but of rewriting it as an action that forms part of collective political consciousness (Anzaldúa 1987; Dulfano 2015; Eber 2012; Harlow 1992) as well as of decolonial imaginaries (Pérez 1999). The physical act of writing helps to form the context through which collective identities are generated. When the everyday world becomes naturalized and the global relations of domination are not as evident, having to think about the past collectively and interpret lived experiences in order to generate a written text, regardless of its length, becomes a practice that names acts of exploitation and possible alternatives. Thus, research founded on this space of decolonizing dialogues requires anthropologists to be attentive to the implications of the division of labor described above and to design methods that question the effects of reproduced dichotomies.

Venezuelan scholar Beatriz González Stephan describes how, in nineteenth-century Latin America, the invention of the "other" was legitimized through the act of writing. Constitutions, urban etiquette manuals, and grammar books were all used to produce "appropriate" Latin American citizens, in contrast to "second-class" citizens. Writing thus became an exercise that responded to the need to organize and classify so as to implement "civilizing" mechanisms attached to "modernity." This sits in direct contrast to those mechanisms located exclusively in the realm of the oral, which were thus excluded from modern capacities (González Stephan 1995; Nahuelpan 2016). Such expressions of coloniality resurface when indigenous culture is read as exclusively within the realm of the oral tradition, a legacy partially upset by the actions of the men and women interviewed who insisted on incorporating the process of writing as part of the implementation of research methodologies. Similarly, it is important to pay attention to the ways in which the Zapatista support bases delimited the interview space, primarily through the use of silences and filtered spheres, such as the preparatory meetings to which I was not invited, as well as the use of language as a barrier between that which was rendered accessible to me and that which was delegated as an arena for parallel objectives. The actions of the women and men who participated in the interviews thus signaled the limits of a committed research exercise, given that even though the process itself may be collaborative, this text and its sentences are, ultimately, my own interpretations.

Such limitations, however, also suggest new possibilities. To recognize the actions within silences implies directing the analytical gaze not always to the "data" collected but rather to the process itself since the act of narrating aspects of a shared history in the context of an interview is immersed in complex webs of power. Rendering visible these relations and critically analyzing them is a fundamental step in developing transformative decolonizing practices. An analysis of this nature also emerged as part of the discussions undertaken with the autonomous council based on a review of the transcribed material.

The Interview as Testimony on the Knowing-Doing of History

The priorities and activities of the autonomous council constantly shifted, contingent on local political conditions, agricultural cycles, and the national political context. Though for months I attempted to discuss my progress report with the council members, more pressing concerns prevailed and my document continued to lie at the bottom of the pile until finally we met to discuss the content of my first round of interviews.

Mauricio arrived late to our fourth meeting. In contrast to the younger council members, such as Juan Miguel and Santiago, Mauricio was at that time in his late forties, a Tseltal man with a long trajectory of participation in the spaces created by the Diocese of San Cristóbal and who tended to transmit an air of wisdom as he spoke. I was finishing my third cup of coffee that morning and was feeling frustrated with the thought that the meeting would once again be postponed.

"An apology! There is much work to be done! We never finish!" Mauricio explained after he arrived as a way of apologizing on behalf of the other two men from the council who could not attend due to other priorities. "We have to divide the work. Down there [in the Tzaconejá River valley] some *priistas* want to screw us over because they want to get their hands on some of the lands we reclaimed."

We spoke briefly about the political situation of the region and the work of the autonomous government. After exhausting the introductory themes, we both took out our copies of the interviews and placed them on the table. Mauricio raised the central topic of our meeting: "We read the interviews and they are fine. You only have to make a few changes and correct several things," he said, without clarifying who read the interviews or how they had agreed upon the observations. He opened the folder to reveal pages with lines underlined in blue ink.

I was a bit nervous since I was unsure what they would think of the transcriptions. I did not know if the autonomous council would suggest changes that censored the content of the interviews or if they would want to present only one version in order to narrate a homogeneous story. I had conflicted feelings about both possibilities. On the one hand, I refused to write an official Zapatista history on the project of autonomy, but at the same time, I was committed to their political project and did not want to write anything that could have potentially negative effects or put their activities in jeopardy under a heavily militarized state.

I prepared to make the necessary corrections. Flipping from page to page, I jotted down a few changes, corrections of specifics of the history of peasant organizations prior to the EZLN or of local political events. They were minor details. However, three corrections that Mauricio suggested stood out due to their implications for the representation of history.

Mauricio opened the document to one of the women's group interviews. In almost all the communities, the women spoke of the Mexican military incursions in 1994 and 1998 as critical events in their political formation. In 1998, groups of women blocked the road with their bodies and a few sticks and stones. Confronting the military tanks and the soldiers was without a doubt one of the most sharply recorded memories of recent years. Mauricio read aloud one of the descriptions narrated by them. "See, on page 53, here it says that they felt fear when the soldiers arrived. You need to take out fear and put rage."

I immediately responded in anger. "Why do you want me to take out the word 'fear' if that is what they felt? I can't change how they describe their own experiences!" I imagined that perhaps the change in words was a way to present Zapatista women as martyrs defending their communities, thus eliminating the complexities and ambiguities that defined the moment. Mauricio retracted the comment and reflected in silence for a while before answering:

Well, it is because fear paralyzes. If you only put fear then it's as if the soldiers defeated them. It is as if the soldiers instilled fear so that no one would do anything, which is what the government wanted. But it wasn't like that. I think they also felt rage, because if not, they wouldn't have acted or defended themselves. They threw stones at soldiers and sent them packing, that is why it was rage.

I too fell into a pensive silence before responding: "Let me see if I understand you. You are saying that if it is only fear, then it is as if they were merely victims because fear paralyzes? However, rage mobilizes? And by adding rage it is a way of explaining that they also acted in this situation. Is that it?"

Mauricio explained that that is roughly what he meant. He moved on to a second point. "Also, we saw that often in the interviews the *compañeros* said that people from the outside came to teach." Mauricio pointed to the contribution of a man on page 73: "'They came and they opened our eyes.' That is what it says. But that isn't true because someone else can't come to open your eyes. You open your own eyes." He physically demonstrated such an action by lifting one eyelid with his index finger. "We have reflected during many years on our own experiences and history in order to understand our oppression. If with these words you are going to write a book, then you need to change that they came to plant ideas." He turned the page to communicate that he was continuing with the same theme while moving on to another point. "It is okay that we talk about these other people," he said, referring to religious workers, solidarity groups, NGOs, individuals, and organizations that have played different roles over the course of the past thirty years in the region. "They are part of our history. But if we are to talk about the autonomous municipality, then we need to be in the center of the story. The government and many people write about us—how should I say it? Well, they leave us to the side."

"Do you mean when they write about indigenous people and peasants as if they were people who can't think for themselves but rather must have others come to tell them what to do and what to say?" I asked, to which he responded:

Yes, what is important is to put us at the center of the story. The obstacles, the errors, how we respond to them, all that needs to be written down. That is why history is important, it tells us what happened, but it also helps us reflect on how we should proceed. The important thing is to emphasize that we are those making history.

This conversation stayed with me for several days. At a superficial level, the change in wording seemed a minor point. However, when placed in light of the daunting task of engendering alternative sociopolitical relations, I could see that Mauricio, as a member of the autonomous council, was making a critique of the diverse hegemonic representations of Zapatista community members as indigenous, rebel, political actors. The production of knowledge about indigenous peoples in Mexico during the era of Vogt and Tax centered on representations of them as living outside of time and history, isolated in premodern communities. More than six decades later, this discourse continues to permeate the dominant constructs of indigenous political actors as incapable of influencing the course of history. Two decades after the Zapatista uprising, the enduring nature of these representations has been both activated and articulated by different state interests during pivotal moments in the movement's history so as to discredit the rebels' actions. Since the uprising, mass media outlets have published declarations that peasant farmers lack the political maturity to organize a movement of this magnitude, that foreigners and politicians from the urban centers manipulated them, or that it was the Catholic Church under Bishop Samuel Ruiz who planted the idea to organize (Legorreta Díaz 1998). If the foundation of the social movement had been made up of *mestizo*, urban, middle-class men, this argument would not have found traction in the commonsense opinions of a significant sector of the population. By proposing to reconstruct portions of the interviews to identify members of the population as instigators of the action, rather than people who were acted upon, Mauricio was critiquing the discourses that reproduced racialized colonizing knowledge and, in this case, also questioning their political ramifications. His concerns mirror novel research initiatives in Chiapas that have developed methodologies to fuel alternative narratives based on forms of indigenous self-representation (Rus, Rus, and Bakbolom 2016; Kohler and Leyva 2015).

At the same time, Mauricio's desire to challenge some of the words spoken by the individuals interviewed surely had to do with the tensions that exist between the responsibilities and concerns of the Zapatista authorities and those of their support bases. However, Mauricio's comments also signal tensions that exist when subaltern actors attempt to create counternarratives of themselves and their actions.

The way that a story is narrated is restricted by the ways in which that story is received—by who listens to it, how they listen to it, and what they do with the words (Mohanty 2003). I was left thinking that for certain liberal audiences, it is more acceptable to listen to the interpretations of certain marginalized groups exclusively from their position as victims than from their role as historical actors. Documentary films, books, and images abound that represent those who have suffered acts of state repression or socioeconomic marginalization as victims. Uncomfortable with being assigned to rewrite certain interpretations of the past by Mauricio and curious to see whether tensions of this sort might be present in other moments in the interviews, I read the transcriptions again. With a fresh gaze, I noticed that the interviewees debated the same issues mentioned by Mauricio.

Reading all the interviews together, especially those of the women, allowed me to identify the debates and conflicts surrounding the representation of particular historical events. While some used the formal language of the *testimonio* to focus on their suffering and on the repressive acts carried out by soldiers, estate owners, or their husbands, other women punctured these narratives by questioning these very interpretations. The following exchange, taken from my field notes on a 2006 group interview in the community of Zapata, provides an example.

An elderly woman spoke in a pained tone, placing careful emphasis on each word and directing her gaze to the younger women: "Life was very difficult. It was pure suffering. The landowner was the true master. When the men were far away, he would order the adolescent girls to bring him tortillas and he would rape them."

Upon hearing this memory, one of the young women jumped from her seat and with a nervous laugh interrupted: "You shouldn't have tolerated that! If the landowner tried something like that, I would have kicked him and taken off running."

Another woman clarified the situation: "The husbands and fathers picked up the same ideas as the landowner, and the women didn't have anyone to defend them. They all did the same. We didn't have rights. That is why we had so much fear facing the soldiers, the government, and our husbands."

"With the Word of God, that started to come to an end. They opened our eyes," said a third woman, recalling how, starting in the late 1960s, liberation theology in the Catholic Diocese of San Cristóbal de las Casas under Bishop Samuel Ruiz, which they called the Word of God, provided methods that facilitated group discussions about the communities' past.

The reflections continued, shifting to emphasize the women's position of agency. Another young woman recalled,

The women supported each other in the community. That is what my mother said. When I was a little girl I saw the women going to play basketball and I wanted to go with them. My mom would put on pants and she would go to the center of the town with the rest. I saw that they helped each other and between them they showed that they could do things as women. I used to laugh when I saw my mother like that.

One fundamental segment of these *testimonios* is the act of denouncing the experiences of suffering, repression, and collective pain inherited through the years that the estates played a prevalent role in the region. Narrating a *testimonio* represents a mechanism to record collective histories of resistance and repression so as to name those experiences as they circulate in the community. In this sense, *testimonio* can be converted into a medium through which to name, identify, and heal, as part of a process of decolonization (Anzaldúa 1987; Macleod 2008; Saldaña-Portillo 2003; Tamez 2012; Tuhiwai Smith 1999; Velásquez Nimatuj 2015). However, *testimonios* do not exist in a vacuum of power that is outside of interpretive processes and institutional practices; rather, they are restricted by discursive frameworks (Naples 2003). Perhaps the predominant framework in conflict zones, where denunciations of human rights violations form a key part of measures to confront the repressive state apparatus, is that of the "victim-subject" (Kapur 2002). In these cases, oppressed actors are identified and categorized exclusively by their status as victims of the state apparatus, political economic structures, and violence. These debates generated a new category of victim, the victim of culture and customs and traditions (Newdick 2005), where the indigenous woman is a victim of the traditions of her community and for that reason her people should not be granted collective rights.

Highlighting stories of repression and victimization tends to attract the attention of the media, human rights networks, and solidarity groups. For that reason, it plays an important role in preventing further acts of violence. However, I am not suggesting that offering a *testimonio* is an exclusively strategic act. The suffering experienced at the hands of repressive landowners, soldiers protecting particular political and social interests, and corrupt state officials is a reality impossible to negate or to exclude from the act of narrating lived experiences in this region. What I wish to emphasize is that representations of the "victim-subject" reverberate and articulate to liberal global discursive frameworks, which identify marginalized actors almost exclusively as exploited and oppressed or as victims of patriarchal violence and neocolonial processes, dependent on the decisions and actions of others (Mohanty 2003).

Even though only a minority of the women in the group interviews had had contact with journalists or academics, they were familiar with the importance of these discourses. The women situated me, with my pen and notebook in hand, taking note of their words for a public document, as one of the actors that listens to, administers, and reproduces these histories of victimization. At the same time, however, these women demonstrated clear disagreement with those discursive frameworks that limit their capacity for self-representation as agents of their own history. In the intergenerational discussion in Zapata, the women's attempts to emphasize their capacity to intervene in history—by fictitiously slapping the landowner or by struggling against acts of violence—exist in tension with statements of suffering. In this sense, the giving of a *testimonio* as an action comes close to the argument set out by John Beverley:

> If the point of testimonio were simply to represent the subaltern *as subaltern*, victims as victims, then . . . it would be little more than a kind of postmodernist *costumbrismo*. . . . Testimonio aspires not only to interpret the world but also to change it. Nevertheless, how one interprets the world also has to do with how one seeks, and is able, to change it. (2004, xvi)

Beverley locates *testimonio* as part of that agency of the subaltern, as a model to establish new ways of doing politics, producing new political imaginaries as part of global circuits of consciousness and resistance. The women interviewed offered the genre of the *testimonio* as part of these tensions that generate new representations of their history as a people while simultaneously acting as a medium to denounce oppression.

Conclusion

The active participation of the Zapatista support bases occurred in four distinct phases of my research: in deciding to accept the study and establish a format, in defining how information would be gathered, in providing *testimonios* during group interviews, and in evaluating and analyzing the interview transcripts. In this sense, the process itself became just as important as the final product or products. An emphasis on process forced me to be aware of the tensions and power relations at play at any given moment so as to seek to transform those resting on colonial gendered and racialized relations.

Community members emphasized two colonizing realms. First, they critiqued a racialized division of labor that exists between oral and written expressions. Collecting verbal data to later process and make sense of as a written text runs the risk of reproducing a masculine and colonial logic. A traditional research process involves such a division of labor, in which one person freely narrates experiences while another organizes them in a systematic form. By arriving to the interview with a written text, community members challenged this racialized and gendered method. Second, those interviewed pointed to the ways that research exists, not in a vacuum, but rather as conditioned by hegemonic discursive frameworks and by the production of dominant representations. In this light, the women interviewed resisted and transformed narratives of victimization at the same time as they reproduced these through the act of denouncing experiences of violence and exploitation.

Rather than just posing critiques, participating community members modified the methods through which data is collected and transformed the dynamics that emerge among those involved. Of particular relevance in the events discussed in this chapter was their decision to opt for intergenerational group interviews so as to prioritize the circulation and production of social memories as part of their continual political formation. In fact, as I illustrated, such methods redirected the original objectives of the fieldwork by generating a dynamic in which the collective highlighted those events of the past most relevant to them, specifically those that occurred in the time of the *fincas*. This forced me to listen to the effects of these social memories, how they are mobilized in the present and how they serve to unearth particular forms of sexism and racism. It is toward this focus on the time of the estates, their racialized cultural project, and the political tools developed by community members prior to the uprising that I direct your attention in the next chapter.

THREE

Social Memories of Struggle and Racialized (E)states

M acario, a man in his early forties, wrote down his personal history and his reflections on local struggle as a way of substituting for his direct participation in the collective interviews I conducted in the community of Nueva Revolución in Diecisiete de Noviembre in 2006. As a member of the education commission, he spent very little time in his village, only enough to see his family, attend community assemblies, and take care of his *milpa* (a cornfield that usually also has beans and other vegetables growing in it) and his coffee fields. He spent the rest of his days traveling to different communities in the municipality to oversee the autonomous schools or in the *caracol* center taking care of administrative or political matters. Since he wanted to participate in the research process but did not have time to do so, he chose to write his testimony down for me:

> When I was a child, I remember my grandparents suffered a lot, in the es-
> tates we were indentured servants, they didn't have a fair salary, many of
> our grandparents were humiliated by the master—the work was very hard,
> they explained that one week they would get paid, and another week it was
> *baldío* [emphasis in original], in vain the work that is to say they didn't pay
> them anything, besides the good lands were in the hands of the big estate
> owners: our grandparents founded their villages in the hills, there was much
> suffering, when I was a child I remember that I cried when my mother and
> family underwent great hardships and I cried even more when I learned that

my father was a goddam rancher that abused my mama, and since in those days, there was no justice, well the rights of women were trampled on by the bastard landowners and, that to this day they govern badly, the laws were to protect the rich and to keep the poor in a state of injustice.

When I became an adult, I remember that first arrived the Word of God that helped us discover that we are human beings and that we deserve to be treated with dignity and that there was great social inequity and these reflections helped us to begin to organize and unite to defend our rights and struggle for lands and water, the years passed and the bad government never listened to our demands, but every time the wisdom of our people grew more and we started to participate in movements, marches, meetings, it's as if our spirits started to warm up and we started to lose our fear and ignorance and we started to believe that we are all the same and that no one is lesser than the rest.

There was a system of education that followed the road of colonization, anyway, we learned a few things, we learned to search for paths and to make the paths by walking, we participated in the organization Aric [Rural Association of Collective Interest], later we participated in Ansies [ANCIEZ] and later it's as if we found the road blocked and we got confused, because the government also tried to use strategies of political control and what did we know of politics. But through our necessities and the reality that we were living we learned to do politics and we started to reorganize and think of how we are to struggle, what are we going to do, because the petitions for land under the Agrarian Reform were hopeless. Each time we were tricked and there was never any response that would guarantee our demands, the *compañeros* grew tired of contributing to cover costs of the commissions traveling to Tuxtla, there was nothing, only the agrarian backlog increased, more needs, more poverty, we were still *mosos* and the masters were the ranchers and it was as if we were returning to the time of our grandparents, we only obeyed, during election time, they would call us to vote but we never knew for whom we were voting but the ranchers and the rat politicians did know who was their candidate, we only would cover our finger with ink and mark the paper, but to them that was very valid it was democracy, but what democracy if the word NAFTA already appeared, the North American Free Trade Agreement, and what it was no one knew.

Only the great rich knew, ah, but we were learning that there were great transnational businessmen in our country and that they were robbing our riches, stealing our products (and our natural resources), because of the low price of coffee, cattle, and corn and all other types of products, for the poor there were no services, no good education, health, because it wasn't in the interests of the rich, they wanted us to remain in misfortune and in ignorance: but in 1994 when war was declared the panorama changed, the law of the rich wasn't valid, the ranchers left, they abandoned the lands that they had invaded, because those lands were of our grandparents [ancestors], later those of us who were tired of so many lies, by the Agrarian Reform, we occupied those lands and that is how the word of Zapata, that says the land is for those who work it, was honored, now we have a new system for cultivating the land, a *collective system* [emphasis in original] today we have advanced and we have grown in the autonomous education system, in the health system and in the production system, especially in the practice of our autonomy, also in the value that as indigenous peoples we are constructing a new democracy with our self-determination.

Today we continue to grow in our resistance, we continue to open the path, we have alternative projects, with a new model of life, leaving to the side the old neoliberal system.

We continue to organize in:

> Primary education, in three levels. The primary level for the smallest, middle level for those who know a bit and the superior level is for those who can read and write, mathematics and other knowledge.
> Municipal education, is a technical secondary school with knowledge and topics are taught for them to grow and be developed in practice.
> Education for adults, is to teach literacy and reduce illiteracy.
> Natural education, is for those who have their knowledges and wisdom, they share with everyone so they can learn, that is called nature teachers.

For us autonomy is the soul and heart of our resistance in our pueblos, it is a new way of doing politics in construction and in development in democracy, justice and liberty.

Macario handed me the pages early one morning as we were walking to catch the only public transportation vehicle that consistently traveled from one end of the Tzaconejá River valley to the other. Long before dawn, we walked, with a flashlight in hand, as there was no moon to guide us, up the muddy trail that connected the center of his village to the road. It was the rainy season: our rubber boots were covered in mud and I kept slipping steps back as we moved ahead. He told me he had sat down to write his testimony the night before. The process made him recall a series of thoughts and emotions that he shared with me as we walked. He said that whenever he thinks about how he came into this world it pains a part of his heart that has no limits. "When I found out [my mother had been raped], I hated myself and it hurt me deeply whenever I saw her. I wanted to hit or do worse things to the rancher that was my father, but I couldn't. I was scared that he would do more bad things to my mom," he said as we searched for firm earth on which to climb up a particularly rocky section of the path.

Macario continued telling me about himself, that he and his family lived in the *ejido* Lázaro Cárdenas, adjacent to the Yaxolob estate. In 1953, the secretary of agrarian reform granted the twenty-four soliciting indigenous peasant families *ejido* land on a steep, rocky hillside with very little available local water and with soil so thin that their *milpas* grew hardly any corn or beans. Despite the fact that the new *ejidatarios* (members of *ejidos*) had finally been granted the fruits of the 1910 revolution—communal lands to free them from the estate economies—they had little choice but to continue working for their *patrones* (estate masters). Macario's mother was living in the *ejido* at the time. She was no longer an indentured servant, yet the figure of the *mozo*, as the social location that condenses not only economic forms of exploitation but control over the lives and bodies of indigenous people, continued to establish profoundly hierarchical social relations. The act of rape by the *mestizo* rancher is one of the most extreme displays of this domination.

By taking Macario's testimony as a window into a collective interpreted history among Tseltal and Tojolabal Zapatista community members, this chapter unfolds with two objectives in mind. To begin with, it focuses on the economy of the estates as that which condenses racialized orderings of local society, an economy that begins in the mid-nineteenth century, explodes during the Porfiriato, and peaks during the mid-twentieth century, when the *ejido* Lázaro Cárdenas was founded and when Macario was born there. As his testimony suggests, the demise of the estates after the 1970s and the prevalent role of the *ejido* did not dismantle the social relations on which the niche of the *mozo* rested. In fact, his testimony alludes to different moments in his adult life where the image of the *mozo* continued to serve as a grounding point to understand different experiences of exploitation. It is the primary reference point he uses to explain the undignified treatment he and other men from Lázaro Cárdenas were subjected to when soliciting for an extension of their *ejido* from the sec-

1 Cuando yo era niño, recuerdo que mis abuelos Sufrian
mucho, en la finca eran Mosos acasillados, no tenian un salario
Justo, muchos de nuestros abuelos heran humillados por el Patron
el trabajo hera muy duro, dicen que una semana les pagaban
y otra semana era un trabajo Baldio es decir que no les
pagaban nada, ademas las buenas Tierras estaban en manos
de los grandes fingueros Terratenientes; nuestros abuelos Pobleron
en las serranias, abia mucho sufrimiento, yo cuando hera niño
recuerdo que yoraba porque mi madre y mi familia Pasaban
grandes Carencias y mas yoraba cuando descubri que mi Papa
hera un pinche vanchero que se abuso de mi mama, y, como
en ese tiempo no abia Justicia, pues el derecho de la mujer
hera Pisoteado Por los cabrones Terratenientes y, Por los que
hasta ahora mal gobiernan, las leyes heran Para proteger
a los ricos y tener sujetos a la injustia a los Pobres.

ya cuando fui adulto, recuerdo que Primero llego la
palabra de Dios que nos ayudo a descubrir que somos
seres humanos y que merecemos un trato digno y que abia
una gran desigualdad social y estas reflexiones nos ayudo
a empeza a organizarnos y unirnos Para defender nuestros
derechos y luchar Por las Tierras y el agua, pasaron años y el
Mal gobierno nunca escucho nuestras demandas, pero Cada Vez
Mas fue Creciendo la sabiduria de nuestros pueblos y
empezamos a participar en movimientos, marchar, mitines Como
que empeso a calentarse los animos y empezamos a sacar
el miedo y la ignorancia, y empezamos a Creer que
Todos somos iguales y que nadie es menos ante los demas.

2 Abia un sistema de Educación Con un proyecto al camino
de la colonizacion, bueno en fin aprendimos algo, aprendimos
a buscar caminos y hacer caminos caminando, participamos en
la organizacion Aric, luego participamos en la Ansies y luego
Como que encontramos un tope y nos confundiamos, porque
tambien el gobierno empeso a usar estrategias de Control
Politico y nosotros que ibamos a saber de politica. pero
la nesecidad y la realidad que estabamos viviendo, afren-
dimos hacer politica y empezamos a reorganizarnos y a pensar
Como vamos a luchar que vamos hacer, porque las solicitudes
au Tierra a la Reforma Agraria ya no abia Esperanzas
Cada Vez heramos engañados y nunca abian respuestas
que garantizaban nuestras demandas, los compañeros se
cansaron de cooperar Por viajar a Tuxtla de las comiciones
no abia nada, solo estaba incrementando los resagos
agrarios, mas nesecidades mas pobreza seguiamos siendo
Mosos y los amos pues heran los rancheros y nosotros como
que estabamos volviendo al tiempo de nuestros abuelos
Solo ovedeciamos, en Tiempo de elecciones nos llamaban
a votar pero no conociamos por quien votabamos pero
los rancheros y los politicos ratas si sabian quien era
su candidato, nosotros solo nos marcaban el dedo
Con tinta y manchavamos el papel, pero eso ya era
muy valido segun ellos hera la democracia
Pero cual democracia, si ya se asomaba la
palabra T.L.C. Tratado de libre comercio y que hera
eso nadie sabia.

3 Solo lo sabían los grandes ricos, A, pero ya empe-
samos a descubrir que estaban grandes empresarios
transnacionales en nuestro País Mexico, y que estaban
saqueando nuestras riquezas y nuestros recursos naturales, robando nuestros Productos
con los Viejos precios del café, el ganado, el maíz y
todo tipo de Productos, Para los Pobres no abía servicios
buenos de Educación, Salud, Porque no les convenía a los
ricos, querían que siguiéramos en la desgracia y en
la ignorancia. Pero en 1994 cuando se declaró la
guerra cambió el Panorama, ya no valió la ley del rico,
los rancheros salieron, abandonaron las Tierras que
abían invadido, Porque esas Tierras heran de nuestros
abuelos, luego los que estabamos cansados Por tantas
mentiras de la Reforma Agraria, Ocupamos las Tierras
y así se cumplió la Palabra de Zapata que dice
la Tierra es de quien la trabaja, ahora hay un
nuevo sistema de manejo de la Tierra, sistema colectivo
hoy hemos avanzado y hemos crecido en el sistema
de Educación Autonoma, en el sistema de salud y
en el sistema de Producción, sobre Todo en la
Practica de nuestra Autonomia, también en lo que
hemos Valorado que los Pueblos indios sí estamos
construyendo una nueva democracia con nuestra auto
determinación.

4 Hoy seguimos creciendo con nuestra Resistencia, seguimos
abriendo caminos, Tenemos Proyectos Alternativos, con un
nuevo modelo de vida, dejando atrás el viejo sistema
neoliberal.

Seguimos organizandonos en:

Educación Primaria, en tres niveles. Nivel Primaria los mas
chicos, Nivel medio los que ya saben un poco y
Nivel Superior es los que ya dominan lectura y escritura
matematica y otros conocimientos.

Educación Munisipal, es como una s_____ tres técnicos
_____ movimientos, y se enseñan Temas de crecimiento
y de desarroyo en la practica.

Educación Para Adultos, es Para alfabetiza y des-
minuir el analfabetismo.

Educación Natural, es que los que tienes sus
conocimientos, y sabidurias, se comparte con todos
Para aprender, eso se llaman maestros Naturales.

Para nosotros la Autonomía es el Alma y el Corazon
de nuestra Resistencia en nuestros Pueblos, es una
nueva forma de Acer Politica de construccion
y de desarroyo en la democracia, la Justicia y la
Libertad.

retary of agrarian reform as well as the way he explains that their inter-actions with the local *mestizo* elite marked their indigenous bodies as apt only for working and obeying. He identifies a continuation of this role of obedience during electoral periods, when the ranchers would tell the in-digenous people which candidate to vote for. According to the state, he ex-plained, democracy is when the *ladinos* decide and define politics. Though what he wrote was a personal account, Macario recognized his history as a shared experience in the region. In fact, in his opening sentence he used both "I" to refer to the stories of his grandparents and "we" to claim the experience of the *mozo* as his own.

This chapter argues that a rejection of the social niche of the *mozo* figures prominently in the political formation of Zapatista community members, particularly for those generations born and raised prior to the 1994 uprising. As the testimonial discussions among women in the com-munity Ocho de Marzo in the previous chapter suggest, the figure of the *mozo*, and the *mozo-patrón* relationship, is the primary frame through which community members analyze experiences of oppression, not only of the past but within recent fields of power. It is the lens through which community members make sense of the naturalized locations of indige-nous people and *kaxlanes* on a local terrain so as to attempt their unrav-eling. Though in his testimony Macario focused on class-based forms of exploitation, between the rich and the poor, these are marked by what he described as the "road to colonization," and by processes of racialization, as when he equated the *kaxlan* to the *patrón*, and the indigenous popula-tion to the *mozo*.

The second objective of this chapter is to describe the various spaces influencing the political formation of Tseltal and Tojolabal community members who eventually became Zapatista support bases. Macario's iden-tity could have been reduced to a bastard child of the *patrón*, an ambiguous identity that would both mark him as the result of an act of violent domi-nation over an indigenous woman's life and grant him an upwardly mobile position. While we walked that morning, in fact, Macario confessed the conflicted role he held when he lived in the *ejido*. Despite his feelings of self-hatred, some *ejidatarios* treated him as if he were above other commu-nity members. He offered two possible explanations—that his father was a local rancher who held a superior position in the region's social orderings and that his own fairer skin makes him "look less indigenous." In light of these contradictions, he described how he had to forge his own path and come to understand himself under alternative sets of premises as a way to directly confront and transform deep personal shame and pain. What he described in his testimony was a process of collective self-making heavily influenced by the Word of God, the liberation theology–inspired Catholic teaching starting in the late 1960s. He then recognized as central the different peasant movements in which he participated beginning in the 1980s, including the Unión de Uniones Ejidales y Grupos Campesinos Solidarios de Chiapas (Union of Ejido Unions and Peasant Solidarity Groups of Chiapas, known as the Union of Unions) and the Alianza Nacional Campesina Independiente Emiliano Zapata (ANCIEZ, Emiliano Zapata National Independent Peasant Alliance), until joining the Zapatista movement in its pre-1994 clandestine form. The "many things" he learned in these spaces, this chapter suggests, form the collective political consciousness nourishing continuing expressions of social struggle through claims to indigenous autonomy.

In closing his testimony, Macario described autonomy as the heart and soul of the struggle, which begins with the reappropriation of land considered Mayan ancestral territory, followed by what Diecisiete de Noviembre community members define as the three pillars of autonomy: education, health, and agricultural production. The combined set of autonomous practices, Macario stated, affirm their capacity as indigenous people to define the terms of democracy and ways of doing politics as part of what generates the possibilities of a new life, of *lekil kuxlejal*, in contrast to the type of life represented in the figure of the *mozo*.

Tseltal and Tojolabal Zapatistas' accounts of their own history, narrated on the basis of a genealogy of recent struggles, highlight diverse political spaces that affirm their humanity. Macario expressed such affirmation when he said that it was through his participation in the reflection spaces of the Catholic Church that he grew to see himself as a human being with dignity.[1] To create new cultural practices, the Zapatista support bases reinterpreted a range of experiences and memories. Such elaborations effectively require novel social imaginaries. However, the imagination does not arise out of a void but rather rests on material experiences, on what is transmitted and handed down across generations,[2] hence the importance of circulating shared memories of resistance as part of the weaving of alternative genealogies ascribing meaning to current practices of autonomy. New knowledge arises from a toolbox, if you will, that may be used in various ways in different contexts, while at the same time, those very contexts simultaneously transform and condition imaginaries of potential future unfoldings.

I analyze social memories, such as those conveyed by Macario, as part of cultural resignification processes spurred by the act of remembering, memories that are simultaneously separate from, yet interconnected with, official productions of history (Flores 2002, xv). For this task, I borrow Veena Das's (1995) concept of "critical events" to identify the principal fulcrums setting out such a cartography. Das develops the term in reference to experiences that transform the ways individuals interpret their daily lives in relation to dramatic events shifting nation-state projects; incidents situated in highly complex social terrains engender shifts in meaning and subjectivity (6). I would like to pause to clarify two brief points. First, when discussing "critical events," Das refers largely to major occurrences, such as the Partition of India. I use the term not to refer solely to extraordinary or dramatic incidents. A critical moment may be, and in fact frequently is, something much more ordinary and apparently mundane. Secondly, rather than register the effects of these critical events primarily on individuals, I am interested in highlighting the collective appropriation of particular moments in regional history as part of the construction of social significations, in a similar way that Macario identified his experiences as part of a shared memory and claimed the history of life on the estates as his own. Over the course of the interviews, it became evident that it was not crucial to have experienced a particular event in the flesh for it to spark changes in current interpretation; while only the most elderly of community members have lived the life of a *mozo*, their particular experiences form a collective memory that frames a shared analysis of power. As such, I extend the term "critical events" to refer to a social imaginary constructed across generations.

Taking this expanded understanding of critical events as a point of departure, I now turn to the accumulative transformations of local history, beginning with what Macario refers to as the time of the *mozos acasillados* (indentured servants), a time period that reached its apogee in the mid-twentieth century and lost its saliency during the 1970s. The experiences during the era of the *fincas*, the conditions of racialized exploitation, sexual violence, and near slavery, were communicated by the Tseltal and Tojolabal women and men interviewed in order to establish a collective, negative reference point. That is, they placed the subsequent struggles in direct opposition to the conditions of oppression condensed in the figure of the *mozo*. On the basis of this opposition, support bases, including Macario, named and shared different social experiences—in particular, the struggles in the *ejidos*, in the religious spaces set up by the Diocese of San

Cristóbal, and in the various peasant organizations—as expressions of struggle that ascribe meanings to current processes. In this sense, the construction of a genealogy does not reflect a frozen legacy of acts of domination and resistance, but rather one of conscious and constant processes of reflection, of rethinking history alongside historicity (Alexander and Mohanty 1997).

My analysis begins with a two-century history of the Tzaconejá River valley region where Diecisiete de Noviembre is now situated, with an emphasis placed on the unfolding of the estate economy.[3] It then turns to the postrevolutionary period, particularly the subordination of the *ejidos* to the permanence of the estates. The third section focuses on what I describe as a racialized cultural project emerging from the *fincas* and locates three primary tropes used to fix niches for local indigenous people. As I laid out in the introduction of this book, the first trope is one of infantilization, while the second fixes indigeneity to the figure of the *mozo* as a servant born to obey, and the third activates representations of indigenous bodies as ingrained with degenerate cultural values. The three final sections describe the central spaces influencing political formation for local Tseltal and Tojolabal residents: the reflection circles promoted by the liberation theology–inspired Diocese of San Cristóbal under Bishop Samuel Ruiz; two women's organizing spaces, one Catholic and one civil; and the different peasant organizations of the 1970s and 1980s.

The Tzaconejá River Valley: Rebellious *Mozos* and the Expansion of the Estate Economy

The Tseltal communities now in the geographic area of Diecisiete de Noviembre were most recently populated in the 1940s by families who moved there from the Patihuitz valley, located on the other side of one of the mountain chains in the Lacandon Jungle. Other Tseltal families migrated from the municipality of Chanal, while the Tojolabal population originated from the lands adjacent to the municipality of Las Margaritas (Gómez Hernández and Ruz 1992). Still other families are descendants from generations of *mozos* who worked in the region's estates that, in the mid-nineteenth century, *mestizo* landowners founded over land belonging to Tseltal settlements, though records show the existence of a few estates, such as Chiptic (whose land is now part of Diecisiete de Noviembre), as early as 1819.[4] The original founders of what is now the town of Altamirano, however, were Tseltal families who fled the Dominican-managed *fincas* during the last years of the colonial period and staked claims to the land as part of such an act of rebellion.

A letter dated January 2, 1806, documents a new population center, named San Carlos Nacaxlan, founded when "*Yndios baldíos* [indentured natives] that lived on the estate of Santo Domingo, left the estate with the objective of founding their own settlement."[5] In the letter, the priest, Manuel Ruiz, writes about the natives' numerous attempts to establish a village on that land, given that "the object or cause that led them to want to found this settlement was to liberate themselves from the work on the estates. . . . These are the *Yndios* influenced by liberty." On several occasions these Tseltales had requested land, but on receiving no response, they opted to escape and settle on unoccupied fields without permission. A notary certifies that 343 indigenous *baldíos* formally named their village, situated on the banks of the Tzaconejá River, San Carlos Nacaxlan.[6] They used the name of a former estate in the region of Chilón, San Carlos, and added a word made up of *na*—"house" in Tseltal—and *caxlan*—"nonindigenous"—to make San Carlos Nacaxlan, meaning the house of the nonindigenous. That is, in an attempt to ensure the success of their land claim, they disguised their indigenous identity under the name House of the Kaxlan. The tactic suggests an acute awareness of the fragility of their request, which is reaffirmed in a letter written less than a year later to a local colonial government official in Ocosingo:

> We are distraught and inconsolable given that we do not know if we will achieve having our settlement officially recognized, as the *baldíos* [indentured servants] that remained on the Estates of Santo Domingo frighten us by saying that the Gather Administrator has told them that we will never be able to be granted this *pueblo*. This brings us much sadness as our roots, houses, cornfields, and animals are here, and our women and children feel this is where they belong.[7]

In 1815, church census records identify in the entire Ocosingo valley 80 percent of the population as indigenous and 20 percent as *ladino*, with nine estates already in operation.[8] But most of those *ladinos* were in Ocosingo, not in San Carlos Nacaxlan, where there were only two *ladino* families. The fertile valley where the village stood proved of great benefit to those Tseltal families, who generated vast agricultural production. Their success quickly drew the attention of prominent Catholic Church figures. Merely a decade after the Tseltales settled the valley of the Tzaconejá

River, the curia's head notary remarked in a letter summarizing a tour of the broader Ocosingo region that "the Yndios of the new settlement San Carlos are the richest and most fortunate of the entire Tzendal Province," referring to a colonial administrative region that roughly coincided with the territories of the Tseltal population at the time.[9]

From early on, the opportunities this land provided also attracted local *ladino* families. Shortly after the church notary letter, a census identified an increase in their presence, from two to thirteen families living in San Carlos.[10] The quick incursion of *ladinos* meant that the Tseltales' attempt to secure communal lands lasted but a brief time. By 1839, a letter states that *ladinos*, with the help of a land surveyor, had confiscated the fertile lands of the Tseltales: "The *ladinos* took over the best lands to the detriment of the Indians of San Carlos, leaving them in a state of misery."[11] The *ladinos* originally from the town of Comitán de Domínguez forced the indigenous inhabitants to move to uninhabited parts of the valley (Iribarren Pascal 1986). Another letter suggests that the local indigenous population, rather than remaining passive, formed alliances with other communities to try and push out those who had robbed them of their land:

> Indians of Ocosingo, Sibacá, and Pueblos Nuevo San Carlos agree with the rebellion spurred by Indians from the Villa de Chilón against the *ladinos* that had been planned for March. . . . The reason for their rebellion against those who are not *Yndias*, against all types of *ladinos*, is not so much the taxes as the lands possessed by many *ladinos*, to the extent that they no longer have lands to grow their crops or on which to build their homes.[12]

But this rebellion was unable to prevent the de facto appropriation of the Tseltales' land, which was legally substantiated a few years later, when the federal government decreed a series of laws that were designed to deny corporate landholdings of the Catholic Church but that also severely affected indigenous land. Between 1856 and 1863, three laws were passed—the 1856 Confiscation Law, the 1859 Nationalization of Church Property Law, and the 1863 Occupation and Expropriation of Uncultivated Lands Law (Reyes Ramos 1992)—whose impact transformed the social geography of the state, setting the terrain for the rapid expansion of the estate economy. While in 1837 there were 853 plantations, by 1889 this number had nearly quadrupled to 3,159 registered plantations in Chiapas (Favre 1973). Over the following twenty years, an exaggerated stratification unfolded, dividing the local population along class lines and between indigenous people and *kaxlanes*. In 1910 individual rural landowners constituted 4 percent of the population, while indentured laborers accounted for 92.8 percent (Aguilera 1969).

The estate economies flourished as they benefited from the transnational capital interests of the so-called tropical economies. During the 1880s, Chiapas governor Manuel Carrascosa promoted a massive campaign to attract international investment and directed efforts toward introducing potential Chiapanecan commodities at the 1889 World's Fair in Paris (Tenorio-Trillo 1996). Government officials noted that those considering launching economic enterprises in Chiapas were attracted not only to its widely available low-cost land but also to its abundant cheap labor, and the state injected funds to improve necessary infrastructure so as to make the potential investments a reality (Rus 2012). As a result, Chiapas became known for its rubber and cacao plantations, tropical fruits, precious woods, sugarcane, and, most importantly, coffee. Coffee, in fact, quickly grew to take center stage as indicated by figures at the time. According to Chiapas intellectual and politician Emilio Rabasa (1895), during the late nineteenth century, coffee growers annually harvested beans from more than 125,000 coffee plants.

Aaron Bobrow-Strain (2007) notes that the increase in coffee production during the end of the nineteenth century and the first half of the twentieth century went hand in hand with the rise of *ladino* domination in Chilón, in the northern region of the state. In the highlands, by the mid-twentieth century the Tsotsil population similarly sustained the consolidation of estate socioeconomic power, as its population served as forced labor in the coffee plantations of the southern Socunusco region, which borders with Guatemala (Rus 2012). The valley of the Tzaconejá River was not the coffee zone of the Socunusco or the *engachadero* [forced recruited labor] economy of the highlands. Rather, estate owners there dabbled in the different commodities, including coffee and sugarcane, but after the mid-twentieth century, cattle.

Estates expanded through the continued exploitation of indigenous labor as *mozos*, who kept production costs down. This exploitation occurred alongside, and was in fact partially fueled by, state-sponsored citizenship projects spurred by the ideas of the intellectual elite. During the Porfiriato, Rabasa played a pivotal role in developing ideas about the principal problems facing the country, including "the problem of the Indian." Rabasa wrote, "Three million Indians, morally and intellectually inferior to those of Moctezuma's time, without personality or any notion of such a thing, with no common idea or feeling that connects them to the conscious portion of the population, was the legacy received from the dead colony to the new nation" (1921).

According to this intellectual, indigenous peoples threatened rational components of society—the motor required to achieve modernity. Despite alleging a scale of inferiority expressed in cultural deficiencies that hindered the country's progress, Rabasa firmly upheld the liberal philosophy that underpinned the ideology of *mestizaje*, the cultural and biological mixing of European and indigenous people in Mexico, and asserted that no racial distinctions existed in the country. This ambiguity between the enduring permanence of racial ideologies and liberal *mestizaje* thought is reflected in the juridical frameworks of the time. Though Chiapas state laws marked no distinction between indigenous and *mestizo* citizens, they concealed racialized codes that sustained and reproduced social hierarchies. In 1858, the articles of the second constitution of Chiapas on labor, treasury, and education referred to indigenous people by omission. Article 13, paragraph 8, established that "exercise of the rights of citizenship are suspended by the status of domestic servant" (cited in Gall 2003, 80).

By the beginning of the revolution in 1910, thirty-seven estates existed in the broader Tzaconejá Valley, many of which continued to exist to some degree until the Zapatistas took over land in 1994, such as the estates Jobero, Gran Poder, Porvenir, Yaxolob, San José la Unión, Buenavista, Mendoza, Tzaconejá, and El Amolar.[13] Though the revolution enacted land reform through the establishment of *ejidos*, estate economies continued well into the latter half of the twentieth century.

Postrevolutionary *Ejidos* as Satellite Villages

The most significant legacy of the Mexican Revolution for indigenous peoples and peasants was without question Article 27 of the Mexican Constitution. The article rendered the state responsible for undertaking a territorial reordering and established normative frameworks as well as procedures for the *ejido*, for the agrarian community, and for private property. The legal reform converted land into a social right to the extent that it allowed for the expropriation of large estates to create *ejidos* as collective property under the tutelage of the state to be granted to peasant farmers for their use and enjoyment. The *ejidatarios* held inalienable, nontransferable rights to *ejido* lands.

However, in southeastern Mexico the landowning class obstructed the effective implementation of the ideals and demands of Zapata until the 1940s, thirty years after the revolution began. While in much of the rest of the country, peasants and indigenous people struggled to dismantle the landowning class, in Chiapas a counterrevolution defended the interests of the *ladino* elite (Reyes Ramos 1991). At the conclusion of the revolution, the landowning class maintained their hold on local state power, which allowed them to halt the distribution of land and protect their own economic interests. State legislation sought to take advantage of the contradictions that existed between federal and state agrarian laws in order to preserve estate properties and convert the obligation of agrarian reform into a matter of buying and selling land (Aguilera 1969). State agrarian laws restricted indentured laborers from requesting land. Their supposed lack of rational ability, combined with their "mental backwardness," continued to mark a dividing line between the social categories of *mestizo* and indigenous person, as those in the latter were classified as "incapable" of seeking their own land. At the same time, estate owners maintained the right to choose the area of land they wished to retain, as well as the right to parcel it and sell it.

They also invented different formal and informal mechanisms to avoid losing control over their properties, including exchanging their lands with family members and close friends; legally subdividing their properties among children, spouses, and other relatives; and generating a wall of complicated paper trails so as to avoid the confiscation of their estates (Bobrow-Strain 2007, 97). In terms of figures, the legislation succeeded in distributing only 46,600 hectares in the decade of the 1920s, which contrasts with a figure ten times higher two decades later (Reyes Ramos 1992, 51).

In a heavily politicized climate spurred by the leadership of the Mexican Communist Party, the state government was forced to amend agrarian laws that limited the effective implementation of Article 27 in Chiapas. The 1934 Agrarian Code granted indentured laborers the right to request lands previously belonging to the estate owners (García de León 1985, 172). It was following this decree that a group of almost a hundred Tseltal families began to organize at night in the mountains to strategize how to be granted an *ejido*, a collective objective achieved in 1945, when they founded what is now called Morelia (previously known as Victórico Grajales) as the first communal landholding in the Tzaconejá valley. The owners of the Tzaconejá and Buenavista estates, Mauro Yáñez and Amado Castellanos, respectively, took advantage of their right to choose which plots of land they would relinquish and granted the families 3,237 hectares that had the poorest soil. Other estate owners in the valley, such as the Castellanos, Ruiz, and Kanter families, soon followed suit, ceding plots so as to allow the founding of *ejidos* such as Rancho Mateo, Rusia, and La Florida without losing control of the most fertile sections of their properties. Table 3.1 shows the thirty communal lands in the Altamirano municipality, which include twenty-nine *ejidos* and one agrarian community, as well as the dates they were founded, the number of hectares of land on them, and the original number of beneficiaries. As the table illustrates, only two of the *ejidos* were founded in the 1940s and two-thirds were founded in the 1950s and 1960s. Five of the *ejidos* were legally recognized after 1994 as part of government attempts to contain the profound political crises resulting from the EZLN uprising.

The majority of these *ejidos* were founded on hilltops or on small plots that acted as satellite villages and sources of cheap labor surrounding estate properties. The map that emerges is one of racialized segregation linked to the relative productive capacity of the land, which parallels the social geography resulting from the land reforms in the mid-nineteenth century. Then, indigenous people were cleared off their lands and forced to move to uninhabited areas. This relocation created a ring around the town of San Carlos where the *ladinos* moving from Comitán settled; a century later, estate owners still maintained control over the hearts of the fertile valleys, while the indigenous peasants' *ejidos* created a belt supplying temporary labor in a "monopoly-marginal producer relationship" (Reyes 1992, 63).

Descriptions of life in the *ejido* Lázaro Cárdenas serve to illustrate the racialized geography emerging from this local version of the postrevolutionary agrarian reform. As Macario explained to me, the *ejido* his parents and grandparents founded was located on the most of a mountain, where the soil was too thin and rocky for cultivation. Although the local population no longer lived on the *fincas*, their infertile land impeded their ability to ensure basic levels of subsistence. While in other regions of the state, such as the highlands, Tsotsil farmers would migrate for months on end to work as day laborers in the coffee fields of the Socunusco region (Rus 2012), in the Tzaconejá Valley, the relationship between indigenous communities and *ladino* estate owners was much more intimate, both geographically and socially. In the case of the men of Lázaro Cárdenas, they had little option but to walk two hours each day to work on the Yaxolob ranch, the property of Mario Yáñez. While some elders recall having

Table 3.1. Founding date, size, and number of beneficiaries of *ejidos* in Altamirano municipality

Ejido/agrarian community in Altamirano	Year founded	Original area (in hectares)	Number of original beneficiaries
Morelia (previously called Victórico R. Grajales)	1945	3,237	98
Rancho Mateo (previously called Joaquin Miguel Gutierrez)	1948	1,158	29
Rusia	1950	670	21
La Florida	1952	762	32
San Carlos Altamirano	1952	6,060	140
Belisario Domínguez	1953	1,880	38
Lázaro Cárdenas	1953	1,457	24
Puerto Rico	1953	865	24
El Triunfo	1954	681	unknown
Puebla	1954	2,030	29
La Grandeza	1954	2,257	38
Venustiano Carranza	1954	1,312	35
Agua Escondida	1961	2,399	26
San Luis Potosi	1963	1,670	32
San Marcos	1964	1,410	34
Victórico R. Grajales	1964	860	20
Luis Espinoza	1965	1,940	47
San Miguel Chiptic	1967	1,773	20
La Candelaria	1968	1,841	29
Las Delicias	1968	2,060	32
Nueva Virginia	1969	964	28
Guadalupe Victoria	1969	1,319	20
San Isidro	1978	620	26
Caltillo	1984	1,308	48
La Laguna (agrarian community)	1988	1,221	175
Santa Cecilia Pedregal	1995	757	25
San Francisco	1997	1,633	22
Los Bambues	1999	1,267	48
Ojo de Agua	2002	96	20
Santa Rosita	2003	80	20

Source: National Agrarian Registry, Mexico City.

grown sugarcane in the fields of Yaxolob, most of the activities later centered on taking care of cattle and producing milk and cheese.

Not only was securing food staples a source of constant concern and anguish for these families, so too was access to water. Women from Nueva Revolución who grew up in Lázaro Cárdenas described to me how they obtained water from a small well, which gradually began drying up until they could collect only drops at a time, a task that required several hours of patient collection in the early morning to secure enough for daily tasks. Most of the time, the women were unable to draw sufficient quantities, so in the afternoon they would send their children to the hillside caves for water. There, using a gourd, the children collected water from the small pools produced by the condensation of water on the walls and ceilings of the caves. Only through these means could the families of Lázaro Cárdenas survive.

The lack of access to water became so severe that securing this vital liquid took precedence over the search for more arable land. In the late 1960s, the men requested an extension of the *ejido* that would grant them access to the Tzaconejá River. However, all the land surrounding the river belonged to the Yáñez family. Yáñez not only refused to grant them access to the water source but responded through explicit threats of sexual violence. Elifonso, from Nueva Revolución, recalled his exact words: "If my sons rape your girls, that is no longer my problem. It will be your fault for sending them to the river. So it's up to you, because you know what men are like, they can't help themselves." The words of the estate owner reflect the deep ties between territorial control and sexual violence, the racialized and gendered expressions of domination similarly highlighted by Macario in his testimony. This is an aspect I will explore further below, when I discuss the racialized cultural projects emanating from the estate economies.

In the same way that Macario narrated the countless visits to the office of the secretary of agrarian reform to request an extension of their *ejido*, Elifonso's narrative also rested in part on these costly trips to the state capital, Tuxtla Gutiérrez. Instead of responding to their petition, however, the state officials, Elifonso described, further humiliated them through partial responses that in essence only exacerbated the situation:

What we wanted was land, but the [agricultural] engineer tried to buy us off with a hole in the ground up on the hills. He dug the hole to collect rainwater. The horses and cattle drank from it. We washed our clothes there, and cleaned the children's dirty diapers there. We used the same water for bathing ourselves and for drinking and for preparing the *nixtamal*.[14]

As the descriptions of life in Lázaro Cárdenas suggest, although the *ejido* model succeeded in redistributing a certain amount of land in the valley, hence providing Tseltal and Tojolabal populations the possibility of freeing themselves from their status as *mozos*, it had a only relative impact on the rationale underlying the social distinctions between indigenous people and the *kaxlanes* as this continued to be expressed through a racialized division of labor. In this section, I described two aspects that sustained such divisions. First, the redistributed land was of poor quality and did not meet subsistence needs, meaning the local population was forced to continue working on the estates to survive. Second, laws created loopholes used by the landowning elite to affirm control over their properties and hence maintain their position of privilege. In the following section, I turn to a third realm, what I refer to as the racialized cultural logics of the estate economies.

The Racialized Cultural Project of the Estates

Scholarship points to how the relationships between Mexican landowners and their workers transcended strictly labor dynamics to include a complicated web of personal ties (Bobrow-Strain 2007; García de León 1985; Gómez Hernández and Ruz 1992; Rus 2012). Toledo (2002) refers to this shared terrain as the culture of the *fincas*, where individuals lived with profoundly unequal relations of power as if they were natural and thus they went largely unquestioned. The testimonies offered by Zapatista community members point to the ways this cultural project emerged heavily racialized, generating a violent cohesion sustained by the participation of all involved actors. Although the estate owners tended to develop strategies of interaction with their indentured workers in terms of the binary of paternalistic generosity/mandatory obedience (ibid.), these dynamics were sustained through violence as they were founded on rigid social relations of domination. Though I recognize that social reality is much messier, I analyze this racialized project through the constructed binary of *mestizo* estate owner/indigenous *mozo*, for such a dichotomy inscribes particular attributes onto bodies.

Agustín is a man who lived most of his life in Morelia, though he was born on the Buenavista estate, where the new Zapatista settlement, Zapata, now stands. Agustín, who was around age seventy when I interviewed him, narrated for me the different stages of his father's childhood through the changing tasks the owner of Buenavista ordered him to carry out, the first being to feed and look after the owner's animals. As he grew older, he took on different chores:

> [At] fourteen or fifteen he would bring the water on donkey-back. Then he was given a machete, and started to clear out the cornfields, or carry wood needed to heat barrels of cane juice and turn it into brown sugar. And so he grew up. But there was no pay. You asked for beans and corn, and what you owed went down on an account. When Day of the Dead came round, the boss turned up to hand out sandals, hats, machetes. He "distributed" goods to his people. But the debt remained. The gift was a debt. My father told us all about how they suffered and I didn't want to forget it. Before, we would come across the old folks in the street and they would talk about how they suffered. They said they couldn't take it anymore.

The *mozos*, such as Agustín's father, were almost exclusively indigenous families and individuals whose lack of access to land forcefully channeled their limited life options toward the role of the indentured servant. In exchange for a small plot and a house, indigenous men typically worked three days for the landowner, those days that Macario labeled as working *baldío*, for nothing, and what Agustín describes as when "there was no pay." The three remaining workdays were dedicated to their own *milpas*, while often on Sunday the peons were invited to "voluntarily" contribute to the maintenance of the landowner's property. In the case that *mozos* received a wage, it tended to dissolve in the *tienda de raya*, the company store, as the only available option to purchase goods.[15]

Both mestizo as well as indigenous intermediaries—such as cowboys, overseers, and *caporales* (foremen)—were socially situated above *mozos*. According to the narratives of elders in Diecisiete de Noviembre, an indigenous intermediary partially lost an indigenous identity as a result of an upwardly mobile position of relative authority, that is, when he reached a position where he could give orders. Juan, from San Pedro Guerrero, noted, "For this reason, sometimes the one who treated us worst was the *caporal*, who was indigenous, but because he spoke Spanish he got on better with the owner and sometimes he thought of himself as a *kaxlan*." If the rancher recognized a child of his *mozo*'s as his own, that would potentially offer his offspring an ambiguous heightened position. Though rarely treated as the legitimate children of the ranchers, these people remained above the other *mozos* yet in socially subordinated roles, as was the case of Macario. Further up on the social scale were local *mestizos* who interacted with estate owners though they did not work for them directly, as they were small business or even small property owners. In rare cases indigenous people became small private property owners, including ex-peons who inherited land from their *patrones*.

At the top of the social tiers, the figure of the estate owner prevailed as *the* masculine authority, who appropriated himself the role of the father, managing the workers on the estate as if they were his family. As a paternal figure, he punished, disciplined, and forgave while at the same time deploying apparent generosity toward his *mozos*, whom he treated as children (Bobrow-Strain 2007). A well-oiled formula ingrained the social dynamics through which estate owners disciplined their workers so as to ensure that they were efficient workers, at the same time demonstrating "generosity" by granting the peons loans, resolving their internal conflicts, and responding to their family needs. In essence, estate owners' role as paternal benefactors hinged upon the continued infantilization of indigenous peons. They reinforced their authority through a clear dichotomy established between what Toledo refers to as those who "know how to work" and those who "know how to govern" (2002, 137). In this regard, the wife of an estate owner in the region of Simovojel explained that

> anyone who had a ranch needed to know how to give orders . . . and given that the husband knew how to give orders, his woman also needed to know because when the husband wasn't there, the woman of the ranch needed to give orders. In general, in the ranches they rang the bell and the peasants would come to find out where they were to go work. (in Toledo 2002, 141)

The landowning elite similarly controlled local political administrative power, often forming part of the state apparatus by dominating local government offices, including those of municipal president, congressional representative, and judge. State formation and estate interests were far from uniform or seamlessly fused, but rather they engendered a disputed terrain of local elite power. As Heraclio from Nueva Revolución explained to me, when it came to local political elections, the *finca* owners

> fought among themselves, but to see who controlled the Party [Institutional Revolutionary Party]. The biggest struggle was between Mario Kanter and

Pepe Castellanos. They clashed with each other. Each named their candidate for municipal president and got their people out in support. But once the votes were cast and the position occupied, we were all forgotten. . . . We allowed ourselves to be drawn into their conflicts, because we really wanted the best one to win.

As Heraclio's description illustrates, regardless of the multiple internal conflicts among estate owners and the state, from the point of view of the *mozos*, or, subsequently, from the viewpoint of the *ejidatarios* who worked on the estates, landowners and state officials formed a virtually impenetrable dominant block.

While the landowning class occupied the naturalized position of those who govern and give orders, the position of the *mozo*, in turn, was defined by the capacity to work for others. This niche of servitude was secured upon birth and reinforced through the expected role of obedience, including showing due respect and humility to all those in a higher social position. The equation of their existence wholly with working was reflected in the *testimonios* of both male and female workers, who narrated their lives on the estates through the splitting of their days along a series of chore slots, as if a set of labor activities wholly defined who they were, in a way similar to how Agustín described his father's childhood through shifts in tasks at Buenavista.

Women interviewed narrated how their days began with hulling corn and preparing the *nixtamal* for tortillas, then grinding salt stones for the cattle and horses, followed by making tortillas and coffee for the *patrón*, only to later cook his meals and wash his clothes, then return home to feed their husbands as well as wash their children's clothes. At the same time, this role of servitude, with its expressions of forced obedience, fused with accounts of sexual and domestic violence. They analyzed the complex relationship between landowning *kaxlan* men and the indigenous men of their households, and then delved into internal family gender dynamics. When referring to life on the *fincas*, women argued that they "had two bosses: our husbands and the master." Women reflected that they had no one they could turn to, or who would defend them, because there were no other such actors—such as the progressive church or centers for human rights that came later—and because there were no alliances to be had with *mestizo* women. As Eufrosina from Ocho de Marzo explained, "The mistress was no different. She mistreated us when we worked in the kitchen or looked after the animals. She let her husband do what he wanted with us [rape indigenous women]." The role of servitude broke any possible act of solidarity among women.

In the *testimonios* of Eufrosina, Macario, and Elifonso, sexual violence, as a control mechanism on the ranches, occupied a constant yet silent presence. Many narratives alluded to memories or threats of sexual violence, such as those about when the young women had to take the tortillas to the master; when the estate owner made threats concerning what might happen if they went to get water from the river; and "when a girl wanted to marry, the first to take advantage was the master." Feminist researchers indicate how sexual violence in a racialized context represents the recolonization of the indigenous subject and an intimate colonization that "degrades the sexuality of indigenous women, affecting how they understand their own bodies and experience their spirituality and their being" (Blackwell 2007). Sexual violence represents a symbolic reconquest of an entire people through the forced control of women's reproductive capacities (Smith 2005, 55).

Both intimate expressions of domination and strict division of labor reflect the ways in which a racialized cultural project resulted from a rigid separation and vertical classification of particular bodies and lives. Dehumanizing or "nonhumanizing" practices figured prominently in marking such distinctions. Zapatista community members made constant reference to the punishments and other acts of humiliation that made them feel like animals. Cristóbal, an elderly man living in Morelia, spent his childhood as an orphan in the La Laguna estate, property of the Ruiz family. Together with a half dozen other children who had lost their parents to illness, he had a series of specific household duties under his responsibility each day. He recalled,

I had to mop, sweep, and take out the bedpans every day. And look after the animals. I was responsible for the owner's monkey. Damn monkey, it had more to eat than I did! I was stuck with that monkey. Then I realized that it hated chicken shit so much that it stopped eating. So I covered it in chicken shit. It wouldn't eat anything and died. That's how I got rid of that job. . . . One day they made me carry a huge box and I couldn't. I ran off. But the boss caught me. Bastard! He strung me up in a tree to punish me. I was only ten or twelve years old then.

On numerous occasions the women referred to memories of physical violence and pain inflicted on the body, such as the beatings dealt out to them in the kitchen of the "big house" for having prepared "yellow" instead of "black" coffee that did not meet the standards expected by the landowner's wife. They also recalled their burnt fingers from having to prepare a huge amount of tortillas each day for their *patrón* and his family and the punishment for errors in their tasks, such as being forced to kneel on hulled corn until their knees bled. Men emphasized the humiliation caused by having to walk for days from Altamirano to Comitán carrying their employers on seats on their backs as if they were beasts of burden (a common practice I analyze in greater depth in chapter 6). They also recalled excruciating pain after working so many hours each day. Rarely did the feeling of hunger subside, to the point that when there were no more tortillas, they would search for fruit that had the same consistency to eat.

Men and women interviewed also made frequent reference to the insults the *kaxlanes* directed toward them, insults that often invoked a dirtiness attached to their bodies, such as *indio apestoso* (stinky Indian) or *indio pata rajada* (Indian with cracked feet). The lack of hygiene, as an expression of biological decay, acted as a marker of permanently inferiorized bodies. Artemio, from Ocho de Marzo, remembered the procedure for entering the "big house," in his case the property of the Castellanos family:

We had to be washed. We had to clean our skin before entering the hall. If we didn't, we weren't allowed to go anywhere near them. When it was time to collect our wages, the *kaxlanes* provided the money through a window. It was just big enough to put their hand through; the Indians weren't even allowed to go inside. They don't want an indigenous person to come close because they say we stink.

Local *mestizo* elite pointed to the lack of cleanliness of the indigenous body so as to prevent close contact between the *kaxlan* owners and the *mozos*. Dirtiness, thus, was not the result of toiling all day under the hot sun, but was used as a kind of permanent marker on the skin, as the sign of a body in an inevitable state of degradation. As the above statement suggests, even after bathing, indigenous workers were not allowed to get too close to the *kaxlanes* because of their "smell." While the postrevolutionary Mexican state highlighted, as part of its *mestizo* nation-building project, the elevated civilizations of the Mayan and Aztec empires, the indigenous descendants of these civilizations were marked through these forms of decay. In contrast to the promise of the state that through cultural alterations such degradation could be reversed and incorporation was possible, estate owners activated such tropes so as to establish an inherent separation from their peons, an inferiorizing distance required to avoid physical or cultural contamination.

Beginning in the 1970s, a combination of factors, including shifts in global economic interests, Mexican state neoliberal reforms, and pressure exerted by growing peasant movements in Chiapas, led to the demise of the estate economies (Rus 2012). This, however, did not dismantle the racialized cultural projects described above. While national and international changes generated unfavorable conditions for the estates, their outright dismantling became a focal point of diverse organizational spaces, including peasant organizations, women's groups, the liberation theology–inspired Diocese of San Cristóbal, and later largely church-sponsored NGOs. Zapatista community members interviewed drew from these political spaces key reflections that allowed them to name the injustices they suffered on the estates in a discourse that blended a class-based analysis of exploitation with racialized expressions of domination. They began to question why as indigenous people they were treated as if they had been born to work for others, and why others were controlling their bodies and their lives. As Macario emphasized in his written testimony at the beginning of this chapter, in light of dehumanizing socioeconomic relations, they struggled to affirm their humanity. The next sections of this chapter focus on the unfolding of these political spaces.

The *Tijwanej* and Collective Actions through the Word of God

In response to tutelage dynamics and corporatist state ties that helped maintain the cultural project of racialized domination in Chiapas, the Catholic Church, under the leadership of Bishop Samuel Ruiz García, played a prevalent role in fostering spaces for critical collective self-reflection resulting in concrete community action. Liberation theology, specifically a version developed by Ruiz called "Indian theology," committed the Catholic Church in Chiapas to promoting the idea that indigenous men and women could and would become the subjects of their own destinies (Morales Bermúdez 2005). Ruiz arrived in the Diocese of San Cristóbal in 1959. He slowly turned his religious service to social justice for the poor, a transformation that crystallized in 1968, when he attended the Conference of Latin American Bishops held in Medellín, Colombia. Nourished by Marxist analysis and dependency theory, the bishops at this conference concluded that structural factors created conditions of poverty in Latin America. As a result, they promoted a renewal in the Catholic Church by preaching the importance of overcoming economic and political obstacles as part of the liberation of the poor. From that year on, the Diocese of San Cristóbal transformed the modality through which it preached the Bible.

Prior to 1968, the indigenous catechists in the diocese taught the Word of God through the *nopteswanej* method, which in Tseltal means "he who makes the other understand." As part of the shift in priorities of the diocese, the new method was based on reflection and a politics of listening referred to as *tijwanej*, "taking what is found in the word of the other" (Leyva and Ascencio 1996, 403). The role of the catechist centered on the study circles after mass on Sundays. His or her main responsibility consisted in facilitating reflection so as to encourage, provoke, and stimulate a direct correspondence between the Word of God, local living conditions, and community actions.

Fray Pablo Iribarren Pascal, who made a pastoral visit to the region of Altamirano in 1986, took notes during his visit that provide a window into the resulting types of reflection circles. Upon arriving in the community Sociedad la Victoria, he recorded a group discussion on what life was like on the El Tulipán *finca*, from which followed discussions on the actions of the estate owner, Pepe Castellanos. Village members pointed to the lies of Castellanos and how he promoted the destruction of the forest. They then moved on to a new point, the primary issues facing women in the community. The women identified difficulty accessing a water source close to their houses as their main problem and then named how it affected their daily lives. They had to walk long distances to a river or creek, which made washing clothes an all-day endeavor, and their family income suffered because their husbands used their meager resources to travel to the National Indigenist Institute to solicit a water system for their *ejido*.

After mass the next day, the catechists read a passage from St. John on the Resurrection and then asked community members to divide into four groups and reflect on two questions: What does the passage say? What does the resurrection of Christ teach us of our current circumstance? Iribarren's notebook records the responses: "With the death of Jesus, the Disciples organized and struggled to follow the path of Christ, so too we must organize better . . . organize among the poor to overcome the suffering caused by the rich . . . organize the Word of God to defend ourselves as the poor and help the sick" (Iribarren Pascal 1986, 9).

Elders such as Anselmo, from Morelia, recalled in interviews with me that in the mid-1960s priests from the parish of Ocosingo arrived to the region, first visiting the *ejidos* of Morelia, Lázaro Cárdenas, Jalisco, and others. "I can clearly remember when they arrived," Anselmo said. "It was in 1967. That was the first year we prepared the fields for cattle grazing. It was an important moment for autonomy." With his words, Anselmo established a direct corollary between community decisions that affected daily life decades ago and decisions being made in the current Zapatista struggle. He highlighted the fact that at the time, group discussions led to founding of production cooperatives, along with collective cattle grazing, both of which increased agricultural production, leading to a subsequent decision to refuse to continue working on the estates, in this case for the owners of the Buenavista ranch: "The priests taught us that we are going to work for ourselves, not for the rancher. We aren't going to ask anyone's permission anymore. But we will do so secretly, because if the *kaxlanes* realized what we were doing, they would take away what is ours." Anselmo recalled with pride that community efforts resulted in building the primary school and establishing an adobe workshop, where they manufactured the bricks that still sustain the houses of elders such as Agustín. He then described the *ejidatarios'* other achievements:

> [We] opened up cattle grazing fields, installed a water system, built the school and the church. . . . My brother Sebastián was one of the three elders killed by the army on January 7. He helped organize the cooperative. . . . It was so much work. Finding a solution to the problems showed us that we are worth something, that we are not dead.

Anselmo associated "not being dead" with demonstrating a collective capacity to enact changes that alter daily living conditions. Such affirmations later became the basis for enacting life politics through autonomy. He pointed to the community members' building their own houses with material they sourced themselves and increasing subsistence agricultural production so as to break away from the niche of the peon. In this sense, he located community decisions partially promoted through the *tijwanej* method as situated against dominant inscriptions of infantilization, of *ajvalil* (master-governor) actions that label indigenous community members as not being quite adult enough, as not quite human enough, and thus incapable of influencing the unfolding of history. The *tijwanej* method is central to current cultural politics in Zapatista autonomous municipalities; in chapters 5 and 6, I note its influence in multiple spheres of Diecisiete de Noviembre. The women interviewed identified and added to this genealogy their participation in two women's groups, one civil and one religious.

CODIMUJ and AMMAC: Women's Heart Praxis and Political Action

Ernestina and Cristina are childhood friends who were entering their seventh decade of life when I interviewed them. Both women began participating in women's Catholic Church spaces in the 1960s, which in the 1990s transformed into the Coordinación Diocesana de Mujeres (CODIMUJ, Diocesan Women's Group). Ernestina became one of the first catechists in the Tzaconejá valley. In 1963, when she was still a teenager, her parents sent her to be in the first generation of students at La Primavera religious school. Cristina joined not long after, so their involvement in diocesan women's organizations spans several decades. Interviewed in Morelia, the two women identified the activities of CODIMUJ as a key platform for the broader processes of political and social action. In light of their extensive experience, I asked them to reflect upon women's organizational processes in the region. Ernestina recalled,

> My father was one of the first to go to San Cristóbal as a catechist. For three months he was there, and when he came back he asked me if I wanted to go and study with the sisters. . . . I agreed and in total three of us went. There I learned Spanish, I learned about the suffering of women. We came back to teach the girls to cross themselves.

The diocese was just beginning to take an interest in women's issues and agreed to found the religious school, an initial platform for what would later become CODIMUJ. This history is narrated in the book *Con mirada, mente y corazón de mujer* (*With a woman's eye, mind and heart*), published to commemorate the first ten years of the diocese women's project and more than three decades of the church's support for women (CODIMUJ 1999). In the book, the nuns who initiated CODIMUJ acknowledge that in the 1960s and early 1970s, the activities they carried forth with indigenous women negated their agency by focusing exclusively on measures to alleviate individual conditions of extreme poverty. They worked with women, but without methods focused on women's rights, let alone from a feminist perspective. Rather, CODIMUJ's initial approach promoted women's right to choose a husband, in rejection of the practice of arranged marriage.

Figure 3.2. Tseltal women and their children playing a round-about game during a popular-education workshop for women in the Zapatista municipality Taniperla, Caracol III, 1999; photo by Francisco Vazquez

At the beginning of the 1980s, the reflection circles became a permanent space for Tseltal and Tojolabal women as CODIMUJ formally integrated them into the structure of the diocese, particularly in the "Tseltal region" and in the "southeast region." Those coordinating activities heavily influenced local women's priorities in Altamirano. Women decided to organize production collectives, a task that required visiting neighboring communities, holding women's meetings, and encouraging women to form their own groups. Ernestina remembered that at the time, the women in Morelia wrote songs and performed plays with social-political messages: "One of the songs clearly said that if we are talking about justice, praying is not enough."

Though the women participated in marches, provided logistical support, and took care of the land while the men left the community to engage in political action, the vast majority of peasant organizations at the time lacked a platform for women. The sole space available to them in the 1980s remained the church. In this context, and as a result of critical internal discussions, CODIMUJ expanded upon methods referred to as "see-think-act" and added spaces for women in community activities. Subsequently, the nuns refined the method to prioritize a collective praxis technique, which involved analyzing the Word of God with a "woman's mind, eyes, and heart." Reflections on the basis of personal and collective experiences continued, not as an end in themselves but as a platform for triggering critical discussion about current social conditions based on the specific ways in which women think, see, and feel (Santana Echeagaray, Kauffer Michel, and Zapata Martelo 2006). In Tsotsil, Tseltal, and Tojolabal philosophy, the heart is the organ that records states of being on the basis of both emotions and rational capacities. In fact, the expression for asking a person "How are you?" may be translated as "What does your heart say?" Listening to the heart is thus what enables observation, analysis, and action. In her research conducted in the municipality of Bachajón, Tseltal scholar Patricia Pérez Moreno traces the relevance of the heart in Mayan thought, quoting one person she interviewed who eloquently stated, "The heart is the way to be-exist-do-think of the Tseltales, the wisdom of our mothers–our fathers, the honest-clarity in our words" (Pérez Moreno 2012, 110).

The method of thinking-seeing-feeling as women converged with this central component of Mayan philosophy so as to acknowledge a shared condition as indigenous women, to seek answers in a higher being, and to act to transform living conditions. In turn, the method entails remodeling the role of the individual, who is no longer regarded as a passive object of welfare actions but as an actor who defines her daily life. The year CODIMUJ set this method in motion, Ernestina was named coordinator of the Tseltal region.

In the late 1980s, the Asociación Mexicana de Mujeres, Asociación Civil (AMMAC, Mexican Association of Women, Civil Association), an interregional women's platform aimed at sparking political organization, was founded. In workshops, AMMAC advisors encouraged group discussions based upon methods that generated reflection on everyday reality, such as analyses of media stereotypes of indigenous people. The participants reflected on the lack of images of *mestizo* Mexican women, let alone of indigenous peasant women, in discussing why the media primarily represent white-skinned women from apparently affluent backgrounds (advisor to AMMAC who asked not to be identified, interview by author, May 2007). The facilitators of these workshops aimed to trigger these women's ability to name structural conditions of oppression in their daily lives so as to enable concrete actions to alleviate them. AMMAC facilitators sought to promote a shared analysis of articulated forms of oppression based on economic exploitation and on the assumption that, in the countryside, capitalist relations are less evident than in the urban context with the working classes; within that invisibility, indigenous peasant women are virtually forgotten. In addition, the reflection methods operated with the underlying assumption that indigenous peasant women are active agents of change and can therefore participate in struggle through multiple spheres.

The emphasis on praxis emerged through the spheres of the production collectives promoted both by AMMAC and by CODIMUJ. Indeed, Ernestina and Cristina, along with women interviewed in other Zapatista communities, acknowledged the central importance of both organizations in their political formation. With a smile, Ernestina recalled,

> We were out and about a lot. We had to go see how the collectives in the other communities were operating. We started walking to villages like Belisario Domínguez, and La Laguna, to see how the collectives were getting on. There were four of us women. We took some older women with us too. We came in order to teach. The government harassed us. Officials would turn up and ask, "What are you doing?" We would tell them we were working in a collective, planting vegetables in a plot. The government would always harass us in any case. "Why are all the women together? What are they doing?" They would watch us suspiciously.

Cristina continued:

> We didn't think we could go out and talk, because when it [broader peasant mobilizing in the region] began, it was made up of all men. But then as women we began to participate, because we began to work in the collectives. The government didn't like it, we would see the soldiers, the helicopters, the airplanes go by.

In both women's memories, the activities of AMMAC and CODIMUJ merged as part of one overall impetus of political formation. When I asked Ernestina and Cristina about the differences between the two spaces, Cristina replied, "I think they are the same; or at least, not different. It doesn't matter because the meetings were almost the same. They were about talking about women's suffering and struggling to change things." The principal difference between the two political spheres centered on stated objectives: while AMMAC held an explicitly political position of social struggle, CODIMUJ promoted reflection in order to indirectly advocate for social change, but not as a part of more formal organizational processes. However, it should be recognized that while the ideological, ethical, and political intentions of the two spaces may have diverged, the ways in which participating women interpreted and granted meaning to their experiences within AMMAC and CODIMUJ were closely intertwined. For them, the production collectives in the two organizations and the spaces for collective reflection served as central components in their political identity and engendered changes in their everyday lives, as Ernestina described:

> Before [the organizations were founded], women would not talk. They covered their heads in church and one didn't know if they had understood what was said during mass or during the Word of God. But in the collective, though at first they were embarrassed to participate, eventually they learned. It was there where we learned to talk.

Her friend added,

> We have no schooling, we don't know how to read or write. But we saw the truth with our own eyes. We learned with our own eyes. We learned as a group. . . . I told the women, we can participate as well. Each Monday we met to talk and work together as women. When we worked together, our hearts were lifted.

While most women in the Altamirano region participated both in AMMAC and in CODIMUJ, shortly before the uprising they fell under pressure by church officials and male community leaders to choose one or the other. Ernestina chose AMMAC, while Cristina remained with CODIMUJ. However, by then both women were participating clandestinely as Zapatista support bases, an affiliation neither abandoned. Shortly before the uprising, the AMMAC and CODIMUJ collectives redefined their political activity, including politicizing their domestic chores, a development that I analyze in detail in chapter 5. These were processes that unfolded parallel to the involvement of the men in a range of peasant organizations.

When the Struggle for Land through Peasant Organizations Is Not Enough

> We saw how the times were changing. First we realized that the PRI [Institutional Revolutionary Party] didn't care about us. When the local municipal governments were elected, everyone cheered in the streets of Altamirano. But then they [the politicians] would forget about us. We realized that they used us for their own purposes. The first important thing that happened [in the municipality of Altamirano] was the situation with the sawmill. There was this guy Sebastián, an indigenous man, who took the position of [*ejido*]

commissioner and then became the owner of the sawmill. He oppressed the workers, paid them next to nothing. The municipal president at the time was called Carlos Frey. He and Sebastián fought among themselves. They dragged us into their dispute. At the time we were with the J. Manuel Altamirano peasant organization that was part of the CNC [official government National Peasant Confederation].

These are the words of Simón, a forty-year-old Tseltal man. In the community of Zapata, a group of fifteen men including Simón met in 2006 to talk with me about the organizational processes in which they participated prior to joining the EZLN. The interview brought together two generations of men who had held positions of authority in local organizations. Discussion centered on what they had learned from these organizations, including how each political space expressed its demands over the years. Simón identified one of the most significant local events in the political formation of the men of his generation. It was 1980, Chiapas was seething with peasant movements (Harvey 2000), and those in the Altamirano region were unknowingly fueling local government interests seeking to incorporate potentially dissident organizations into state priorities.

A historical watershed in Chiapas had occurred six years earlier, during the 1974 Indigenous Congress, organized by the Diocese of San Cristóbal on the invitation of the state governor, Manuel Velasco Suárez. For the first time, over 1,500 indigenous representatives met to discuss their living conditions and forms of exploitation, to establish contacts, and to explore the possibility of creating a network. The Indigenous Congress played a crucial role in stimulating the organizational processes of the various regions in Chiapas. The preparations for the congress began with preliminary meetings at the local and municipal levels. After the event, the diocese coordinated a series of follow-up activities that operated under the assumption that the Indigenous Congress, rather than a one-day event, had been the beginning of an ongoing effort that "enabled the delegates to make progress, to engage in documenting the issues they face, to set up official services such as an agrarian delegation, an indigenous newspaper in the five languages, and a study of the exploitation of coffee growers" (Diócesis de San Cristóbal 1980). In fact, documents show that the two major peasant organizations in Chiapas, the Unión de Ejidos Quiptic Ta Lecubtesel (Union of Ejidos United by Our Strength)—which became the Union of Ejido Unions and Peasant Solidarity Groups of Chiapas, or Union of Unions, in 1980—and the Unión de Ejidos Lucha Campesina (Ejido

Union of Peasant Struggle), emerged as part of continued efforts to implement the agreements of the Indigenous Congress (Morales Bermúdez 2005; Diócesis de San Cristóbal 1983).

The Quiptic, legally established in December 1975, grouped together eighteen *ejidos* in the Lacandon Jungle valleys of Patihuitz and San Quintín, in the municipality of Ocosingo. In January 1977, the organization established a transportation, production, and purchasing cooperative. In the early 1980s, the more than seventy-five *ejidos* and twenty villages in the organization centered their political demands on resolving agrarian conflicts through the Ministry for Rural Affairs and improving the marketing of their agricultural products, especially coffee (Diócesis de San Cristóbal 1983).[16]

The first peasant organization in the Tzaconejá River valley was J. Manuel Altamirano, founded in 1976 and made up of twenty-nine *ejidos* (Iribarren Pascal 1986). State representatives attempted to set up this organization as one that appeared independent from state institutions but that bolstered government interests by drawing local populations away from the dissident mobilizing spurred by the Indigenous Congress. The same state representatives created the National Indigenist Institute, which promoted the formation of political cadres also for the purpose of weakening independent peasants' organizing efforts, a goal achieved through the active participation of indigenous leaders throughout the valleys, including Sebastián Santiz, the Tseltal leader from the municipality of Altamirano who ultimately founded J. Manuel Altamirano (Gaspar Morquecho, director of the NGO Chiltak, interview by author, January 2008). For some of the current members of the autonomous government, the political activities of this organization represented the first major intercommunity effort to struggle for land in the Tzaconejá River valley. Pánfilo from Zapata, a representative of Diecisiete de Noviembre's agricultural production commission when we spoke in 2007, recalled that "it was an organization created by the government itself. We didn't know at the time; we thought it was a way of getting ahold of land."

As the above narration describes, Sebastián Santiz engaged in a political power struggle with the municipal president, Carlos Frey. Santiz operated a sawmill as part of his commitment with the J. Manuel Altamirano organization. The business generated employment at a time when lumber was one of the leading sources of income in the region. As soon as Carlos Frey took office as municipal president, he immediately entered into a political dispute with Santiz over the profits generated. According to Pánfilo, both politicians "took advantage of the divisions between Tojolabales and Tseltales, and each sought the backing of one group: Santiz the Tseltales and Frey the Tojolabales." The conflict reached a crisis one day when male community members violently clashed with sticks and stones in the center of the town, with a toll of one dead and several wounded.

The men who participated in the events now remember the incident with a combination of humor and shame as one of the clearest examples in recent history of the manipulation of individuals by the interests of the local government and the *kaxlan* elite. Indeed, they do not remember Santiz as an indigenous man so much as someone who transcended this category to become a "politician" who took advantage of the ethnic divisions in the region to pursue his own economic interests. The men interviewed acknowledged that they joined together so as to expand the limits of their lands and market their products, but that at some point they found themselves embroiled in the power struggles of political stakeholders. Thus Pánfilo claimed that "J. Manuel Altamirano worked to counteract the demands of the Union of Unions [which was formed as a result of the Indigenous Congress]. It concerned itself with soliciting agricultural projects to make money, sell coffee, and obtain livestock. However, it was only a distraction [from more transformative political objectives]."

After the "sawmill dispute," some *ejido* members joined the Quiptic and continued to participate in land struggles so as to expand the *ejidos*, including those of Lázaro Cárdenas and Morelia. At the same time, others requested that new *ejidos* be established, while continuing to seek new ways to market their products. Elifonso, from Zapata, recalled,

> All kinds of problems began to arise, and for each problem we tried to find a way to try hard as indigenous people. We turned to the Union of Unions as a new way for the indigenous people to deal with the government. We tried to obtain land. . . . It was the young people who had no land, and the government offered no answers. "No, tomorrow," "the official is busy," "come back tomorrow"; that's all they said. And they got tired of going back and forth.

Another man, Salomón, interjected before Elifonso could finish, as if he wanted to draw attention to the lessons learned rather than the obstacles. Salomón explained their organizing process:

> [It] was step by step. The next was Quiptic, and our work progressed. With the Quiptic, what we learned is that you can be united. You can hold demon-

strations and do everything necessary to get what is yours. The move to the Union of Unions was a bigger step. Everything was on a larger scale, it was on a regional level, and progress was being made.

By "be[ing] united," Salomón was referring to their different levels of participation in the structures of both peasant organizations, including the coordination processes, the nomination of the delegates, the communication of information, and the assembly discussions. The peasant groups organized by valleys, where the inhabitants of each *ejido* or *ranchería* would discuss the problems they faced and make proposals to be put forward by the delegates at the regional assemblies of the two organizations. The proposals that were enacted at these assemblies were the ones that were seen as most viable in the light of the goals and strategies of the organization, and they centered on three strategic pillars: land, financing for agricultural production, and the marketing of coffee. This organizational makeup united the communities of the Lacandon Jungle valleys so strongly that Xochitl Leyva has referred to them as a "jungle commons" (2002, 60). Via a regional advisor, the agreements established by each of the six regional assemblies were presented at the General Assembly of Delegates of the Quiptic, which was the highest authority (Leyva 2002). Though not all the unions of *ejidos* followed the same methods, Quiptic members maintained spaces for critical reflection on past peasant struggles, together with an analysis of the current situation. Around this time, peasant organizations' demands included greater control over agricultural products, including access to markets, subsidies, and technical assistance (Harvey 2000, 143). Some of the men interviewed, such as Salomón, identified this change as part of the thinking they now associate with Zapatista autonomy. As Salomón put it,

> Up until the 1980s, the struggle was about land. Later, the organizations began to demand other things they needed because they realized that having a little bit of land wasn't enough. We needed better markets and support for our products. That was when we saw that, even once we had won all this, they still don't respect you [as indigenous people]; that's why the struggle for autonomy began.

In 1989, a dispute in the Union of Unions—which in 1988 had become known as the Asociación Rural de Interés Colectivo Unión de Uniones (Rural Association of Collective Interest Union of Unions)—based on political differences between the advisors and involving power struggles between them and the EZLN led to the foundation in 1991 of a new organization, the Alianza Campesina Independiente Emiliano Zapata (ACIEZ, Emiliano Zapata Independent Peasant Alliance). In the same period, some sectors of the community treated the women's AMMAC platform with suspicion, as they believed that the separate organizational process provoked divisions between the women and the men. As a result, in 1992, AMMAC merged with the ACIEZ. Subsequently, as part of the mobilization for the five hundred years of resistance on October 12, 1992, the organization took on a national character, becoming the Emiliano Zapata National Independent Peasant Alliance (ANCIEZ). By then, most of the population living in the *ejidos* in the municipality of Altamirano had joined the clandestine ranks of the Zapatista Army while openly participating as militants in ANCIEZ.

As part of the demonstrations held across the continent on October 12, 1992, ten thousand indigenous peasant farmers marched through the colonial streets of San Cristóbal. They carried placards protesting against the reforms to Article 27 of the Constitution, against the North American Free Trade Agreement, and against government policies they claimed "aim to wipe us out." Brandishing bows and arrows, they shouted, "Time to put an end to five centuries of oppression!" According to reports from that day, a gathering of such magnitude in the colonial city had not been recorded since the presidential campaign of Lázaro Cárdenas in the 1930s. Women interviewed recalled proudly that an AMMAC leader spoke on the need to struggle against women's oppression (Klein 2015). Upon arriving at the Santo Domingo church, two young men climbed the plinth of the statue of the conquistador who founded San Cristóbal de las Casas, Captain Diego de Mazariegos. Using sledgehammers, they succeeded in knocking it to the ground, where the people smashed it to pieces, the moment captured by photographer Antonio Turok. Zapata resident Simón recalled how

in 1992, the ANCIEZ held a major demonstration. People arrived in groups of 300 or 400. There were a lot of people. The government saw that the people were gathering strength. When there were demonstrations in San Cristóbal, the people insisted on going. We sent ten people from here, but they wanted to send more. To show our strength; we were truly united.

With their participation in ANCIEZ, the men of Zapata concluded a political trajectory of more than a decade of participation in different peasant organizations in the valleys. They believed that this accumulation of experience taught them the potential of their organizational capabilities. At the same time, these men emphasized that they learned to use novel political tools to negotiate with, and place pressure on, public officials, while escaping the corporatist and tutelary position that had been allocated to indigenous peasants. Simón and Salomón pointed to the fact that through the peasant organizations, they acquired knowledge about the inner workings of the state and the attitudes of public officials. Their experience of the bureaucratic processes required for requesting extensions to *ejidos*, the deceit of the engineers, and the complicity between the town hall and the ranchers led them to join the EZLM and struggle through the terrain of autonomy.

They acknowledged that on the basis of these negative experiences with public officials as well as the advances made under self-government, they broadened their definition of struggle to include not only land but also control over the different phases of production and marketing of their products. Meanwhile, they redefined the terms in which state officials stereotyped them as indigenous people. In the community of Zapata, the men's final recap of events concluded with the following words from a man named Juan: "And that was how the ideas for how to pursue our struggle were sown. . . . And well, things change, but the struggle goes on. . . . The way we organize ourselves changes when history changes, though the struggle remains the same."

Conclusion

As this chapter explained, the practices and meanings of autonomy partially emerged from historically contingent expressions of resistance in the region now known as Diecisiete de Noviembre. The collective reflections and the accounts narrated above suggest that the appropriation, use, and reinterpretation of these multiple political experiences arise from the diverse arenas of struggle in the recent past—from the spaces of the *ejido*, the Word of God, AMMAC, CODIMUJ, J. Manuel Altamirano, and the Quiptic. The presence of other actors not mentioned in the interviews but who have played a significant social and political role in the region should not be forgotten: these include the San Carlos hospital, which since the 1960s has provided health services in Altamirano, and various NGOs that since the 1980s have become involved in social- and economic-development projects in the communities. The combined cultural and political influences provide analytical tools that Zapatista community members are able to draw from so as to name different manifestations of oppression and exploitation.

In this chapter, I suggested that although after the 1970s the estate economies were largely dismantled, this did not in fact result in the dissolution of their racialized cultural project. As part of the naming of oppression and exploitation, community members highlighted in their narratives particular tropes that portray indigenous people as suited only to work for others, as perpetual infants in need of paternal benefactors, and as people whose bodies are continually marked through biological and cultural forms of degeneracy. In the following chapters, I analyze the practices of autonomy in light of the racialized tropes that fuel color-blind neoliberal policies. I focus on Zapatista agrarian reform as a series of cultural practices seeking to unravel the localized division of labor and historical tendencies to reconcentrate land in the hands of nonindigenous elites; women's production collectives as directly confronting the eugenics-inspired antipoverty development programs centered on addressing cultural forms of degeneracy; and decision-making practices under *mandar obedeciendo*—governing while obeying—as fragmenting the dichotomy between those destined to govern and those destined to obey. I shall begin with the first of these in the next chapter.

FOUR

Zapatista Agrarian Reform within the Racialized Fields of Chiapas

rnestina sighed deeply as she placed a tortilla on the *comal* (griddle) while speaking to me one evening in 2005. The smoke from the stove obscured the sadness and worry in her gaze. She was concerned about her son. "Mario went to work in Playa del Carmen twelve months ago, saying he'd be back in two, and there's no sign of him. Not a word, not a message." She was sixty years old and had dedicated the last few decades of her life to "the organization," as she referred to the EZLN. As women's coordinator, she was in charge of the production collectives and also served as a figure of authority in the region. "I joined the struggle for my children to have land and a better life," she explained.

The new generation represented by Ernestina's seven children does not live under the same conditions that gave rise to the Zapatista movement. Though there is more than enough land to farm, many young people choose to abandon "the struggle" and no longer work the fields. They labor for three or four months in the state of Tabasco or on the Riviera Maya in Quintana Roo in order to purchase most of their corn and bean supply for the year instead of maintaining a life of subsistence agriculture. Her youngest son, Mario, is a Zapatista. He inherited the family plot on the Morelia *ejido* yet in 2005 was traveling to the Caribbean every four months to earn a living as a construction worker in the tourist zone, only to return after two months to tend to the *milpa*. The family spent the 2,000 pesos (200 US dollars at that time) Mario saved during his weeks at the construction sites on corn and building materials, as their thirty-year-old wooden-board house was gradually falling apart.

When the EZLN announced a "red alert," what the rebel army defines as a delicate political conjuncture that requires taking drastic measures to protect its territory and civilian support bases, in the summer of 2005, the hundreds, if not thousands, of young Zapatistas who were living far from their villages were told to return immediately.[1] Mario did not respond to the summons and missed so many assemblies and collective responsibilities in Morelia that he was in danger of being expelled from "the organization." I could tell that knowing the very real nature of this possibility generated a deep anxiety in both Ernestina and her husband, Fabricio, yet despite their efforts, they were unable to locate their son.

The scene was very different that evening on Fifth Avenue, Playa del Carmen, on the Riviera Maya: The main thoroughfare of the tourist destination was lined with luxury stores, bars, restaurants, and open-air lounges decorated with soft, flowing fabrics and sofas, all in pure white. The crystalware tinkled with the movement of ice cubes submerged in liquor. Men drove convertibles at slow speeds while observing the bronzed skin of women strolling along the sidewalks. The average cost of a hotel room per night was 1,400 pesos (about 140 US dollars), and dinner for two was 800 pesos (80 US dollars).

Three streets away, there was a "little park" that was a meeting point for the construction workers who migrated there from the south of the country, from Tabasco, Yucatán, Veracruz, and above all from Chiapas.[2] The small plaza was surrounded by low-cost clothing stores and eateries such as the Gómez taco shop as well as stands selling fresh juice and lime-flavored lollipops. Everything cost three pesos. The sound of *cumbia* music emerged from the Tres Hermanos shoe store.

Saturday night was a time of rest for a few and of arrival for most. Men from all across the state of Chiapas met in this plaza. Few women undertook the journey. The complexity of political projects underway in Chiapas faded away here, reducing each individual to little more than a poor indigenous peasant in search of employment.

The intensity of the social activities taking place in both arenas increased as the night advanced, reaching a peak in the early morning. On Fifth Avenue, tourists celebrated the sea, sun, and sand. The exotic "Mayan route." In the little park, the four hundred men who had arrived early in the night multiplied to over a thousand. They played basketball, met old acquaintances, transformed backpacks into pillows to sleep on the grass or on the concrete, and, above all, they waited. A man from Palenque approached me to convey how he felt: "Here they treat us like mules. Hup! Hup! Hup! Faster! Work faster. Move it! We're not animals. But if you don't obey orders, you don't get paid."

At dawn, the men were already waiting for the contractors who arrive there in search of cheap labor. Those lucky enough to be hired immediately were driven to the construction sites for new tourist hotels. On the side of the highway closest to the beach, construction workers were building the Playa del Sol resort. On the other side, hidden among bushes three hundred meters down a dirt road, lay the makeshift camp where the majority of the workers stayed. Four galleries made of cardboard sheeting served as dormitories for over a thousand individuals. At the entrance to this compound, half a dozen guards stood watch. A notice read, "Show your ID card on entry. Have your belongings ready for a full search. Entry prohibited during work hours, from 7 a.m. to 7 p.m." There was a canteen a hundred meters away. Each meal there cost seventy-five pesos. At the small convenience store within the compound, the workers bought their drinking water since the tap water provided in the camp was not potable. The cost of everything the workers bought was taken from their weekly wages, a tab system that reminded me of the *tiendas de raya* (company stores) run by the estates decades ago.

A few years earlier, Antonio, a Tojolabal man from Diecisiete de Noviembre, had worked for three months on a similar site. He was so angered and humiliated by the experience that he kept a diary of his impressions of the exploitation as well as racial segregation that he and his fellow workers were subjected to.

I wrote about how my cousins lost their jobs. Before returning to Chiapas, they wanted to see the Fifth Avenue for themselves and went for a walk there. But the police arrived and threatened them. They told my cousins that if they didn't get out of the area they'd get beaten. That street wasn't a place for them; it was for the *kaxlanes*. There, at Playa del Sol, I thought a great deal about how we are treated as indigenous people. And about how difficult the struggle for autonomy is. However much you work, sometimes it isn't enough, and you are forced to go searching for jobs, even though you know you will be mistreated.

Such was the case of Mario, Ernestina's son. Despite having enough land, his family barely managed to get by, so he felt his only alternative was to leave to earn a wage. Over a year passed before Ernestina learned what had happened to her youngest son, her *kox*, in Tseltal. He was accused of a theft he did not commit and spent twelve months in jail, until the site foreman paid his bail. Another year passed before he could pay off the debt accrued with his former employer. During these two years, from 2006 to 2007, the family's finances deteriorated since there was no one else to help Fabricio work the land. Most of their other male children had left "the organization," and the remaining sons no longer lived in the *ejido* Morelia. Fabricio was able to keep up with the labor of caring for the coffee plants, which is less labor intensive, but not with that required in the cornfields. The price of corn rose in the local market, while the price of coffee—their sole source of income—fell once again. Ernestina said that her son had paid off what he owed, but he had not come back because he had gotten used to a life "where everything is purchased." He lost interest in the land. In her kitchen, Ernestina continued to await his return.

This chapter focuses on the struggle for land and territory as expressed in the possibilities and decisions of two generations of Zapatista community members, reflected in the lives of Ernestina and Mario. Before 1994, during the period in which the EZLN clandestinely organized and Ernestina made the decision to support the rebel army, the Mexican countryside underwent profound transformations as a result of neoliberal policies. The legal reforms opening the door to the privatization of communal lands and the dismantling of agricultural subsidies and programs, such as the coffee marketing board, represented the most significant changes. Against this backdrop, Ernestina's generation supported the 1994 armed uprising, the immediate result of which was the occupation of lands. In the case of the Altamirano and Ocosingo valleys, this led to a substantial increase in the area of arable land now managed by the Tseltal and Tojolabal peasant farmers, indeed more land than was required for the immediate needs of the local population. Two decades after the uprising, the Zapatista families in Diecisiete de Noviembre continued to have more than enough land to farm. For that reason, the land and territory commission as well as the agricultural production commission sought new economic markets for various products, though ironically the principal commodities remained those that had previously sustained much of the estate economies: coffee and livestock.

This chapter considers the effects of Zapatista land reform and agricultural production by situating current processes in historical trajectories so as to argue that Zapatista support bases effectively altered a local racialized division of labor whereby indigenous Tseltal and Tojolabal peasants had been historically situated within the niche of the peon. In doing so they transformed local political and racial geographies rendered visible through what I suggest is one of the most heavily disputed arenas between the color-blind neoliberal state and indigenous political actors: the relationship between landownership and political enfranchisement. In this disputed terrain, Zapatista cultural practices engaged in a fundamental struggle to redirect the effects of state agrarian policies for their own cultural political purposes.

At the same time, however, local social orderings were both shaped and limited by global racial economic forces, as the pressure to migrate as day laborers to the Yucatán Peninsula illustrates. In this sense, indigenous peasant farmers such as Ernestina's family continue to be subjected to neoliberal policies, even when their daily lives take place in consolidated projects of autonomy. As Antonio described through his experiences as a construction worker in Playa del Carmen, regardless of racialized unsettlings achieved through practices of autonomy, globalized tropes continue to attempt to resituate or restabilize indigenous bodies into the niche of the peon. In this light, the shifts in racialized geographies brought on by Zapatista land tenure and agricultural production both represent central contributions of Zapatista indigenous autonomy as well as pose one of its greatest challenges, or perhaps even limitations. The increase in migration, whether seasonal to the Riviera Maya or for extended periods to the United States, clearly reflects how global political and economic changes significantly shape the possibilities of deep social transformation in the autonomous communities.

This chapter is structured around the following questions: To what extent do neoliberal political-economic policies reflect the continuity of a racialized and gendered division of labor in rural Mexico? In what ways have the decisions undertaken by the men and women of Diecisiete de Noviembre affected land use and distribution as part of an autonomous political project? What alternatives emerge from within the tensions reflected in the family life of Ernestina and Mario?

In attempting to respond to these questions, the first section of this chapter details logics behind the certification of land titles under the Programa de Certificación de Derechos Ejidales y Titulación de Solares Urbanos (PROCEDE, Program for the Certification of Ejido and Land Ownership Titles), as it represents new rural-development interests. In the following sections, I detail the processes of Zapatista agrarian reform, together with the role played by the land and territory commission of Diecisiete de Noviembre in resolving agrarian conflicts, as aspects of self-government closely linked to the redistribution of natural resources. In turn, I analyze the implications of this process for the constitution of a sense of territory as central to struggle for *lekil kuxlejal*. Finally, I reflect on the potential and limitations of the Zapatista agrarian project when confronted by shifting racialized flows of the global economy.

PROCEDE: Land Tenure and Neoliberal Logics of Governance

A mile from the Caracol IV administrative center, a narrow dirt road leads to the top of a hill, to the "big house," the ruins of a residential building that previously belonged to estate owner Agustín Kanter. In the surrounding pasture, support bases built the autonomous secondary school, its classroom buildings and dormitories. Murals depicting everyday life in the villages adorn each of the wooden structures. More than fifty boys and girls between the ages of twelve and fifteen study, play soccer, participate in cooking activities, and live together here.

Of the "big house," only the foundation and broken brick walls remain. Students enjoy lounging on the grass growing among the ruins so as to enjoy the view of the Tzaconejá River valley. To both sides, a chain of mountains stretches out to the horizon, with two main peaks located at a middle distance. According to local legend, these peaks are Sakil Huitz and his lover, who greet each other at a given hour of the day. For a few seconds the lady reveals the golden treasure she conceals among her skirts. The surrounding land, which prior to 1994 was mostly cattle pasture belonging to a handful of landowning families with last names including Castellanos, Urbina, Kanter, and Solorzano, is now a patchwork of cultivated fields, dotted with trees, that are in the hands of some twenty Zapatista settlements and are among the thousands of hectares[3] occupied across Zapatista-held territory, representing decades of collective struggle pursued through multiple political strategies. There are ten more settlements on the other side of the town of Altamirano, which, added to the *ejidos* that are Zapatista sympathizers, total thirty-five communities in the autonomous municipality. Zapatista autonomy began with this land redistribution that inevitably transformed the local geography.

In this region, support bases took over at least twelve ranches to establish the new settlements, each of which is home to between seven and twenty families. As for the land in the valley that does not belong to "the

Figure 4.1. Partial remains of the house on the former estate of Pepe Castellanos in Ocho de Marzo, Diecisiete de Noviembre, 2005; photo by author

organization," the support bases did not force all landowners to leave their ranches in 1994. A few, particularly the small property owners, remain in the region and contribute in different ways to the municipality, whether through community or in-kind work, as determined by the *caracol* assembly each year. In 2008, for example, a *mestizo* man who owns twenty-four hectares informed the Zapatista authorities that his contribution that year involved helping with the preparations for the municipal celebrations and donating firewood for the autonomous secondary school's cafeteria.

While agrarian-based disputes existed prior to the 1994 uprising, these, rather than subsiding, have in some ways escalated. In the Altamirano/ Diecisiete de Noviembre region some of the former estate owners continue to demand the return of their property, while small landowners, both indigenous and *mestizo*, continue to live in the valley despite facing multiple forms of political pressure. Peasant and indigenous organizations, some aligned with the Zapatistas, sometimes have highly antagonistic political positions and claim rights to the same plots, using acts of violence and intimidation to pursue their goals.[4] Furthermore, other local political actors (accused of having links to the political class, the police, and even the armed forces) combine legal mechanisms and acts of repression to try to wrest lands away from the Zapatista municipalities.

Despite these political tensions, the transformation of the local land-scape from cattle pastures to cornfields is undeniable, as the view from the ruins of the Kanter house depicts. Change is even more evident if we compare the current makeup of the valley with the last two hundred years of agrarian history in the region, as detailed in the previous chapter. Such a historical vantage point renders visible how Zapatista land tenure and agricultural production have radically altered the local racialized division of labor that rested on the figure of the peon and on the tendency to concentrate the most fertile lands in the hands of a few *mestizo* elite families. In this chapter I analyze the government land-tenure program PROCEDE without losing sight of this long-term racialized geography, as an expanded temporal frame is central to rendering visible its racialized implications for indigenous peasant farmers.

Recall that beginning in 1988, the effects of neoliberal economic policies brought about juridical reforms aimed at land privatization and produced drastic cutbacks to social services and farm-subsidy programs, all of which helped set the stage for NAFTA. An orthodox neoliberal model considered the *ejido* a source of uncertainty that hinders private investment and considered people who collectively owned lands to have limited access to the loans required to increase productivity.[5] At the beginning of the 1990s, the World Bank recommended particular reforms of the *ejido* model, to which the Mexican state responded by amending Article 27 of the constitution in 1992 to, essentially, put an end to land reform (World Bank 2001). The state transformed the agrarian revolutionary figure of Emiliano Zapata from a symbol of "land and freedom" to one of "freedom and rural justice," "freedom" in this case meaning, as Lynn Stephen (2002) notes, the freedom to choose the future of *ejido* lands. *Ejidatarios* acquired the right to sell or rent their parcels, to hire laborers, and to use their property as a guarantee for loans. Meanwhile, they were no longer obliged to work on their own plots and they acquired the right to join forces with investors. In legal terms, the *ejido* was essentially transformed from social property to a commodity.

To facilitate this process of commodification, the Mexican government created three new institutions: the Secretariat of Agrarian Reform (SRA), the Office of Special Prosecutor for Agrarian Affairs, and the National Agrarian Register (RAN). At the end of 1992, the government created PROCEDE "to provide legal certainty to ownership of the land, regularize land rights, resolve boundary conflicts, and grant certificates of ownership" (Procuraduría Agraria 2006). PROCEDE operated by means of a complex coordination between the Office of Special Prosecutor for Agrarian Affairs and the RAN, together with Instituto Nacional de Estadística y Geografía (INEGI, National Institute of Statistics and Geography). The SRA coordinated the program, while the special prosecutor provided advice to the agrarian centers and the RAN registered and certified land parcels. Article 56 of the 1992 Agrarian Law created the legal framework and granted new powers to the *ejido* assembly as the highest decision-making body in the *ejido*. To enter the title-granting process, *ejidatarios* required the approval of half of their assembly plus one vote. Subsequent assemblies would set out the boundaries and assignation of the lands, whether individual or for collective use. According to the official documents, the changes in land tenure had four objectives: to define the rights of the *ejido* owners; to enable access to loans and to planting crops with higher yields; to create the conditions of security and stability needed to attract public and private investment; and finally to improve governance (Procuraduría Agraria 2006).

PROCEDE operated in three phases: the first was based on the decision of the *ejido* assembly to effectively enter into the process of land demarcation; the second led to the certification of individual or joint use of the property; and the third and final phase resulted in the full title to individual property. By the time the program ended in 2006, the results illustrated a strong resistance to transforming communal lands into individual property, especially in states with large indigenous populations, such as Chiapas, though the results were mixed in terms of those *núcleos agrarios* (communal agrarian lands that include both *ejidos* and *comunidades agrarias* [agrarian communities], which are indigenous collective lands recognized as existing prior to the Mexican Revolution) that entered into the first phase of PROCEDE. Of the 31,480 communal agrarian lands at a national level, 28,755 completed the first phase of PROCEDE, accounting for 91 percent of the total. However, only 3,115 communal agrarian lands, or 10 percent of the total, completed the final phase of individual land titling (RAN 2007). Chiapas was far below the national average. Agrarian statistics for 2006 from the special prosescutor's office indicate that 74 percent of the 2,944 communal agrarian lands in Chiapas initiated the certification process (INEGI 2006). However, only 22 communal agrarian lands there completed the final stage of PROCEDE, constituting less than 0.01 percent of the total (RAN 2007). This contrasts sharply with states such as Guanajuato, where 21 percent of communal agrarian lands became individually titled properties.

By 2006, in the municipalities of Altamirano, Las Margaritas, San Andrés Larráinzar, and Ocosingo, four key municipalities in the conflict zone, 40 percent of the communal agrarian lands had entered the first phase of the certification process. RAN records for Altamirano list a total of 30 communal agrarian lands there, 29 being *ejidos* and 1 an agrarian community.[6] Of these, the following 10 entered into the initial phase of PROCEDE and none continued into the final phase: Rancho San Mateo; Rusia; Puerto Rico; Venustiano Carranza; Agua Escondida; San Marcos; La Candelaria; Nueva Virginia; Saltillo; and La Laguna. These figures substantiate an argument made by Ana de Ita (2005) before the end of the program that *ejidatarios* largely accepted the certification process simply to avoid conflicts, to clarify the *ejido* boundaries, and to increase participation, all of which strengthened social relations within the *ejidos*. These goals acquired greater significance than the rent or sale of private lands. Such forms of tacit resistance do not mean that mining interests or other megadevelopment projects are not impacting indigenous lands and territory. To the contrary, both state and private investments are resulting in the dramatic dispossession of indigenous lands throughout the country.

The interest of indigenous and peasant communities to avoid internal conflicts or conflicts with other *ejidos* is key, as we shall see further below, given that while holding out the promise of greater clarity in ownership as one of the main objectives of PROCEDE, government agrarian institutions failed to prioritize resolving thousands of agrarian disputes. Within the vacuum left by the state, one of the central activities of autonomous government representatives in Diecisiete de Noviembre became precisely the resolution of land conflicts.

I would like to return to the last stated objective of the program described above—to improve governance—to reflect upon its underlying racialized logics. This last aim represents a significant shift in federal priorities. As governmental multilateral institutions' documents illustrate, during the decade after 1992, the goal of agrarian reform consisted of eliminating state protection mechanisms so that market supply and demand could dictate new alternatives, including releasing the labor force in regions where peasant farmers were principally engaged in subsistence agriculture and providing the motivation to grow higher-yield crops. However, by 2001 there was a major shift in priorities. Government documents highlight the importance of transforming land tenure through agrarian certification not only as part of economic reform but also to facilitate new political processes, particularly to strengthen governance. This presupposes a close link between privatizing land, improving individual capacity for action resulting from market opportunities, and administering social-conflict resolution procedures (Deininger 2003). At the same time, the new emphasis responds to adjustments promoted by neoliberal policies that, after 2000, tended to prioritize strengthening governance, including encouraging citizens to effectively respond to the interests of the market and the new role played by the state in relation to the market (Schild 2013). The shift toward governance is reflected in a World Bank study of the property regime in Mexico, which indicates that one of the first changes made in the ejido was to "strengthen self-governance of the *ejido*," allowing it to "choose . . . its property rights regime," and to recognize "the legal personality of the *ejidos* and the ability of the assembly to autonomously regulate internal matters" (World Bank 2001, vi).

The priority placed on the certification of property as a requirement for citizen participation and for social stability acquired even greater relevance in Chiapas. The EZLN opposed PROCEDE, and it was not the only organization to do so. Peasant organizations such as the Rural Association of Collective Interest, the Emiliano Zapata Independent Peasant Alliance, and the Independent Center for Agricultural and Peasant Workers took similar positions, demanding that state representatives reach agreements with organizations rather than with each *ejido* individually (Reyes Ramos 2008). In this highly politicized context, official institutions prioritized particular definitions of social stability as fitting into the new mechanisms of governance, including limiting the political power of many of these peasant organizations and ameliorating agrarian conflicts.

During an interview with me in June 2005, Martha Cecilia Díaz Gordillo, the special representative for the SRA in Chiapas, emphasized the importance of reaching "social stability."[7] During the administration of Governor Pablo Salazar (2000–2006) in Chiapas, Díaz Gordillo was responsible for resolving agrarian conflicts. Rather than seeking to resolve the thousands of small-scale agrarian disputes between *ejidos*, the SRA during the Fox presidential administration identified key agrarian "hot spots" across the country and designated special representatives to resolve these large-scale conflicts in several states.[8] One of the most significant was the case of Montes Azules in the Lacandon Jungle, a conflict that began decades earlier, during the Echeverría administration (1970–1976), when 614 hectares were granted to the Lacandon indigenous community in spite of the fact that 4,000 Tsotsil, Ch'ol, and Tseltal families had already migrated into the jungle and established settlements in the same territory; the decision led to deep social unrest, which culminated in the creation of the Unión de Ejidos Quiptic Ta Lecubtesel peasant organization (Harvey 2000). In order for PROCEDE to enter this area of the Lacandon Jungle, the SRA first needed to resolve the still-running agrarian dispute of Montes Azules. When interviewed, Díaz Gordillo referred to this case as *the* hot spot that impeded overall shifts in land tenure in the region.

In relation to the program's stated objectives, Díaz Gordillo believed that "PROCEDE did not increase access to loans or to the economic markets. Its greatest contribution has been to the internal life of the *ejidos*" and to the generation of broader definitions of the concept of democracy. According to the special representative, the reorganization of land tenure led to improvements in the level of governance on two counts: within *ejidos* and in terms of citizen participation more broadly. As to the first, she acknowledged that the state's role in the *ejido* system encouraged passivity and dependence, with a paternalistic relationship whose effects continue to permeate peasants' relationship to the state. She explained that "peasant farmers are used to receiving subsidies from the government, not from the private sector. This is a tradition still alive today. They feel that even though they've received the title to their lands the government still has to provide money or support. This culture still hasn't changed."

Díaz Gordillo's explanation highlights the negative effects of a tutelage state-peasant relationship. However, rather than recognizing the role of state policies in engendering such deeply entrenched dynamics, she blamed indigenous peasants themselves for culturally reproducing infantilized attitudes of dependency. In fact, the public official used the term "tradition" to evoke just how deeply she considers these practices to run. Díaz Gordillo then continued to explain that indigenous and peasant performed passivity combines with the lack of democratic practices in the *ejido*, given that political power is concentrated in the figure of the commissioner, the state's immediate interlocutor. She argued that culturally enacted forms of dependency coexist with antidemocratic, internal-community "traditional" practices. This second aspect of Díaz Gordillo's argument finds a partial normative explanation given that prior to the reforms, *avecindados*, those who live in the *ejido* but are not formally *ejidatarios*, either because they are children who did not inherit rights or because they moved to the settlement, had no right either to express their opinions or to vote, despite working *ejido* lands and living in the village. Díaz Gordillo indicated that the government's purpose in distributing property certificates was to transform this culture of dependency by encouraging greater citizen participation. Later in the interview, Díaz Gordillo clarified that participation is spurred by property title since it

> alters the relationship between the people and those in power. We have observed that when people lack a document, they are fearful of what may happen. So with the land certificate, they have more power. Delivering these certificates to everyone is a form of spreading democracy within the *ejido*. With the reform to Article 27, the assembly becomes the highest authority, in place of the commissioner.

According to the SRA special representative's argument, the property owner enjoys clarity about what he or she owns and can thus take decisions about his or her well-being as well as about the options set out by market interests. Political power is no longer concentrated in the figure of the commissioner or any other local political leader, such as a teacher or a priest, because each individual has the right to participate in decision-making processes. Following the same line of argument, the certification process spurs democratic practices among *ejidatarios* since it alters culturally inscribed "traditions" of dependency and diminishes a concentration of power. To foster these new attitudes, government representatives negotiate directly with the *ejidatarios* through their assembly and refuse to allow peasant organizations to join the discussions or to take part in the decision making. According to Díaz Gordillo, as well as other state officials interviewed as part of this research, the security granted by a land title strengthens participation not only within the *ejido* but also within wider society; on a small scale, these changes reflect broader aspects of new forms of citizen participation in democratic processes as a whole. During the interview, Díaz Gordillo cited laws of supply and demand as motors behind greater democratic practice. The ejido assembly, with a mandate of three-quarters of the votes, can vote to sell, rent, or seek investment or alter land use to cultivate higher-yield crops. The decisions increase participation by members of society and give them greater responsibility over that which affects their well-being.

Two key conclusions may be drawn from this interview. First of all, PROCEDE reflected broader neoliberal logics since it operated under the assumption that a land title both promotes self-government in the *ejido* and encourages entrepreneurship and independence in peasant subjects. These are the corrected "cultural habits" and social practices prized by the state. However, at the same time the state exercises, and indeed reinforces, its role as a promoter of these new types of citizens, it virtually eliminates its capacity to administer land and resource redistribution, except in the cases of "hot spots," such as Montes Azules. As a result, mechanisms that regulate indigenous peasant farmers are delinked from the redistribution of natural resources among the population.

Secondly, implicit in these priorities is the assumption that liberal principles of property and citizenship lead to better governance: land titles generate a greater sense of security and foster *ejidatarios'* active participation. Both the *dominio pleno* property regime (when individual private titles are issued) and the initial stage of landownership certification (when a cartography is presented) facilitate the insertion of peasant farmers into the alternatives provided by the market. In this fashion, different actors become "stakeholders," meaning that they can establish relationships of joint investment or joint responsibility with the private sector, including contracting out their agricultural activities. Such changes in property regimes facilitate new democratic processes as part of a broader neoliberal framework, that is the rationale. In light of this model, support bases interviewed in Diecisiete de Noviembre drew attention to the impact of neoliberal agrarian reforms by evoking racialized (neo)colonial relations and offered alternatives to property regimes and political participation.

Zapatista Agrarian Reform

> The people from the Agrarian Reform think that democracy comes from individual land titles, but they've got it backward. It is true that the *ejido* didn't let everyone participate and that the commissioner was a spokesperson for the government, but taking away collective lands is not the solution—it's the problem. There is no democracy when the few can buy the land. Democracy is when there is land to work.

This was the reaction of Juan Miguel during a group interview in which I shared information gathered on PROCEDE and on the priorities of the Office of the Special Prosecutor for Agrarian Affairs. Following my interviews of state officials, I continued to reflect on their underlying liberal assumptions that suggest private property necessarily leads to greater social stability and citizen participation. I was left thinking about how such rationales operate through an apparently level playing field. However, when present-day arenas are viewed in light of historically engen-

Figure 4.2. Women, their faces covered to identify them as Zapatista members and to protect their identities, in Cinco de Mayo, Diecisiete de Noviembre, 2006; photo by author

dered expressions of *mestizo* privilege, as detailed in the previous chapter, this apparent horizontal terrain turns heavily slanted as it resituates indigenous peoples in subordinated positions, rendering them vulnerable to conditions of dispossession. I was interested in further discussing these issues with Zapatista authorities.

It turned out that this was the sole topic that they showed any interest in discussing. After a number of failed attempts, we managed to meet, members of the autonomous council, of the honor and justice commission, and myself. At first light, Hortensia, María, Sara, Juan Miguel, Antonio, and Santiago arrived to a corner of the large wooden auditorium in the *caracol* compound to talk about the coordination between the different commissions and the council. I was interested in hearing how their stated responsibilities translated into concrete daily activities and meanings posited onto the practices of autonomy. This interview did not arouse much enthusiasm. Excess work, the damp cold of winter, and a thick mist that confused night and day defeated any attempt to raise our spirits. As we sat huddled on wooden benches surrounding a makeshift table and drank lukewarm, heavily sugared coffee, I asked questions, to which they responded at best with brief answers, making for a rather dry, monosyllabic interview—until the issue of agrarian reform surfaced.

Toward the end of our conversation, I presented the principal points on PROCEDE that I had gathered from public documents and a summary of the interviews I had held with public officials. Given the snail-paced conversational dynamic of the morning, I was surprised by the extreme level of collective enthusiasm on the subject. Santiago, Antonio, and Juan Miguel moved forward in their seats and stopped drinking their coffee to listen to the description of my interview with Díaz Gordillo and much of the official content of PROCEDE described above. Santiago interjected, "I think that PROCEDE and taking away the *ejidos* are made to continue forcing indigenous people out [of their lands]. That is why we have our own agrarian reform."

A lengthy discussion of their Zapatista agrarian reform ensued, among the men in particular. Forgetting about my presence for a moment, they began talking rapidly in Tseltal. I understood enough of the conversation to know they were discussing the way the *ejido* system had been implemented in the region and the fact that government representatives had come in past years to non-Zapatista *ejidos* to encourage communal landholders to enter the process of land titling. Santiago shared rumors as to which *ejidos* in the region of Altamirano had accepted PROCEDE. They discussed among themselves details of some of the recent agrarian dispute cases between non-Zapatista-aligned communities and then compared those conflicts to the dynamics in the new Zapatista settlements. Although they contributed limited thoughts, the three women on the council for the most part followed the conversation with an air of deep concentration. In general, the council representatives situated the autonomous activities coordinated by the land and territory commission in direct opposition to the objectives set out in the official documents.

At that point, Juan Miguel offered the comment quoted above in order to both agree with state representatives on the lack of collective participation internal to *ejido* affairs and simultaneously critique government decisions to then do away with the *ejido* on a whole. He then questioned the premise on which democracy is defined, arguing that state policies that seek to privilege those already in positions of power as well as reconcentrate wealth and access to resources are in their very essence antidemocratic as they activate historical exclusions of indigenous people. Though PROCEDE may not have been as effective in spurring land privatization in organized indigenous regions as it was intended to be, this does not mean that subsequent reforms, in energy and mining policies as well as in private investment, have not resulted in the accelerated dispossession of indigenous and peasant lands.

Since the early 2000s, numerous megadevelopment projects have posed direct threats to indigenous lands and territories, including mining projects; projects to exploit new energy sources, such as hydroelectric dams, fracking operations, and wind farms; and large infrastructure projects such as superhighways. These are what the indigenous lawyer Francisco López Bárcenas refers to as the "new routes of plunder" (2011, 181). López Bárcenas points to legislative reforms such as the Expropriation Law, the National Water Law, the Sustainable Forestry Development Law, the Mining Law, and the Agrarian Law as establishing legal justification for either the expropriation of lands or land privatization through different modalities including direct property sales, the renting of lands, and private concessions. Some of the most well-known indigenous struggles against these megadevelopment projects include the Consejo de Ejidos y Comunidades Opositores a la Presa la Parota (Council of Ejidos and Communities against the La Parota Dam), which since 2003 has opposed the hydroelectric dam in La Parota, Guerrero; the opposition by the Wixarika (indigenous Huichol) communities since 2011 to the twenty-two mining concessions granted by the Mexican government to the Canadian company First Majestic Silver Corporation in their sacred land of Wiricuta; the Yaqui tribe's struggle against the aquaduct La Independencia, which would essentially divert a large percentage of the water from the Yaqui River and would directly affect surrounding valleys; the Asamblea de Pueblos Indígenas del Istmo en Defensa de la Tierra y el Territorio (Assembly of Indigenous Peoples in the Isthmus in Defense of Land and Territory), which is against fourteen wind-energy projects that would take away more than 1,500 hectares of indigenous communal land; and the struggle of the indigenous Otomí community San Francisco Xochicuautla, in the state of Mexico, against the construction of a superhighway that would expel them from ancestral lands

In fact, the sole point Juan Miguel as well as other autonomous government representatives shared with the government position was that the *ejido* model, as implemented since the administration of Lázaro Cárdenas in the 1930s, no longer represented a viable solution for indigenous peasant people. This critique drew my attention, given the publicly strong opinion of most indigenous and peasant organizations that the *ejidos* encapsulate political demands. I asked the autonomous government representatives to explain why they criticized the *ejido* model, especially since the communal landholdings are so vehemently defended by indigenous and peasant communities as their central victory of the Mexican Revolution. Antonio responded, focusing his explanations on the ways that the state monitored and limited participation in decision-making practices:

> The government would come to the assemblies to see how we made decisions and to check that only *ejidatarios* were involved—because the *avecindados* weren't supposed to take part in the assembly. The women didn't take part either—only the men. We depended on the government. We had to ask them for everything, though they never delivered. The commissioner did what the Agrarian Reform people told him to; he was just their spokesman. We've seen that this doesn't work.

In most of the group interviews I held during fieldwork, other men offered similar opinions and included three additional critiques of the *ejido* model. The first was on the role played by the state in regulating *ejidatario* participation and the heightened passivity that ensued. To be *ejidatarios* and to receive government "support" required showing loyalty to the political party in power. In contrast to Díaz Gordillo's arguments, which placed the blame for a dependency relationship on indigenous peasants' "cultural habits," Antonio and other Zapatista community members emphasized that unequal power relationships with a corporatist state set the terms for clientelistic ties. The second critique was on the limited level of male participation, largely reduced to voting in the assemblies. These votes, in turn, tended to reinforce the opinions or interests of the commissioner, who acted as an individual interlocutor between the *ejido* and state institutions, a role that lent strength to the continuation of local *cacicazgos* (bossmen in positions of political-economic power). The inertia concentrating power in the figure of the commissioner existed in direct proportion to the exclusion of virtually all women in the *ejido* as well as all male *avecindados*, who lacked the right to participate in the assemblies. The third criticism concerned the quality of the *ejido* lands, as most existed on the hilltops or on the margins of those fertile lands that remained occupied by the estate owners.[9]

At the same time, autonomous government representatives held heated disagreements with government officials as to the reasons behind the model's ineffectiveness, as well as the solutions posed. On this point, autonomous government authorities insisted that the right to collective lands remains an unwavering demand of the Zapatista support bases, along with the majority of indigenous and peasant organizations around the country.[10] Throughout my research, all those interviewed constantly reiterated such a claim and tended to further stress the issue by describing the importance of the cornfields in their daily lives. Such an emphasis led me to ask, what is the role of an autonomous government in ensuring access to the land so that Tseltal and Tojolabal community members can harvest their *milpas*?

When Juan Miguel emphasized in the opening quotation that democracy is ensuring that indigenous people's land permits them an agricultural life, he linked collective political participation to resource distribution. At the same time, he invited a historical reading of racialized structural conditions of inequality so as to highlight the implications of current state land policies for indigenous people. In doing so, he signaled that self-government and resource distribution lie at the heart of Zapatista politics. They initiate the practices of autonomy, and, as the following sections illustrate, figure prominently in generating a feeling of belonging as part of constructing a sense of territory that partially unravels racialized hierarchies. The struggle for *lekil kuxlejal* has as a central pillar the collectives' relationship to a physical locality, which connects them both to their ancestors and to the possibility of future generations.

The 1994 uprising provided the historical conjuncture to de facto exercise Zapatista communities' right to collective lands as well as to implement their own brand of agrarian reform, first through direct action, the armed uprising as part of a political-military strategy, and subsequently through the exercise of autonomy. In the new settlements, I would often sit in the afternoon light outside people's homes or in the center of the community to have informal conversations, as it is a time of day when daily activities dwindle, leaving time for contemplation. That is how I spent one afternoon in Pancho Villa, a community situated on a flat pasture near the Tzaconejá River, with mountains all around (see fig. 4.3). Most residents here are originally from S__ F_____, an *ejido* nestled on a rocky slope, where one has to walk around boulders to get from one house to another. Though not practical for daily activities, the rocky land served as an effective refuge when *ejido* members faced off against police forces as part of peasant mobilizations in demand of additional land prior to the uprising. Zapatista elders continued to live on their *ejidos* while their children settled on the valley floor that had previously belonged to the Urbina family, specifically the ranches El Trébol and El Jobero.

On that afternoon I sat on the grass outside the home of Manuel, until Nacho saw us chatting, walked over, and joined the conversation. We had finished the group interviews the day before, when we spoke at length of

Figure 4.3. Community members in Pancho Villa, Diecisiete de Noviembre, 2006; photo by author

the regional changes spurred by the activities in the autonomous municipality. It was clear to me that they had continued to think about this issue and wanted to pick up the conversation. Given our vantage point of the entire village, both Manuel and Nacho pointed to its physical changes. They recalled the cattle pastures of the Trébol and then remembered the emptiness felt on these lands after 1994, when the Urbina family left and never came back. Manuel remarked that "they left the livestock and everything. Urbina came back only once to try and buy the tractor he had left. We told him no, it was useful for the municipality. It is the same tractor we still use today."

They recalled the exact date that they and other young people in their early twenties or late teens took their belongings to settle and build their homes on these lands: February 26, 1996. The date chosen by Zapatista authorities to coordinate the founding of new settlements throughout the region was exactly ten days after the signing of the first round of the peace talks of San Andrés. Founding these new villages became a concrete material expression of what the rebel army signed on paper. Manuel and Nacho recalled that 1996 was the year when all the new settlements founded their villages, it was a year dedicated to demonstrating how increased political power by indigenous Zapatistas could effectively shift terms of engagement with the state. In essence, it opened the possibility to affirm politics as centered on *kuxlejal*. Nacho, in his midthirties when we talked, recalled how they had moved onto these lands and started to work the fields:

When we drew up the list of who was going to live here, we were twenty-six or twenty-eight families. We measured out the streets and the house plots. Some couldn't handle it and they started to leave. At the time, the agreement was that everyone could take whatever land they thought they could work. After a few years, we measured out the fields in one place, and then the next year, in another place. Now we operate a land-rotation agreement to avoid exhausting the soil.

Since that time, the autonomous government has granted lands to those support bases and to non-Zapatista peasant farmers (not exclusively to indigenous people) who agree to respect the terms and regulations established in the EZLN Revolutionary Agrarian Law, which stipulates that "the lands affected by this agrarian law will be distributed to landless peasants and to agricultural workers as collective property for the formation of cooperatives, cooperative societies, or production collectives, that must be worked as a collective" (EZLN 1993a). The regulations include rejecting all government programs, participating in community and municipal activities, including in collective agricultural work, and agreeing to other Zapatista responsibilities. The Zapatista Agrarian Law was subsequently incorporated into the regulations of the autonomous municipalities. According to those interviewed, the requirements to work on the recuperated lands in Diecisiete de Noviembre included agreeing to three main criteria: the prohibition of alcohol consumption, the obligation to participate in collective work, and the obligation to send children to Zapatista schools in rejection of official public schools.

In the first years of the autonomous municipality, members of local *ejidos* whose inhabitants are not exclusively Zapatista support bases, such as Venustiano Carranza, Lázaro Cárdenas, Puebla Nueva, Puebla Vieja, and Belisario Domínguez, accepted the invitation to join the new settlements. Despite the enormous efforts required to keep up with all the activities and obligations in these communities, the opportunity proved attractive to those families for a number of reasons. To begin with, the new Zapatista communities ensured land for at least the future generation and their children. The land on the valley floor proved much more fertile than what they could access for their *milpas* in most of their *ejido* lands. Such high quality soil promised production that could potentially meet the subsistence needs of families so they would not have to purchase corn for part of the year, as was the case in most communities.[11] However, over the

Figure 4.4. A girl working in the women's vegetable garden collective, *ejido* Morelia, Diecisiete de Noviembre, 1999; photo by Francisco Vazquez

years many returned to their original communities because of economic problems, the need to migrate in search of other sources of work, and the exhaustion that sometimes resulted from being part of the resistance, as it meant rejecting government-led projects and taking part in numerous collective activities as part of the ongoing construction of the new centers. Alejandra Aquino (2012) points to these factors, more than political differences, as the reason community members in the La Realidad valley abandoned the ranks of the EZLN.

Over the years, the gradual erosion of political support proved not to be the unidirectional tendency. A decade after the uprising, individuals from the *ejidos* or from small private properties would enter the autonomous council office asking to join "the organization," which would allow them to move into the new settlements. In early 2008, for example, I documented that an average of two families per week were asking to join the Zapatista villages. This political reaccommodation of families in the region reflects attempts to maneuver amidst an extremely complicated political field constructed in part by limited economically viable options.

Here I would like to return to Ernestina and her son Mario to highlight how the political densities on which the Zapatista agrarian reform rests affect families. As I described at the beginning of this chapter, Ernestina and her husband, Fabricio, are *ejidatarios* in the community of Morelia. As legally recognized communal land members, their family has the right to work agricultural parcels and access communal areas, such as forested hills, for their personal use. At the same time, as Tseltales, they have participated all their lives in rituals that ask the land's permission to plant and harvest the *milpas*, as well as granting offerings to the spirits for a balanced rainy season that ensures abundant crops and sets the foundation for individual as well as collective health and well-being.

The couple raised seven children, though only some will officially inherit *ejido* lands. Concern about having land use for their children's future was one of the aspects that Ernestina and her husband remember prioritizing when they decided as a couple to join the clandestine political-military organization years prior to the uprising. Land, however, was not their only concern. During the countless conversations I held with Ernestina and Fabricio over the years, they would recount the beatings family members were subjected to by local *kaxlanes* and the manipulation of indigenous communities on the part of local political figures to further personal interests. Ernestina would refer to her largely positive experiences in the catechist boarding school to contrast humiliating interactions with local estate owners or their families in Altamirano. The sum of these lived experiences drives home an important point: while land redistribution, the ability to work the land and define the use of that land, including how it is to be respected and honored, may be one of the most evident expressions of community commitment to the Zapatista struggle, this reason is inextricably linked to a rejection of everyday racialized expressions of inferiority. Implementing the Zapatista agrarian reform and participating in the normative systems regulating autonomous agricultural practices translate into very concrete ways of unraveling the local fusion of racism to labor exploitation.

That is not to say that no forms of subversion or resistance existed prior to the Zapatista agrarian reform in the region. The *ejidatarios* of Morelia, for example, recall how, long before the uprising, community members agreed that both *ejidatarios* and *avecindados* would participate in the assemblies and make decisions, regardless of the formal rules on paper. Those sons unable to formally inherit land would work the family fields anyway and participate in communal responsibilities. Though virtually no women participated in the public space because few of them were *ejidatarios*, women such as Ernestina recall discussing in the home the decisions that their husbands would convey in the assembly. At the same time, rather than family parcels clearly delineated, virtually all the *ejido* was considered communal land. Families had general areas where they grew corn, though these were respected more out of long-term habit than because of what was legally recorded on paper. Thus, critiques of the *ejido* system, as expressed by autonomous government authorities, do not exist in a void, but rather emerged through low-volume acts of nonconformity and subversion prior to these families' joining the rebel army; the daily challenging of power over time then fused into high-volume political enunciations as part of the practices of autonomy.

When I stayed in Morelia, I would often go with Fabricio early in the morning to gather firewood for use in the family kitchen. While we walked up and down narrow, cleared paths interspersed with corn or coffee plants, Fabricio would point out that a certain family typically grew their *milpa* in a particular plot, and would then point out where the *milpa* of another family was located. In general, families shifted use of particular areas in multiyear rotations that permitted some land to lie fallow while another field grew corn, so as to avoid depleting the soil of its nutrients. The forested areas we wandered through to search for dry trunks or branches on the ground was for everyone to enjoy as long as they respected assembly decisions as to the type of usage. This kind of assembly decision making in Morelia in fact reflects a tendency in many *ejidos* with a large indigenous population, particularly in the southern regions of Mexico.[12]

In the case of Morelia, assembly decisions do not always result in clear-cut regulation of community practices, given that the *ejido* is politically divided. Two assemblies, both the assembly made up of Zapatista supporters and the one aligned with political parties, implement decisions concerning land use. While at times the collective decisions converge in their agreements, often this is not the case. One of the regulations generally accepted regardless of political affiliation is that firewood may be collected as long as it comes from a fallen tree or from already dried trunks or branches. The assemblies forbid families to cut down a living tree for firewood. In contrast, a point of contention exists in regard to the use of agricultural chemicals and fertilizers; Zapatista normative systems prohibit the use of chemicals, while that is not necessarily the case for the rest of the *ejido* members.

Similar practices of communal land use continue as part of the new Zapatista settlements. As Nacho described in our conversation in Pancho Villa, no individual family owns a particular plot of land, nor does any family have a specific plot assigned to them. Instead, upon arriving in the village, family members walk through potential sites for their *milpas*, trying out different areas of the new community until settling on those that most please them. After the first few years of working the land, each family establishes its own routine, respected in large part by the rest of the families, though in the cases of overlapping interests, the land and territory commission intervenes.

In 1996 the *ejido* of Morelia underwent a profound political split, with many Zapatista sympathizers leaving the movement, shifting the political balance that until that time had weighed heavily in favor of those aligned with the rebel army. One of Ernestina's sons, Eugenio, would later form part of that contingency, opting to return to the *ejido* and align himself with the assembly antagonistic to the Zapatista movement. Though I never had the opportunity of speaking directly to him about his decision to leave "the organization," his parents accused him of drinking too much, which violates Zapatista regulations. Between alcohol and the organization, he chose the former. Fabricio frequently expressed deep anger at his son's decision to abandon the results of their struggle. Aquino (2012) notes that for Ernestina's generation, the emphasis they placed on struggling to leave the life of a peon on the estates makes it incredibly difficult to understand, much less accept, that their children might opt to temporarily or even permanently migrate to other states in Mexico or to the United States in search of employment.

One day I arrived at the couple's home to find Eugenio drinking coffee with them in the kitchen. I noticed there was no more corn from last year's harvest piled in the corner of the kitchen. Ernestina was making tortillas using store-bought Maseca cornmeal while they waited for Mario to return from the state of Veracruz, where he had traveled for a month to earn enough money to allow them to purchase sufficient corn until this year's harvest. I noticed the air was tense, but since I had already entered their home, I had no choice but to join a conversation that immediately switched upon my arrival to talk about fairly mundane affairs such as the weather, how my parents were, and when they would come again for a visit. Once his son left, Fabricio flew into a fit.

Eugenio's decision to leave the organization, despite having participated as an insurgent in the rebel army, generated a strong family tension as his parents could not understand why, when there was finally land for all their sons in the Tzaconejá valley, he did not want to work the land. "Eugenio only wants to drink, he doesn't want to work anymore," Fabricio remarked bitterly. He held a deep resentment toward his son, not only for leaving the organization and for spending much of his free time in a drunken state, but for joining those residents of Morelia who had returned to practices appeasing government officials. Today he was also enraged that the *ejido* assembly had let government officials enter, something they had not allowed in years:

> The *licenciado* arrived to tell the *ejidatarios* that the *avecindados* can't participate in the assembly, and even though that was *usos y costumbres* [tradition] by now, for some reason this time they agreed. Before the organization that is what we would do. They [the *licenciados*] would come from Tuxtla, they would arrive to monitor and ensure that those who voted were only those who had the right to vote for being legally recognized *ejidatarios*. But later the *ejido* didn't let them enter and all who lived in the *ejido* voted. It has been a long time since we let the *licenciado* come in.

Fabricio's anger illustrates the widespread resistance to and rejection of surveillance by state officials and their regulation of internal decision-making practices linked to land tenure, as emphasized by Juan Miguel and other autonomous government representatives. At the same time, and in contrast to PROCEDE, which dissolved the state's ability to administer land reform, the principal functions of the autonomous Zapatista institutions consist of stimulating land redistribution as part of broader processes reconstituting indigenous territories. Indeed, were we to imagine the autonomous council as the government of a nation-state, one of its key tasks would be to ensure that state institutions promote a more equal redistribution of natural resources. The next section describes the role of the land and territory commission of Diecisiete de Noviembre as that which continues to oversee land distribution as well as resolve land disputes. It does so in a disputed terrain where the SRA prioritizes resolving hot spots rather than the thousands of small-scale, not-as-dramatic conflicts between and within *ejidos*.

The Autonomous Land and Territory Commission amid Gaps in Neoliberal Agrarian Policies

Zapatista land reform exists under highly precarious and volatile conditions, given that—first of all—the occupied lands exist in a legal limbo. The corresponding government institutions have not compensated all the original landowners, despite the fact that they have not had access to their land for more than twenty years. The situation of legal ambiguity highlights the potential threat of eviction, leading to a perpetual uncertainty that rises and subsides depending on political conjunctures. While, during the early years after the uprising, support bases feared incursions by armed forces, later conflicts have occurred primarily with non-Zapatista peasant and indigenous organizations that have established their own land claims (Cerda 2011). Since 1996, in Caracol IV, peasant organizations including the Organización Regional de Cafeticultores de Ocosingo (ORCAO, Regional Organization of Ocosingo Coffeegrowers), the Rural Association of Collective Interest, and the Emiliano Zapata Independent Peasant Alliance have asserted their right to lands currently under Zapatista control. At different times some local indigenous peasant leaders have formed alliances with former landowners who hold out hope of recovering their original properties. Early in the Calderón administration (2006–2012), the reactivation of these peasant groups—in some cases accused of being paramilitaries—generated new conflicts. In Caracol IV, the political and paramilitary activities of the Organización para la Defensa de los Derechos Indígenas y Campesinos (OPDDIC, Organization for the Defense of Indigenous and Peasant Rights), above all in the autonomous municipality of Vicente Guerrero, have sparked the greatest tensions. Led by the Tseltal Pedro Chulín, from the *ejido* Taniperla, OPDDIC was officially a development organization for indigenous people who lived in the state, but it was accused of receiving military training and maintaining close ties with elected representatives from the Institutional Revolutionary Party, taking it close to the definition of a paramilitary group (see Hidalgo and Calabró 2006). When I interviewed members of the *junta de buen gobierno* in July 2006 about the activities of OPDDIC in Caracol IV, they identified the presence of the group in the non-Zapatista community of La Laguna, as well as in the town of Altamirano and in the politically divided Morelia, information that the leader of the organization himself confirmed when I interviewed him later that year. According to Chulín, OPDDIC opened legal proceedings to lay claim to lands occupied by Zapatista support bases, as documented in the autonomous municipality of Vicente Guerrero (Cerda 2011).

Within this highly polarized terrain, the *junta de buen gobierno*, the autonomous council, and the respective commissions shifted their priorities. While during the first decade after the conflict, their main tasks involved placing settlers in the newly founded communities, measuring out plots, and establishing the rules for collective labor, later their principal functions encompassed resolving land conflicts, defining settlement boundaries, and resolving disputes with other peasant organizations as well as between those peasant organizations operating in the region. In 2007, Trinitario, a member of the land and territory commission, assessed the situation as follows:

> What we deal with most in the offices are land conflicts. Sometimes the new settlements have problems when people don't want to work in the collectives or participate in community work. We need to give guidance. Sometimes there are problems between different villages. Right now, there is a serious conflict between two communities that are fighting over a riverbank. They want it for their livestock and don't want to negotiate to share it or divide it equally. Other times, different organizations bring their problems to us. For example, the people from CIOAC [the Independent Center for Agricultural and Peasant Workers] came to ask us to help them to resolve a land conflict between their own groups. And sometimes people from the *ejidos* come and ask to join the new settlements. As part of the autonomous government, we deal with all of this.

Why is there so much conflict in the region? Several factors converge, the first being the historical backlog of agrarian disputes that the SRA special representative, Martha Díaz Gordillo, identified, wherein state agrarian institutions granted *ejido* titles with overlapping perimeters. At the same time, conflicts exist between *ejidos* and some of the small property owners in the region. Underlying aspects have to do with the future: pressure to decide on potential cornfields as new generations grow and have less access to land. While these aspects reflect tendencies in other parts of the country, in the case of the conflict zone of Chiapas, additional layers add to the complexity. Politically divergent peasant organizations have established their own particular claims to the same lands taken after 1994. An additional aspect has to do with the very strategies of counterinsurgency in the region. Many subtle and not so subtle attempts to generate political divisions revolve around access to resources. Morelia, for example, lacks stable, year-round access to water. So as to draw political support, between 2004 and 2006, Luis H. Álvarez—who was named by the federal government to be the coordinator of the dialogues for peace in Chiapas, in which position he was responsible for attempting to reestablish contact with the EZLN leadership and reopen the peace talks of San Andrés (neither of which he achieved)—promoted options that included drawing water from springs in distant *ejidos*.

A decade after the uprising, land-dispute resolutions took center stage. I suggest that the shift in priorities reflects how the autonomous government essentially responds to, fills, and in fact redirects a vacuum left by the Mexican state after 1992. As Trinitario explained above, land conflicts formed a central aspect of their commission activities. Documents posted by the autonomous government in Diecisiete de Noviembre attest to this. In 2005, the honor and justice commission printed a report of its annual activities as part of the autonomous government report of the tasks undertaken during a twelve-month period, beginning with September 2004. These reports, some written by hand, others printed on computer paper, were posted on the wooden boards on the walls in the main auditorium, and I read them and took notes on their contents. The documents of the commission centered on a five-month period in which the representatives registered twenty-nine cases, eleven of which were presented on January 25, 2005, alone. Given that throughout my fieldwork I verified that on average twenty cases arrived at the honor and justice commission office per week, the posted report must be understood as a sample of the kinds of cases presented rather than an exhaustive list.

In this 2005 registry, seventeen cases involved individuals belonging to non-Zapatista communities or to political parties, while twelve cases involved Zapatista support bases. These figures coincide with my personal observations, as each time I sat outside the autonomous government's offices on the days when the representatives resolved cases, more than half of the cases involved non-Zapatistas, including individuals and organizations who maintained significant political differences with the rebel movement.

Of the twenty-nine cases, ten referred to disputes or common crimes internal to the community, including the theft of livestock, gossip, and unpaid debts. Nine cases were related to domestic disputes, including cases of separation, infidelity, child support, and the nonpayment of alimony, as well as a case in which a man accused his wife of witchcraft. Additionally, the posted report registered five cases related to violations of the municipality's regulation prohibiting timber felling. Two cases registered did not fall under the honor and justice commission's jurisdiction. One of these was a consultation in which the authorities of a non-Zapatista community visited the offices to seek advice on how to organize women's collectives with a government project start-up fund of 25,000 pesos (2,500 US dollars at the time). The other was a request for a permit to fell trees. It is unclear why these cases were registered as part of the activities of the honor and justice commission, perhaps because this commission's functions often converge with those of the land and territory commission and the autonomous council. Finally, the report registered one case of extortion in the offices of the Public Ministry. The individual who suffered the offense sought out the honor and justice commission and requested that the Zapatista authorities accompany him to the Public Ministry to obtain information regarding a criminal investigation that had supposedly been initiated against him and that served as the pretext for the extortion. When I interviewed members of both the honor and justice and the land and territory commissions, they explained that while this report provided a snapshot of the types of disputes and conflicts resolved at the municipal level, the cases can be grouped under three main categories: agrarian disputes, which are the most frequent, followed by family disputes, and then by complaints issued against official institutions, primarily the Public Ministry. These will be further analyzed in chapter 6. The remaining types of cases are in fact less common.

At the level of the *junta*, only three types of cases are resolved: agrarian conflicts associated with the region's former landowners, issues involving multiple peasant organizations, and cases that are not able to be resolved at the municipal level. In their 2005 report (also posted on the wall of the auditorium in Morelia), the *junta* representatives detailed their mediating role in ten cases, eight of which related to agrarian conflicts. Seven of the entries detailed correspond to agrarian disputes between support bases and non-Zapatista organizations or communities. According to the posted report, the only case exclusively involving Zapatista members was brought before the *junta* because it involved an agrarian dispute between communities that fall under two different *juntas*, those of Caracoles III and IV.

After offering this broader map of conflict resolution, I am interested in focusing on the agrarian disputes and on the role that different levels of the autonomous government play in their resolution. At the community level, the honor and justice commission intervenes when Zapatista support bases fail to comply with the regulations in the new population centers. Similarly, the commission responds to non-Zapatista families' requests to become Zapatista sympathizers, in which case the land and territory commission offers them the opportunity to work and live in one of the more than twenty new settlements. In cases of land distribution among families who are Zapatista support bases or those who decide to join the organization, or land claims by former owners, the autonomous government is responsible for making decisions and carrying them out by means of complex dynamics that require the participation of a range of authorities at both the municipal and the *caracol* level, including the *caracol* assembly, the *junta*, the autonomous council, and the land and territory, honor and justice, and agricultural production commissions.

Trinitario identified conflicts between communities as a second tier of mediation. A large percentage are the result of unclear demarcations of villages' territorial boundaries, partially the result of the historical inefficacies of the SRA and the Office of Special Prosecutor for Agrarian Affairs in Chi.

At a third tier, autonomous government representatives respond to claims and petitions made by landowners whose property the Zapatistas confiscated and distributed. Some of these ex-estate owners turn up at the council center to request the return of a few hectares of their lands. In 2004 and 2005, a former landowner from Altamirano traveled to the *caracol* compound on several occasions to request two to three hectares of his original property. Initially, the man met with the autonomous council, but the municipal authorities declared that a decision on a matter of this nature did not fall within their jurisdiction, so they turned the request over to the *junta*, which in turn decided that the *caracol* assembly — as the highest decision-making body—needed to decide on the request, which was subsequently rejected.

At the same time, Zapatista authorities attempt to mediate between different peasant organizations. Zapatista support bases prioritize resolving cases that involve land disputes which in turn helps to improve relations with indigenous peasant organizations. In an interview, Armando, a member of the honor and justice commission, explained that this priority heightened in importance during the latter half of Governor Salazar's administration, particularly between 2005 and 2006, when conflicts over land intensified. In fact, land-dispute cases presented to the offices of the autonomous government played a central role in easing old tensions, preventing the emergence of new antagonisms, and reestablishing alliances with those same organizations that tended to distance themselves from the Zapatistas. Such strategic goals were evident in the Zapatista authorities' 2005 report. The first case described referred to a land dispute between EZLN support base communities and ORCAO, an organization previously sympathetic to the Zapatistas' political agenda. By 1999, the two organizations had fractured their political ties, which was later reflected in attacks in the community of Cuxuljá. In 2004, a conflict surfaced between ORCAO and the new Zapatista population center Primero de Enero, when members of ORCAO enclosed the "recovered lands" with barbed wire. In a context in which the frictions between the organizations was increasing, *junta* representatives considered it politically relevant to resolve, or at least to contain, the dispute rather than to continue fighting over two hectares of land. The report stated, "We reasoned with the *compañeros* so that they would hand the land over to our brothers from ORCAO and not fight over two hectares." The same concern for improving social and political relations was manifested in a second case, in the community of Santa Rosalía, part of the municipality Miguel Hidalgo, a site of struggle between several political actors since 2004. A third case involved an agrarian dispute between two factions of the Independent Center for Agricultural and Peasant Workers that, at one point, had so many political problems with Zapatista support bases that one of their members went so far as to kidnap one of them.

These cases reflect the ways in which the Zapatista justice system replaces the SRA and the Office of Special Prosecutor for Agrarian Affairs at a local level. The different actions on such highly disputed terrain represent a Zapatista-bred alternative to the corporate model of the *ejido* and a response to the liberal options of private property and neoliberal governance implicit in the PROCEDE program. Over the past twenty years, the autonomous government of Diecisiete de Noviembre has implemented practices based on numerous decisions on the Zapatista agrarian reform, including on land use and agrarian conflict resolution. These alternatives sketch out a social path that differs from the one generated by color-blind neoliberal agrarian policies as it attempts to revert historical forms of racialized inequality. The point I want to emphasize is that the void left by the neoliberal state has been occupied in this region, not by the economic market but by the collective actions of the land and territory commission, together with the autonomous council and the *junta*. The Zapatista support bases gained access to the fertile land in the valley and established regulations for taking joint decisions over its use and distribution, both of which represent essential aspects of broader claims to autonomy in a given territory. The notion of territory in itself needs to be understood as creating a sense of collective belonging in a particular locality as a central aspirational element for *lekil kuxlejal*. How does this sense of collective belonging emerge?

A Territorial Sense of Belonging

The first aspect of belonging to a particular territory evident to me during my fieldwork was the role of agricultural labor. A sense of belonging to "the organization," and, as a result, to the territory under its control, was created on a daily basis by men's and women's constantly working the land. By this I mean the daily labor in the fields, along with the activities needed to maintain the production collectives—whether they be coffee, honey, livestock, crops, or banana plantations—as well as the community activities required to sustain the villages—building the church, cutting the grass between the houses, or clearing the pathways of weeds, along with countless other tasks. Daily life as a political endeavor is shaped by a collective engagement with the natural environment, which in turn shapes a sense of territorial belonging. The theorization of the political as *kuxlejal* politics, linked to a sense of identity and to community participation, initially emerges from the actions carried out in agriculturally based labor activities.

Such activities are intensive and are divided into family as well as communal work. For example, in the new settlement of Zapata, the men have designated Mondays and Tuesdays as the days to work in the agricultural collectives, including taking care of livestock, coffee fields, and beehives, while setting aside Wednesdays and Thursdays to care for their own *milpas*, so that Fridays and Saturdays they can once again labor in the agricultural collectives. Women's activities tend to be more evenly distributed on a daily basis, between household chores, gathering firewood, and taking care of their own vegetable gardens, activities interspersed throughout the course of the day; the women set aside at least two afternoons a week to participate in their collectives, including making bread and working in communal vegetable gardens. Sunday is a day of rest.

The fact that collective agricultural activities make up such a large percentage of the time spent on labor and that families have sufficient land to farm does not mean, however, that small-scale stratifications are absent. In Zapata, the community set aside communal land for more than two hundred head of cattle to graze. Though the production collective takes care of all the livestock, the cattle are individually owned. For families, owning enough cattle increases assets, improving their ability to withstand costly unexpected situations such as a medical emergency and helping to offset drops in the price of coffee or other commodities. How many cattle a particular family owns thus reflects their wealth in relation to other families. Another indicator of wealth is a family's investment in apiculture, honey being a relatively stable source of supplementary income. Those families that lack either, or that do not have enough male children to work the fields, or, as in the case of Fabricio and Ernestina, have sickly family members who require constant medical attention, sometimes lack sufficient crops to ensure year-long subsistence. For many of these families, seeking other sources of income becomes a necessity, including offering their labor for contract fieldwork on other Zapatistas' *milpas*. These internal, albeit small-scale, hierarchies generate tensions as well as uncomfortable sentiments, as expressed in the following comment by a community member: "What makes us sad and feel uncomfortable is when other Zapatistas come asking for a source of income. Some pay them as peons for 40 pesos a day to work the fields. It makes us sad because it is as if they were *mozos*."

At the same time, working the land requires political participation, in the form of membership in the Zapatista organization; in turn, political participation is achieved through productive activity. It is labor activity that grants a support base the right to be in the assemblies and to engage in decision-making processes. If a member of the autonomous municipality stops working in the collectives or in the family fields, or fails to engage in other community work, he or she may lose the right to take part in the community and municipal assemblies. In some cases, such as that of Mario's more than twelve-month absence from Morelia, lack of effective participation may lead to expulsion from the occupied lands or from the Zapatista assembly. This labor-based relationship goes beyond the model of the *ejido* that held sway prior to the Article 27 reforms. I described above that in the *ejidos* before 1992, *avecindados* were formally excluded from the right to participate in the assembly and few women took part, since only a small minority were *ejidatarios*. However, *ejidos* such as Morelia enacted practices dissolving such formal requirements and allowing all community members to participate in the assembly. Such cultural practices continue with greater levels of intensity as part of autonomous municipality practices.

That is not to say that the direct relationship between working the land and political participation is free from complications and contradictions. Distinct values are ascribed to a gendered division of labor and its products. Produce grown for the regional market and staple crops, largely planted by the men, have greater symbolic value in comparison with the produce of the collective agricultural work of the community's women since they are mainly responsible for tasks treated as domestic, such as looking after hens, tending the vegetable plots, and making bread. Solely in the case of handicrafts are sales of products made or grown by women focused on regional—or even national and international—markets. The remaining products are sold within the micromarket of the community itself, meaning they do not receive the same level of recognition and importance.

Families can potentially be expelled from "the organization" and from the new settlements if there is a male absence and the women cannot take over male collective work responsibilities. Such was the case of a woman from a community near Morelia. Her husband left to the United States in search of work in 2007, while she remained at home with no male children to take over her husband's obligations. She was unable to complete the agricultural activities required, though she did participate in the assemblies in her husband's absence. Eventually she had to leave the new settlement and go to work in domestic service for a *mestizo* family in Altamirano. In response to this kind of case, Zapatista women have sought the support of NGOs in San Cristóbal, such as the Centro de Derechos de la Mujer en Chiapas (Center of Women's Rights in Chiapas), in an effort to alter Zapatista accords and open greater space for women's access to land rights (CDMC 2015). Given the level of importance accorded to the connection between the act of working the land and political participation, women in Zapatista communities insist that their working of the land be granted a similar level of value as the males'. This is an aspect of community life that Ernestina and other Zapatista women in political positions as well as other figures of authority insist upon. As we shall observe in the following chapter, it is precisely the kinds of activities the women carry out that give rise to what I view as a key contribution of the Zapatistas to the political.

A stark contrast exists between mechanisms of governance that hold sway under neoliberal agrarian policies and those of the Zapatista practices in Diecisiete de Noviembre. The agrarian policies of the state establish the property title as a kind of filter for mediating between individuals, so as to engender broader social participation. By contrast, in the autonomous municipalities, it is not property titles but rather activities directly related to working the land that underpin the right to participate in community, municipal, and *caracol* assemblies. Working communal lands is what connects the individual to political participation, not the acquisition of a property title; it is what links *kuxlejal* as social-territorial "life-existence" to the political.

Indeed, the action of working the land is embedded in *kuxlejal* politics and plays a central role in the production of meanings associated with indigeneity among Tseltal and Tojolabal support bases. Rather than an inherent relationship to a particular locality, this sense of belonging was forged through generations of struggle for land; it is a sense of belonging felt by indigenous people who have historically and systematically suffered the dispossession of their lands, which were stripped away since colonial times. In Altamirano, the struggle against dispossession and for a sense of place was recorded as early as 1806, when the *mozos* of the Santo Domingo estate fled to form San Carlos Maravlon. It is on the basis of these memories of the struggle for land and for territory that there emerges an indigenous political identity in connection with a specific geographical area, but not with specific plots of land.[13] This historically constructed sense of belonging figures as part of the reconfiguration of the territory understood to be Tzotz Choj, that is, the region under the reign of the Jaguar Bat king of the Toniná Empire, which the Zapatistas used to name the region of Caracol IV.

A sense of belonging similarly emerges from the fruits of working the land and witnessing the transformation of entire areas that two decades before were largely barren. Before 1994, most new settlements were

Figure 4.5. A girl harvesting coffee in Zapata, Diecisiete de Noviembre, 2007; photo by author

pasturelands, and, as Nacho recalled, "everything was devastated; the soil got broken up by the hooves of the cattle and blew away." On average, the soil takes fourteen to twenty years to recover, meaning that for the first few years the inhabitants of the new settlements had meager harvests of corn and beans. However, the production of staple crops improved dramatically after 2007. Between the years 2000 and 2010, a significant percentage of Zapatista support bases succeeded in increasing their production of corn and beans. In fact, in all the new population centers that I visited, families were achieving excess production of staple crops, something unimaginable before the armed uprising. In these communities, most families were harvesting an average of 1.7 to 2.4 metric tons per hectare of corn annually, and the average household of seven members requires 1.5 metric tons of corn. In the Zapatista agro-ecological model fields, which are used to demonstrate the most effective chemical-free agricultural techniques to Zapatista communities, the yield is even higher, with harvests of up to 2.7 metric tons per hectare. These quantities are well above the national average for small producers, which is less than 1 ton per hectare (Villafuerte Solís and García Aguilar 2006).

The progress made toward conditions of food security in Diecisiete de Noviembre is an aspect inhabitants of the autonomous municipality put forward as one of the key achievements of Zapatista agrarian reform.

Access to food security figures as central to unsettling processes of dehumanization and affirms a politics of life-existence as it signifies the capacity of a family to assure their basic needs, a material requirement providing sustenance to the exercise of power. Racialized subordination is difficult to maintain when those involved are the producers of their own food, cultivated on land that belongs to a community as part of a territory declared indigenous and in resistance. Perhaps the principal impact of the increasing level of food security may be observed in the harvest of staple crops between 2006 and 2008. These were the first years that the religious order based in Altamirano stopped selling low-cost corn to the valley communities. In fact, given that the yield was more than sufficient, the new settlements offered sacks of corn for sale to other communities in the region. For many years, the nuns had sold corn to peasants below market price, especially during the "hungry season," a term used by community members to refer to the three to four months a year when families would run out of the grain from the previous harvest yet the corn of the subsequent harvest had not yet ripened. Thanks to the nuns' efforts, for decades many Tseltal and Tojolabal families in the Altamirano municipality maintained minimum subsistence levels. However, by 2006, such support was no longer required by the majority of Zapatista families.

At the same time, however, these changes—visible in the sacks of corn and beans stored by families in Diecisiete de Noviembre—also signal the potential limitations of the social-transformation potential of the autonomy project. The efforts made by the support bases to secure their sources of food, to learn and establish new agro-ecological techniques, and to seek alternative markets in spaces such as the fair-trade market for coffee run up against the limitations defined by global economic policies. Even though the families in the new population centers are able to achieve a surplus in the production of staple crops, the other articles they require for household consumption remain subject to the fluctuating prices determined by global markets. Proof of this is the fact that, in real terms, it is more economically viable to work three months as a construction worker building hotels in Playa del Carmen than to spend an equal amount of time cultivating the fields. Some scholars, such as Daniel Villafuerte Solís and María del Carmen García Aguilar (2006), argue that peasant vulnerability to highly fluctuating prices of key national and international commodities, accompanied by a failed state agricultural policy, generates conditions that pressure indigenous and *mestizo* peasants to abandon their fields in search of work elsewhere, be it in other regions of the country or in the United States. As evidence, these authors point to a strong correlation between the second crisis in world coffee prices in 2003 and an increase in migration flows to other regions of Mexico and increasingly to the United States. The effects of this crisis in fact pushed Mario, Ernestina's son, to begin migrating, first to Veracruz and later to the Riviera Maya (ibid.).[14]

These are the economic and political challenges that lead to the decisions of young people like Mario to migrate seasonally to Playa del Carmen rather than staying on the land his parents fought for under the Zapatista banner. To complicate matters, new generations do not necessarily aspire to the same political goals as their parents (Aquino 2012). The existing tension is present in the decisions of men like Mario, in comparison to other Zapatista community members in the secondary school who claim as their own the generational struggles over land and critically identify with the experience of community members on the estates as that which marks racialized forms of labor exploitation.

Conclusion

This chapter focused on Zapatista agrarian reform as a point of departure in the struggle for autonomy and *lekil kuxlejal*, a collective existence lived in relation to the earth; for the possibility of ensuring access to food for the present and for future generations; and for the perpetual honoring of that land, which feeds communities. I have described how the land and territory commission of Diecisiete de Noviembre, along with the autonomous council, plays a crucial role in ensuring that self-determination links land redistribution to collective forms of decision making. As this chapter has illustrated, a constructed sense of territory within Diecisiete de Noviembre surfaces as part of working the land ... ing and land that grants Zapatista community members the right to participate politically in the autonomous municipality. The combination unsettles the racialized trope of the peon whereby indigenous people are reinscribed as destined to work for those who possess the "adequate cultural" traits to render natural resources productive as part of the agricultural exploitation of the land.

In this chapter, I analyzed PROCEDE both as a program designed to facilitate individual land titling and to increase its productive value as well as to improve state governance and as part of broader historical forces linked to state projects that propel a reconcentration of lands in the hands of private or foreign interests. I demonstrated how the Zapatista agrarian reform in Diecisiete de Noviembre has played the fundamental role of keeping both PROCEDE and other legal/illegal privatizing initiatives at bay. As this chapter illustrated through a discussion of increased migration patterns, this does not mean that autonomous territory is removed from the sway of global political economic forces. To the contrary, while Zapatista agrarian reform may be one of the most significant achievements of the autonomous municipalities, it also faces the most limitations. Zapatista agrarian reform is thus located at a crossroads marked by both the possibilities and the limits of indigenous autonomy, a crossroads on which hinge other key political arenas in Diecisiete de Noviembre. In the following chapter, I turn my attention to the women's production collectives.

FIVE

Women's Collectives and the Politicized (Re)production of Social Life

As representatives from the communities stood around discussing municipal affairs in the esplanade facing the Caracol IV auditorium, a dozen women walked, machetes in hand, along the path that crosses in front of the building. They disappeared behind the building toward the collective vegetable gardens of Zapata and Morelia. In the auditorium's shadow, the women weeded, harvested radishes, and prepared the ground to sow carrots, working in a silence punctuated only by sporadic conversation and laughter. This activity requires a few hours of their time each week, often followed by a women's meeting. After many years, such tasks have become part of a set cultural routine.

Micaela related to me that what the women have now come to understand as a tradition is in fact their own achievement, years of substantial effort. At the end of the 1980s, a group of young women, together with those from Ernestina's generation, who left their villages to study for the first time in the catechist school visited communities in the Tzaconejá River valley on foot to explain to other women the importance of working together outside their homes and to create discussion groups. Ernestina remembered that the landowners at the time observed them with suspicion.

Micaela recalled that one of their initial achievements consisted of organizing the first women's basketball match in the region. In the *ejidos*, the men of the valley adopted the game as a daily entertainment after

Figure 5.1. Women tending to their collective vegetable garden, *ejido* Morelia, Diecisiete de Noviembre, 1999; photo by Francisco Vazquez

working the fields. As part of their newfound collectives, the women decided they wanted to play a sport as well. They organized a game but had no pants to wear while playing, so they borrowed their husbands' or fathers'. Micaela described how, instead of catching the ball as it flew through the air, the women at first would leap to the side in fright to avoid being hit by it. She laughed as she told the story, awakening the interest of her daughter, Amalia, who found it strange that something considered so much a part of the everyday had been taken up so recently, when her mother was in her twenties.

Since she was a girl, Amalia had accompanied her mother to work in the collectives, an activity she recalled with pride as she described them as spaces where women learn, work together, share thoughts, and discuss their lives. She remembered that on one occasion, the women debated how to address the domestic violence that one of their *compañeras* suffered. Another time, they decided to assist a woman whose husband was preventing her from getting involved in community affairs. When a political mobilization arose, they held meetings to prepare for it and sometimes used part of the collective's funds to cover travel costs. On the basis of the activities of the production collectives, Amalia offered her interpretation of autonomy, explaining that in her view, "autonomy is to create a new life; it is the struggle for life."

The activities carried out by the women from Morelia and Zapata appear at first glance to be a trivial affair, a hobby or a minor source of income to meet community expenditures. However, through her interpretation, Amalia inverted the apparent insignificance and presented a theory of power, a way of doing politics that has emerged from these spaces located literally on the edges of the assemblies and major events. The resulting praxis hinges on the politicization of household tasks in community spaces. In this chapter, I follow the same explanatory line taken by Amalia to illustrate the ways in which the inseparability of politics and everyday life as a claim of *poder ser*, the power and ability to be, surfaces from the activities of the Zapatista women's collectives in Diecisiete de Noviembre. I argue that these very tasks of social reproduction sustain fundamental aspects of the Zapatista autonomy project.

At the same time, while avoiding a cause-and-effect analysis, the intention of this chapter is to demonstrate how Zapatista women's praxis destabilizes and profoundly alters the category of the indigenous woman on which central aspects of the Mexican state rest. The activities concentrated in women's production collectives offer alternatives to the gendered and racialized governing rationale of the neoliberal state. Scholarship on Zapatista women explores how indigenous activists challenge the state's use of gendered categories to regulate indigenous subjects. It also questions the definitions of culture deployed by some feminist actors who attribute to indigenous identity inherent associations with violence toward women (Blackwell 2012; Forbis 2006; Hernández Castillo 2001; Speed 2008). Maylei Blackwell describes how "organized indigenous women's groups challenged the gendered logic of racism used by the Mexican government to co-opt women's rights in its arguments against indigenous autonomy — specifically in relation to indigenous law, commonly referred to as *usos y costumbres* (practices and customs) (2012, 705). These studies focus primarily on the role of law as a contentious sphere of struggle.

To these contributions and theorizations, I offer an analysis of the gendered and racialized constructions of social-development programs as expressions of neoliberal governing logics. Specifically, I examine the effects of such policies since the late 1990s through the most significant anti-poverty program in Mexico, which during my fieldwork was called Oportunidades (Opportunities), a program that regulates the social-reproduction activities of women by providing an economic stimulus in exchange for alterations of their social and cultural habits. A number of studies illustrate how the privatization of social services, as part of the first generation of neoliberal policies, affects women, above all those living in racialized poverty who are responsible for care work as well as for administering a limited amount of resources (Staples 2006; Topouzis 1993; Ward 1990). In this context, Oportunidades sought to regulate the social-reproduction activities of women so as to maintain certain levels of social stability.

In turn, we cannot speak of neoliberal governance in terms of its homogeneous, uniform effects, but rather in terms of how these are produced in specific locations. In the case of the highlands and the Lacandon Jungle regions of Chiapas, the neoliberalization of social relations occurred alongside the militarization of daily life. The contradictory articulations between development and security policies simultaneously regulated and fragmented the social-reproduction activities of women by acting both on and against their bodies. In this chapter, I demonstrate that such articulations are not coherent effects, much less cohesive ones; rather, they operate among a series of ambiguities symptomatic of a racialized state. I argue that such an analytical framework allows us to understand in greater depth how the effects of social-development programs and of counterinsurgency practices articulate through the *securitization* of social-reproduction activities as part of neoliberal development policies, that is, they become a target of state security (Buzan, Waever, and de Wilde 1998).

To set out these arguments, this chapter is divided into the following sections. The first details the activities in the women's collectives that engender the politicization of everyday life. To understand its implications, it is necessary to situate Zapatista female praxis in relation to the different feminist strands of the past thirty years in Mexico, the subject of the second section. The following two sections focus on how Zapatista female praxis engages these currents of thought, as well as how it ingrains specific meanings to notions of the political in Diecisiete de Noviembre. The fifth section focuses on the Oportunidades program. In interviews, female support bases note the effects of this program in a context marked by the almost permanent militarization of everyday life. I take these observations as a starting point for setting out how militarization, at different moments in the Chiapas conflict, has targeted women's biological- and social-reproduction activities. Finally, I offer reflections on the implications of this biopolitical context for *kuxlejal* praxis.

From Female Empowerment to the Politicization of Everyday Life

On the pretext that it was too nice a day to be inside, the twenty women I met with decided to sit on the grass in the middle of Siete de Enero. There, we discussed the generational changes that have marked women's activities in the region, first in the *ejidos*, at a time when the remaining estates still shaped local socioeconomic relations, later in the spaces provided by the Catholic Church, and then through subsequent transformations resulting from the responsibilities of autonomy. Despite the extensive range of women's activities, the conversation maintained as a focal point the production collectives, returning time and again to what is evidently a fundamental aspect of women's political formation. At their homes, the women explained, they raise chickens, sometimes rabbits and ducks, they cultivate a kitchen garden with vegetables, and they grow fruit trees. They spend several hours every day grinding corn for the kilograms of tortillas eaten each day by their families. When they have the resources, they build a bread oven. These women explain that it is through their production collectives that these activities emerge from the spaces of their homes and yards to form part of the different spheres of the village. At the same time, family tasks are largely transformed into activities that bring together the women of the community as a whole. During the group interview, Alicia enthusiastically recalled that they founded the first women's collective in Siete de Enero in 1996, during the preparations for the Intercontinental Meeting for Humanity and against Neoliberalism held in the five *aguascalientes*, hence pointing to the ways that mass public events also shaped local political practices:

> We had no money. So we organized and went to the inauguration of the *aguascalientes* and the Intercontinental Meeting, and we sold *atole* and *tamales*. We made three hundred pesos [US$300] and that enabled us to set up the store. . . . Later we started the different collectives: bread, bananas, vegetable collectives, and just recently we bought the mill with the proceeds of the store. . . . Thanks to the collective we provide the bus fares for the human rights promoters, and the other promoters. If it weren't for the money from the collectives the women wouldn't have been able to stick to their *cargos* [political responsibilities].

The production collectives raise a small amount of revenue, which the women then invest in a collective fund to use to cover the costs of female political participation and to support families in the event of emergencies, such as unexpected medical costs. Such activities are certainly not the most visible, nor are they those most associated with the Zapatista autonomy project, where the assemblies, the *juntas de buen gobierno*, and the political actions in defense of land and territory tend to take center stage. Moreover, in terms of agricultural production, the cooperatives connected to national and international markets receive the greatest spotlight, such as the organic coffee cooperatives of Mutz Vitz of the highlands or Yochil Tayel Kinal in Caracol IV, which sell Zapatista coffee, particularly in Europe (Martínez-Torres 2006; Suárez Carrera 2014). Nevertheless, the women's activities, with their own humble collective funds, profoundly impact community dynamics.

Alicia explained that the funds not only support women who are community leaders, supplying them with the resources needed to cover local transportation costs, such as the bus fare to the *caracol* center; in addition, the men, too, occasionally ask for a donation or a loan. She told about how the men approach the women when their own funds are insufficient, but they never dare to ask for money directly. As she described a recent scene, Alicia raised her gaze to the air, imitating the men, who directed their words to no one in particular. "Well, *how* are we going to get ahold of enough money for this? I wonder. Where could the money *possibly* come from?" they asked abstractly. Alicia laughed while describing how the women pretended not to hear them, but later agreed to offer part of what the men needed as if it were an idea that had just magically occurred to them.

The women also discussed the importance of the collectives not only in economic terms but as a space in which to jointly reflect on the different forms of exploitation and oppression they experience as indigenous peasants and as women. During the group interviews, they described how when a woman decides to denounce domestic violence, which is still a prevalent occurrence in the region, other women support her and accompany her in the denunciation or go together to "scold" the husband. In this way, the production collectives are at once platforms for economic solvency and meetings for collective discussion, mutual support, and political formation. Interestingly, it was Armando, the husband of Berta from Siete de Enero, who defined the marked contrast between the women's collectives and parallel men's activities:

> We go and work in the fields, but for the men it is just work. We participate in the assemblies, and that is where we take decisions, where we get involved.

Among the men, we hardly ever discuss our problems. Yet I see that the women do everything as a collective. It's not just work for them, it is a space for discussion, for speaking out, for thinking aloud as a group. And I see that they gain strength from participating in other spaces, it is part of their education, and it opens their eyes.

His words describe women's collectives as pedagogical spaces, in which production entangles with learning. Here, I am referring to the creative sense of production, rather than to a definition associated with accumulation, given that the former emphasizes the generation of new knowledge. In the collectives, economic, cultural, and social affairs become inseparable from life itself. Politics is not something only to be found in public, clearly demarcated spaces, such as the assemblies or the meetings with people "from the outside," but in the very act of living, of reflecting on life-existence, *kuxlejal*, as part of the accumulated exercise of the power to be. From the praxis found in the women's collectives emerges a politicization of everyday life connected to household tasks in such a way that decolonization in autonomy transforms into a collective drive to define the terms for the reproduction of social and biological life. The relationship between the political and daily life is a common theme in different feminist circles. In what ways does Zapatista women's *kuxlejal* politics differ from such strands? To set out in detail these particular ways of doing politics, I first locate the contributions of Zapatista women in relation to different strands of feminist thought in Mexico that share two general characteristics: political education on the basis of experience and the politicization of the domestic sphere.

Beyond the Politics of Experience and the Politicization of Household Tasks

The women's collectives are part of at least two recent genealogies of resistance practices dating to before the Zapatista movement: first, mixed-gender social organizations that, since the 1980s, transformed what were agriculture-related peasant issues into demands as indigenous peoples, and second, what Gisela Espinosa Damián (2009) identifies as different strands of feminist thought in Mexico that influenced women in the highlands and the Lacandon Jungle valleys during the 1970s and 1980s: historical, civil, working-class, and indigenous feminisms. I begin this section with a brief overview of the local tendencies of this second legacy, beginning with the first activities of CODIMUJ, the Catholic women's group that, as discussed in chapter 3, initiated the prioritization of individual female empowerment through a method based on personal experience.

Although the participatory methodology of CODIMUJ seems parallel to the political category of "empowerment" associated with dominant feminist approaches, it differs markedly from the forms of political action employed by the type of feminism Espinosa Damián refers to as historical feminism, which is typically associated with *mestizo* middle-class urban women. It should be remembered that while CODIMUJ was in this first phase of activity, middle-class women from places like Mexico City participated in study groups and discussion circles that frequently used the politics of experience for individuals to share their lives as women and become "empowered" (Espinosa Damián 2009). Scholars such as Ana Lau (1987) describe how these spaces promoted reflections on being a woman as a key aspect in the elaboration of a personal discourse based on the contradictions inherent to experience. Although overlaps may exist with the spaces for collective reflection of the Tseltal, Tsotsil, and Tojolabal women involved in CODIMUJ, I find the following differences: Indigenous women who participate in CODIMUJ tend to seek exchanges that stretch beyond individual consciousness raising; they participate in collective discussions that lead to joint actions, in contrast with historical feminism in Mexico, which largely sidetracks the social construction of feminist projects (Espinosa Damián 2009). At the same time, these indigenous women tend to view gender inequalities as an integral part of intersecting forms of oppression, including economic structures and racialized hierarchies. By comparison, historical feminism, as middle-class urban-based, tends to perpetuate classist and racist attitudes, focusing less on a mass struggle against capital interests and political power and more on personal autonomy and equal rights, particularly on voluntary maternity and against gendered violence (ibid.).

Historical feminism is not, however, the only reference point useful for placing CODIMUJ's method of the politics of experience in a broader context. Since the 1980s, a range of working-class, peasant, and indigenous women's platforms emerged, together with so-called civil feminism, associated with NGOs. Indeed, Espinosa Damián (2009) asserts that a central feature of civil feminism, its focus on methodology, constantly engages with working-class feminisms. The greatest achievements of both currents focus on breaking with the political methods and vanguard notions used by the traditional male left. Both working-class and civil feminism draw heavily on the influence of the Catholic Church by incorporating not only the popular-education methods of Paulo Freire but other teaching methods that arise from social psychology, psychoanalysis, and specialization in adult education through the National Pedagogical University. As we shall see below, through the production collectives Tseltal and Tojolabal Zapatista women not only promote the politicization of household tasks but this reflective pedagogical aspect as well. They appropriate the technique, not as a method to achieve an objective but as the means for engendering new expressions of a political agenda as an end in itself.

A second key aspect of the women's political practices of Diecisiete de Noviembre, the politicization of household tasks, emerged in the late 1980s, influenced by the activities of women involved in CODIMUJ, in local peasant struggles, and in spaces supported by NGOs. A primary element of the "see-think-act" method focuses on resignifying various household activities in order to affirm women's agency and decision-making capacity. As a result, women in the region of Altamirano started production collectives, which were later appropriated and supported by peasant organizations, above all by the women's civil association AMMAC. The focus on politicizing and collectivizing social-reproduction activities is not limited to the valleys and highlands of Chiapas, but is rather part of a broader tendency associated with working-class feminisms in Mexico (Espinosa Damián 2009). At the same time that CODIMUJ and AMMAC promoted women's collectives, productive projects for indigenous and peasant women emerged, together with small credit unions, *nixtamal* mills for grinding corn, markets for the sale of handicrafts, and funds for marketing products. Although peasant organizations and NGOs promoted such programs, government bodies, such as the National Indigenist Institute, largely covered their financial costs. Regardless of specific policy objec-

tives figured prominently in the political formation of indigenous and peasant women. They served as a common reference point and a starting point for their leadership roles. Members of some of the most significant movements of the past twenty years, including Felicitas and Epifania, two women who are leaders of the Coordinadora Regional de Autoridades Comunitarias (Regional Coordinator of Community Authorities) in the state of Guerrero, recalled the importance of participating in production collectives in the 1980s, of growing radishes and raising chickens, as central to their leadership development (Espinosa Damián, Dircio Chautla, and Sánchez Néstor 2010).

The emphasis on the politicization of household tasks, as part of broader organizing processes, reflects a clear influence of Marxist feminism on organized Mexican working-class women. Scholars in this field of study, such as Silvia Federici (2013), argue that the tasks of social reproduction support capital relations. Though neither acknowledged nor remunerated, social-reproduction activities sustain the institution of the family and create the conditions for men to participate in productive work outside the home (Federici 2013). In this sense, the reproduction of the workforce is based to a large extent on activities conducted in the domestic sphere, such as preparing food, washing clothes, administering household finances, and caring for the well-being and health of family members. Though one of the invisible pillars underpinning capitalist logics, such tasks acquire an even greater role under neoliberal development policies. Current global political economic forces restructure the state through disinvestment in spheres that enable social-reproduction activities. In doing so, capital accumulation reactivates, hence generating additional pressure on working-class women, particularly peasants, indigenous, and Afro-Mexican women (ibid.).

Within this broader global context, Tseltal and Tojolabal women from the Altamirano valley fortified social-reproduction activities by creating collectives, hence resignifying household tasks, injecting them with political content, including as the principal spaces for women's education and "consciousness raising." At the same time, they critique the liberal public/private binary, along with its production/reproduction dichotomy, by recognizing that activities outside the "home," such as in the *milpas*, in the hills and forests, form part of that which permits the reproduction of their identity and life as indigenous peoples.

Women from CODIMUJ and AMMAC, many of whom participated as clandestine EZLN sympathizers and militants, played active roles in the women's collectives when the uprising took place. Two years later, in the context of the San Andrés Accords, the political significance of the women's production collectives in Diecisiete de Noviembre took on additional meanings as part of the exercise of autonomy and self-determination. The convergence of these actions forged the politicization of everyday life, which, I suggest, is one of the foundations of the Zapatista autonomy project and is central to understanding *kuxlejal* politics.

Women's Collectives and *Kuxlejal* Politics

Audalia, a Tseltal woman in her midthirties, lives in Zapata, a short walking distance away from the *ejido* Morelia. Unlike villages such as Siete de Enero, whose inhabitants were mostly in their early twenties during the uprising, here the population varies across generations. Audalia played a key role as a women's organizer prior to 1994, following in the footsteps of more mature women like Ernestina. Though she resisted for several years coordinating the women's activities in Zapata, arguing that with her fourth child, she was tired of participating and needed a break, the other women named her, and she had no choice but to obey. She completed the *cargo*, only to then opt to participate in health commission training sessions to learn to be a midwife. I spoke with her a few years later, when I visited the *caracol* center while pregnant. It was evident how much she felt inspired by this new role; we had a lively exchange as she eagerly shared her new knowledge on how to ensure healthful conditions during the breast-feeding stages of early childrearing.

When I stayed in Zapata the first time, Audalia invited me to accompany the women to the vegetable garden. I accepted, and after the group of women finished their morning house chores—making tortillas, gathering firewood, and washing their children's and husbands' clothes—they gathered at the trailhead to walk to the *caracol* compound. The small children of some of the women came along, the younger ones strapped on their backs with a *rebozo*, while those a bit older ran around in circles as we went. "And you still don't have children?" one woman asked in puzzlement. "Don't worry, we can find you a man," another said. Laughing, she added, "Yes, I know just the one, the *tatacux!*" She was referring to an elderly blind man who could hardly stand upright. She pretended to be him, grasping at the air in search of my leg. I protested loudly and played along with the teasing. "It's fine," said a fourth woman, defending my midthirties single status. "You still have some time, and besides, that way you are free to travel and move as you like. There is no man to block your path."

The topics of children and husbands continued as we reached the vegetable fields to begin harvesting radishes and pulling the weeds out of the beds where the women had recently sown cucumbers. It was February, shortly after the anniversary of the day in 1995 when President Zedillo publicly announced the supposed true identity of Subcomandante Insurgente Marcos and released arrest orders for all the EZLN leadership. On February 9 of that year, the military was ordered to enter Zapatista terri-

Figure 5.2. Tseltal women during the Encuentro de los Pueblos Zapatistas con los Pueblos del Mundo (Gathering of Zapatista Communities with Communities of the World), Oventic, Caracol II, 2006; photo by Francisco Vazquez

tory, forcing community members to flee into the mountains, where for weeks they sought refuge. One of the women remembered the harsh conditions of those weeks: her baby was born then near some caves, and her oldest child spent days on end with a high fever, as there was no medicine nor sanitary conditions to improve his health. "Those days were hard, so hard," she recalled with a sigh. "Even after we came back to Morelia and kept on with our house chores, my head would hurt terribly and I couldn't sleep at night."

"Can I take some of these leaves home with me?" interrupted another woman, asking the group. "My daughter has a stomachache and this plant will soothe her." The rest of the women nodded in agreement and kept to their tasks. Some distance away, I heard two women carrying on a conversation, half in Tseltal and half in Spanish. They commented on the screams they had heard coming from a nearby house the night before. "Her husband is drinking secretly at home," one said, "and then he gets all riled up and lashes out at her. We need to do something to make sure he is punished."

"But the *compañera* doesn't say anything," the woman standing next to her said. "I think she doesn't want to cause him problems or maybe she has her eyes closed as to what her rights are."

"It's no excuse, but I think his heart is sad with all the problems of the low-intensity war. I think he needs to have a talking to so he stops treating his wife badly, and then gets help so his heart feels lighter," responded her conversation partner. They walked some distance away and finished talking out of earshot, but I assumed they continued discussing the circumstance as well as the possible responses.

The simultaneous discussions taking part in the production collectives reflect the politicization of everyday life and the praxis of self-reflection as well-established cultural practices among organized women in the Tzaconejá River valley. Though these practices existed prior to the 1994 uprising, the autonomy project led to their fortification and transformation, as discussions forming part of the activities in the municipality—including debates on their political identity as indigenous people, on the implications of merging rebellion with autonomy, and on the meaning of self-determination on the margins of state institutions—resignified political agendas. In this section I focus on three realms directly impacted by the praxis of women's collectives.

The first realm is of social-reproduction tasks as a central pillar of the political. Autonomy, as practiced by the indigenous survivors of successive acts of genocide and attempts by state forces to eradicate their ways of life as a people, contains an immanently political aspect. To live, subsist, and exercise control over the reproduction of life are in these cases political and politicized acts in and of themselves. In this sense autonomy must be understood as a series of *kuxlejal* practices that assert control over material and immaterial conditions—land, territory, individual and collective bodies, local knowledge of health and care—that render it possible to establish a collective identity as indigenous people in a timeframe that extends beyond and behind the present. What I wish to highlight is that the politicization of daily life is concentrated in the actions and reflections of women in their collectives.

Women's political praxis in Diecisiete de Noviembre invites us to locate autonomous struggle not only against the effects of racialized discourses rooted in colonial institutions such as the estates, but from what Rita Segato (2011) describes as the meeting point of the modern colonial patriarchy and the coloniality of gender. This implies understanding the category of gender not as one among several facets to be dealt with but as "a real theoretical and epistemic status, by treating it as a social category capable of shedding light on all other aspects of the transformation imposed on the life of the communities when they are captured by the new modern colonial order" (Segato 2011, 31). Viewed from this perspective, the activities that at first sight seem minor aspects of autonomy take center stage; the politicization of activities traditionally associated with the feminine sphere, and which allow for control over social life, become a type of matrix that grants meaning to the other aspects of autonomy.

A second realm is the critique of the power relations that engender identity and culture. Politicizing domestic activities in a dialectical relationship to processes of collective self-reflection destabilizes fixed meanings ascribed to "tradition" and to "practices and customs." If the autonomy project triggers discussions about the content of Tseltal, Tsotsil, and Tojolabal identities, then the participation, claims, and demands made by women in the municipalities place the power relations that comprise these at the heart of the debates, beginning with the family nucleus.

A few days after I accompanied the women of Zapata to their vegetable garden, I interviewed the women on the history of the region and on their reflections on autonomy. I asked them an open question: What is autonomy to them, and what makes it relevant? They answered that autonomy is a form of self-government and of exercising women's rights. It is important to them since it enables them to keep "alive their indigenous culture" and because it is an expression of *compañerismo*. They believe that autonomy acts as the means to political participation, although they acknowledged that the number of women who regularly speak up at the assemblies remains low. At the end of the session, I asked what aspects of autonomy need strengthening. While the rest of the interview had unfolded with many pauses and reflective silences, on this point many women responded quickly that some traditions need to change:

> We want the men to learn how to prepare their own food. We want them to stay at home to look after the children, so that we women can leave the house. We want them to raise the chickens. And we want them to stop being jealous—sometimes they don't let us participate out of jealousy. They shouldn't reproach the women. They accuse us of traveling [to other villages] and looking for a boyfriend, and they don't let us hold positions in the autonomous government. Men should be punished if they don't defend women's rights.

With this conclusion to the interview, the women of Zapata agreed that the tasks and relationships forming household activities, the value ascribed to them, and their politicization initiate new cultural practices. This in turn transforms gendered identity formation along with the meanings of autonomy (Millán 2014). In this regard, Blackwell invites us to analyze the ways in which women have reshaped the debate on autonomy as a "practice of decolonization that is part of everyday life and community" (2012, 705). Martha Sánchez Néstor, an indigenous Amuzgo leader from Guerrero, makes a similar claim when she declares that autonomy necessarily entails a collective process. Nevertheless, "this does not mean creating a homogeneous group that denies the collective rights of the women in it" (Espinosa Damián, Dircio Chautla, and Sánchez Néstor 2010, 414). Autonomy is both collective and individual, it operates out of an assertion of culture along with the claim to question and modify culture. Autonomy passes through both an individual and a social body, opening the door to collective debates on the content of traditions connected to power and to dominant processes, including the role of the state and of capital.

In contrast to the lives of previous generations of women, who defined life as a series of hardships sustained by their "two bosses"—their estate owners and their husbands—younger women in Siete de Enero emphasized that significant changes had begun to take place in the division of household tasks and in their daily interactions with the men in their families. Alicia stated that although some women continued to be victims of domestic violence, changes in household dynamics had become visible as part of autonomy: "Now our husbands help out with bathing the baby, when before they would never take on women's work." Sofia remarked that another significant change was that the men take on household tasks when their wives go to a course or to take their turn at the vegetable garden. She explained that the men had "learned how to make tortillas and do the washing."

In August 2013, during the celebration of the tenth anniversary of the *juntas de buen gobierno*, I found myself at the *caracol* center with Gabina, whom I have known since she was five years old. At twenty-three, she had four children and was a health promoter in the municipality. She was at the *caracol* center for the celebrations, but beforehand had spent three weeks away from home, between workshops and courses, and a week fulfilling her shift at the clinic. She carried her youngest child, who was still breast-feeding, on her back, while the rest remained at home with her husband, who jointly takes care of the house. She explained that "we are *parejo*, we walk side by side, we support each other equally, and share the struggle together."

I would like to pause here and focus on this issue of complementarity, which is a rough translation of the term *parejo*, since the women often refer to it during interviews, when describing their roles and those of their husbands as part of a search for mutual support. Sylvia Marcos refers to *parejo* as a "Mesoamerican perceptual mechanism" based on a notion of duality that questions and criticizes the power relations with which it is imbued (2011, 112). Marcos discusses complementarity as an aspect of Tseltal Mayan philosophy that constantly resignifies tradition. In a similar vein, Morna Macleod cites the philosophical reflections of Virginia Ajxup, a spiritual guide from Momostenango, Guatemala, who in an interview explained this duality as "the integration of two elements for the conservation and continuity of life, and may be understood as what completes and harmonizes being. . . . They are not contradictory or exclusive, but necessary" (Macleod 2008, 485).

The women interviewed, while referring to this equal sharing that is understood as necessary for ensuring the continuity of life, emphasized the power relations reflected in this search and struggle for *parejo*, rather than duality as an end in itself. Doing things *parejo* means to question, to attend to, and to seek to transform the power relations that generate inequalities between men and women. A group of women from the new settlement of Nueva Revolución reflected on this point during a group interview. Twenty-seven-year-old Yolanda first shared her view that she lives in a *parejo* relationship, one in which she enjoys freedom. However, in other spheres, the men still assert traditional hierarchies, above all when it comes to setting out proposals and making decisions:

> In the assemblies, when the men see that the group is disagreeing with them, or they don't like a particular proposal, they start to make a lot of noise, and totally humiliate us. They make us women feel stupid. It is so frustrating. I've seen how when the women leaders are speaking, the men start to laugh or make a racket.

A third expression of the politicization of life in autonomy is the collective self-reflection as a method operating not simply as a means to social transformation but as an outcome in its own right. By "outcome," I am referring to the practice of discussing a given problem and possible solutions—as the conversation on the case of domestic violence between the women from Zapata above illustrates. In chapter 2, I referred to this collective self-reflection as part of the method that the women placed at the heart of the group interviews. In this sense, engaging in joint critical reflection forms part of their political formation and identity. It is often the starting point for women's involvement in autonomy, as explained by Marisa from Cinco de Mayo: "In the collectives we learned to wake up and understand what our rights are. They help us get rid of our shame, since we all encourage each other to speak up. At home we are on our own, but in the collective we can share words and our eyes are opened. We learn to defend our rights."

Throughout the interviews, women like Marisa used terms like "opening our eyes" and "waking up" as synonyms for becoming conscious, a Gramscian concept often used in reference to the dynamics and methods of popular education. In an earlier section, I signaled that civil feminisms tend to develop methodologies for awareness raising and praxis. The emphasis placed on the act of becoming conscious is based on the assumption that understanding oneself in space and time, in relation to men and to unequal power relations, is a necessary step for women to rename life experiences along with the world that surrounds them, identifying problems and seeking solutions on their own terms. Feminist academics point to the complex ambiguities in the use of the concept, given that workshops and training spaces that pursue "awareness raising" form part of broader social hierarchies and inequalities (Espinosa Damián 2009; Hernández Castillo 2003). The method of "awareness raising" hinges upon the idea that the facilitator possesses knowledge, which the participants lack, hence transferring knowledge rather than generating spaces for the mutual production of knowledge.

When Marisa said, "At home we are on our own," she referred to a tension that exists when some male heads of household, be they husbands, fathers-in-law, or grandfathers, continue to exert pressure as to what needs to be done and how the women should do it. By the act of "waking up" and "opening our eyes," she was not describing the arrival of an external agent who helps women finally recognize their oppression at the hands of men. Rather, she was pointing to the act of awakening as a group process, triggered as well as achieved among women, as a result of collective self-reflection on their roles as indigenous peasants (Rabasa 2008). Such reflection forms the basis for action, a praxis that, Adolfo Sánchez Vázquez (1980) considers, enables the overcoming of a natural and immediate point of view that adopts an ordinary perspective as a result of the habits produced by commonplaces. When a gathering of women dislodges this naturalized point of view, the women connect the interpretations that arise from their own experiences to a creative process transforming an as-yet-incomplete reality.

Over the course of my visits to the twelve communities in the autonomous municipality, I observed the well-established dynamic of collective discussions among women participating in the collectives. In the communities with a long history of these women's spaces, I took note of the fluidity with which they spoke among themselves and the types of interactions the women held with the men, dynamics that contrasted to those visible in the communities that joined the Zapatista organization nearly ten years after the uprising. In these villages, just one or two women took part in the group interviews or activities, while the rest showed open resistance to getting involved; on one occasion, some women even got angry when I invited them to contribute to the group discussion rather than letting just one individual speak.

At the same time, "collective eye-opening" as praxis finds limits and counterweights with other cultural practices, most notably *chisme* (gossip). Audalia pulled me aside shortly after the women's meeting in Zapata to share how hurt she was that despite doing the best she could in her *cargo* and responding to what women in her community assigned to her, a small group of them would not stop criticizing her, saying that her true motive was to be outside of her house so as to go find herself another man. She recognized that part of the process of political formation requires preparing oneself to stand the weight of rumors. Audalia explained that she had learned to be strong and withstand what was said so that she could defend herself without attacking the accusers directly. For women, the most frequent rumor spread is that they accept *cargos* because they have romantic interest in other men. In contrast, the rumors spread about men in similar positions are that they have accepted money from the government or that they have stolen money. One of the main conversations I had with women like Audalia was about how these *chismes* emotionally drained them, leaving them not wanting to participate politically. These conversations were typically held in intimate spaces, in a kitchen, for example. In fact, listening to women describing these problems was part of a central supportive role I played over the years.

Before embarking on the fieldwork for this book, between 1997 and 2000 I worked at the San Cristóbal–based NGO K'inal Antzetik. Hilary Klein and I prepared popular-education workshops to reinforce the participation of women in the autonomous municipalities and in their production collectives. If it were not for this solidarity work, I would not have paid attention to the political effects of women's collective work discussed in this chapter, nor would Klein have highlighted these spaces in her book *Compañeras: Zapatista Women's Stories* (2015). In three autonomous municipalities, we held workshops that combined discussions of women's rights with basic math, accounting, teamwork, and other skills required to strengthen the collectives. These activities do not form part of this investigation, and for this reason, I will not provide detailed information about them. Nevertheless, I consider it important to refer to the reflections I recorded in a journal during that period as they illustrate how this form of collective reflection functions as a pedagogical aspect of productive work.

In one workshop held in Diecisiete de Noviembre in May 2000, a woman from one of the communities led a meeting and asked the dozen or so participants to divide into small groups. She described for the groups the exercises they were to work on, which focused on learning about accounting and calculating the profits of the collectives. Each group decided for itself how to work together, without prior definition. In my journal, I pointed out that there was a great deal of flexibility in the established dynamic and, with the exception of a group in which one woman decided to solve all the accounting problems, to the exclusion of the others, the groups developed a collective dynamic. In one group in particular, a woman who already knew basic accounting explained it to the others, and then each of them solved a math problem to later share with the rest. They advanced rapidly, more so than the team where a single woman chose to solve everything herself. In my journal, I noted that the woman community facilitator used the obvious differences as a pedagogical tool to highlight that "this is how collective work functions; if we all learn from each other, more ideas emerge and we all progress faster."

Such expressions of collective knowledge production led to actions aimed at transforming gender relations within communities and between communities and the state. In 1999, we supported a revolving fund in a number of communities that had recently joined the Zapatistas. There, women discussed for the first time how they wanted to work in collectives and, following a series of discussions and meetings, drew up a set of guidelines that established basic principles for group activities. They defined their agreements in light of two objectives: to improve mutual support and to change their subordinated position as women in the municipality. At the time, only men participated in community assemblies, but the women decided that the entire community needed to approve their decision. They wanted to establish their presence, so they gathered outside the concrete building where the meeting was being held. I recall their nervous excitement as they supported each other to feel brave enough to eventually walk into the assembly space together and request that they be heard. The women presented their set of guidelines, which were later approved by the men. In my journal I wrote that the women undertook this joint action "to show the men that we women have power, too." I later noted a conversation I held with one of the women, who explained that this small action reflected the first lesson of the women's collectives put into practice. She located the women's activities in relation not only to the men of the community but to broader power relations with the state, as "the collectives are for the women to support each other, to be united. They are a space for learning, for defending our rights and for doing our work. The idea is for everyone to cooperate and not go cap in hand to the government." In the next section, I discuss the ways in which such actions affect how women hold autonomous government positions in Diecisiete de Noviembre.

From the Collectives to Municipal Commissions

Marisa, from Cinco de Mayo, is on the honor and justice commission of Diecisiete de Noviembre. Along with the other members, she resolves cases at the municipal level concerning both Zapatista and non-Zapatista community members. Marisa is a strong woman, the only one to show up in the center of her village wearing sneakers slightly hidden beneath her traditional Tojolabal dress. In addition to her *cargo*, she works in the fields clearing and preparing the land to sow corn, weeding, and harvesting. Women in the village mock Marisa, and rumors about her circulate. They say she engages in men's work because her husband's arms are deformed. He is the village schoolteacher, and though he diligently works alongside her in the fields and participates in all other agricultural responsibilities, they say that he's "worthless" because one arm ends at the elbow. That's why she goes out so much, the women whisper; according to the gossip, she takes positions in the municipality to find other men because her own husband is "incomplete."

For two days every month, Marisa goes to the *caracol* center to fulfill her *cargo* as a member of the honor and justice commission. Although this commission is made up of four men and four women, all the men participate every Monday and Tuesday, while only one of the women participates each week, the position rotating among them. The reduced time that they dedicate to imparting justice is reflected in the types of cases they resolve; the commission members do not all participate in resolving the same cases. As stated in the previous chapter, the honor and justice commission resolves three types of conflicts: agrarian disputes are the most frequent, and the second most frequent are domestic cases. In these matters it is common practice for those involved to approach both the state justice system and the autonomous commission to see which of them "issues a better decision." The third type of case involves acts of corruption in the state justice apparatus or involving public officials in the official municipal town halls. In these matters, victims ask the members of the commission to monitor the actions of the institutions and defend them before official government authorities (Mora 2013).

During the period in which I conducted research, I never saw any of the four women on the commission, Marisa, Judit, Carolina, or Ermelinda, participate in the resolution of agrarian disputes. This contrasts with their active participation in cases of domestic conflict, hence reflecting a re-inscription of those gender roles that assign women to the place of the family while men are assigned to issues of land. The men on the commission did not ascribe much significance to domestic disputes, particularly cases related to divorce and separation, and they recognized it as a politicized sphere for the women. The case I shall take as an example is a divorce resulting from infidelity. The Tseltal couple in question had three children of primary school age. The husband became involved with another woman from the same village. The new couple decided to remain in the community, in a house near where the first wife lived. During the hearing to establish the terms of the divorce, the honor and justice commission considered it important for the woman to enjoy her own economic solvency and not to have to depend solely on the monthly alimony payment from her ex-husband. For that reason, in addition to a monthly payment, the commissioners agreed on the transfer of a proportion of the livestock that belonged to both of them, as well as of the beehives they owned for apiculture. However, the man refused to keep up with the agreements. Despite the autonomous council's summoning him on several occasions, he failed to turn up at the municipal offices. A relative remarked that the man showed little respect for the autonomous governing office's moral authority, even though he served as a driver for the municipality.

In an interview, Judit and Carolina indicated that despite the challenges, this type of case serves as the starting point for autonomy. Both they and Marisa argued that it rendered possible reaching new agreements on the types of relations established between men and women. Thus they identified their responsibility not only in terms of conflict resolution, but also in terms of a pedagogical role. The three evoked their years of participation within the women's circles of CODIMUJ as well as in the women's collectives that taught them to listen and offer advice, practices that figure as central in the resolution of conflicts. Judit explained that she had been involved in CODIMUJ and in the women's collectives for much of her life, and as a result it felt natural for her to incorporate the methods she learned there in her *cargo* at the time. She said that serving on the commission

> feels almost the same as working with CODIMUJ because things are resolved in a positive manner. If, for example, you impose a fine or imprisonment on a man, he is not going to understand what he did wrong when he mistreated his wife. Instead, you need to talk. If he doesn't realize what is wrong, you need to explain about women's rights for him to see the error of his ways.

A significant aspect of her responsibilities, Judit stated, included explaining to men why they cannot mistreat women. They have to ask for forgiveness, yet this may prove insufficient if the man pays little attention to the commission's decision or, enacting entrenched gender roles, tries to continue his behavior regardless:

> When a man says it is his custom to beat his wife for failing to cook or clean, we explain to him that this is no custom but a mere excuse for him to continue his *pendejadas* [stupid actions]. That's when the regulations are applied and the man is punished with community work, and he has to continue attending the talks [given by women on their rights].

Judit emphasized that resolving a conflict relating to a divorce also serves to explain to a woman her rights. In this sense, her task is also to generate other ways of thinking and acting between women and men. In these cases, female authorities play a moral role and offer explanations rather than adhering to the praxis of "collective eye-opening." She again connected the activities of the commission to her participation in the production collectives:

> The honor and justice work is like what we do in the collectives. There we try to encourage our *compañeras* and explain their rights to them. Sometimes, however, we explain to the women their rights and they don't understand. . . .

In my village we talk about it. If your husband mistreats you, it's not just for the sake of it or because God has decided it. He has no right to treat you like that. That's why we give the talks to the women, too.

The activities described by Judit, Carolina, and Marisa illustrate the ways in which Zapatista women serving as members of the commissions carry out their responsibilities as influenced by collective methods of self-reflection emerging from the production collectives. Their starting points are these political meanings ascribed to social-reproduction activities, those very spheres that lie at the regulatory center of the most relevant neoliberal social-development program—Oportunidades, the focus of the following section.

Oportunidades and Racialized Development Policies

A line of over one hundred non-Zapatista women in the village of Ocosingo pulled me to its center, until I found myself talking to a group who had traveled there early in the morning from different communities across the municipality to receive their bimonthly payment from the Oportunidades social program. María Adela, a Tseltal woman, approached me to ask why I was there. I explained my interest in hearing their opinions on the program, to which she reacted as if she were speaking to a government official conducting an evaluation or recording a promotional video: "Well, I am *very* grateful to the government, because there is a lot of support for the poor. Our husbands have no land and we have no education, but thanks to the *help* from the government . . ." Tere, her friend, quickly interrupted her to express an opposing point of view:

I disagree. That's the truth. I don't see this as help, they give us just 300 pesos [30 US dollars] every two months and in exchange we are obliged to do everything. To receive the money we have to get our Pap smear tests, we have to go to the doctor, we have to send the children to school: everything is obligatory.

"What are you going to use the money for?" I asked.

"For soap, some corn, beans. We'll receive the check shortly. Then we'll go to the store, take everything home, and our opportunities are over for another two months," she replied. As Tere continued to ironically criticize the program, María Adela changed her original tone, one that I understood had emerged from the role she assumed I represented, and expressed agreement with her friend:

What I don't like is that everything is obligatory. I have to go to the medical checkups and take the other women from the community as well. The doctors mistreat us and insult us. They don't even give us treatment or drugs. And I have to take the kids to school, keep the house clean, and go to talks on health. But I already know about boiling water, I know when my house is clean, and I know that my kids should go to school.

"And in these workshops, do they talk about women's rights, domestic violence, or other issues?" I asked her, as it seemed obvious that if they were attending workshops and were obliged to show that what they were learning was improving their lives, they would also be receiving information about how to transform gender relations.

Tere's response was rather different from what I imagined it would be: "No. All they say is that we should not have too many children. On the one hand, our husbands insist on having more children. On the other, the government tells us we shouldn't have any more. Both of them want to force us to do one or the other."

"And how does that make you feel?" I asked.

"Like we are enslaved, doing what the government tells us to. . . . They want to control us, the program is a way of controlling us as women."

This conversation stayed with me over the following weeks as I continued to observe the women from Diecisiete de Noviembre while they went about their daily activities, working in the collectives and participating in their *cargos*. Two aspects in particular struck me: first, there was a contrast between the type of female subjects promoted by Oportunidades and women's praxis in the autonomous villages, and second, despite the marked differences, I noticed that both focus on women's social-reproduction activities. In this section I am interested in shedding light on the regulatory capacities of the program to emphasize the extent to which women's collectives destabilize particular racialized and gendered neoliberal governance techniques.

Since it was launched in 1997, Oportunidades has been the flagship antipoverty policy of four consecutive federal administrations, beginning with that of Ernesto Zedillo (1994–2000), when it was named Progresa (Progress), followed by those of Vicente Fox (2000–2006) and Felipe Calderón (2006–2012), during which it was called Oportunidades, and continuing in that of Enrique Peña Nieto (2012–2018), when it was renamed Prospera (Prosper). In 2006, the Inter-American Development Bank published advertisements in the country's major newspapers declaring Oportunidades *the* model for combating extreme poverty across the continent. Over the course of my fieldwork, it received the largest budgetary allocation ever seen by a federal program of its kind: 25 billion pesos (250 million US dollars) in 2004, 33 billion (330 million US dollars) in 2005, and 36 billion (360 million US dollars) in 2007 (Ornelas Delgado 2006; SEDESOL 2007). To give an idea of the impact of this program in Mexico, one in every five Mexicans is a direct or indirect beneficiary,[1] and the program has covered every municipality in the country since its seventh year of operation (López Estrada 2011). At the time, Chiapas was home to almost half a million recipients, and together with Oaxaca and Veracruz was one of the three states with the largest number of beneficiaries, according to Sandra Dávalos, regional director of Oportunidades, whom I interviewed in June 2006.

At first glance, Oportunidades appears to be a neopopulist social-welfare program, given that it provides impoverished women fellowships for their school-age children, basic health services, and a bimonthly financial contribution dependent on the number of children attending school. However, to promote development of the family's human capital, the program requires the woman receiving the cash transfer to alter certain cultural habits. In the realm of education, the money received is conditional on her children's attending public school. In the sphere of health, the program offers a specific sum for all family members to attend public health clinics, and the mother is responsible for attending workshops on health and nutrition, making annual visits to the gynecologist, and maintaining her house in acceptable conditions of hygiene. According to government analyses, shortcomings in these areas are the inadequate habits of social reproduction that perpetuate generational cycles of poverty, hence preventing families from gaining access to better opportunities (Orozco and Hubert 2005).

According to the program's objectives, the co-responsibility serves to demonstrate to women that they have the capacity to deal with the problems affecting their lives. This implicit logic suggests that through the alteration of the culture of poverty and the regularization of the sphere of biological and social reproduction, these families will increase their social capital, emerge from conditions of extreme poverty, and effectively participate in the economic opportunities provided by the market. As a result, Oportunidades is a social-development program that is distinct from the welfare policies of populist governments because it is grounded in neoliberal logics of efficiency and risk management among poverty-stricken populations. Such neoliberal programs emerge from the notion that social-welfare conditions improve through human capital investments (ECLAC 2007).

Dávalos described in my interview what she considered one of the most significant features of the program:

> The change in habits and attitudes among the women who take part are most important. I have seen how the women who receive their check every two months take their roles more seriously. They have to share responsibilities for the program to work. This sense of responsibility improves self-esteem among indigenous women. If they fail to attend the health workshops or fail to send their kids to school, they are unsubscribed from the program. . . . I observe that they acquire a level of [civic] maturity because they are able to take decisions about their lives. Oportunidades teaches them they have the power to choose. This is part of building democracy [in Mexico].

Dávalos's response suggests that the program's overriding aim has less to do with increasing economic development of impoverished populations and more to do with reeducating women so that they imagine themselves differently, as active and rational subjects that are responsible for looking after their own well-being, which contrasts with the passive, dependency-creating approach of the populist programs. This change in attitude includes linking human freedom to the development of human capital, and defines autonomy as the ability of the individual to choose between available options and alternatives. While the focus rests on self-management and on empowering women to deal with their own socioeconomic needs, it simultaneously erases any notion of redistribution and even more so any analysis of enduring structural inequalities.

Focusing our gaze on the unequal racialized and gendered fields of power elucidates two aspects central to Oportunidades. Firstly, I would like to situate the emergence of the program in a broader sociopolitical context. Oportunidades—or Progresa, as it was first called—began to operate at the same time as a substantial number of indigenous groups were taking an active role in social mobilizations in demand of their rights to autonomy and self-determination. In contrast to these claims situating indigenous men and women as historical subjects, three successive federal governments—amounting to almost two decades of social policy—responded through a neo-indigenist approach that reinforces a state-indigenous relationship of tutelage. By situating these populations as objects of attention by the state, rather than the collective subjects of rights, Oportunidades perpetuated the racial orderings of Mexican society, even after the multicultural constitutional reforms of 2001. It is partially in rejection of these types of logics underlying state policies that Zapatista communities vehemently refuse to accept any government social programs, including Oportunidades. It bears remembering that although Oportunidades does not specifically target indigenous populations, 80 percent of indigenous people live below the poverty line and thus are beneficiaries of the program. Indeed, of the budget that was allocated to social development of indigenous populations in 2011, 50 percent was channeled into this program (CDI 2011).

Secondly, Oportunidades, along with other cash-transfer social programs, depoliticized feminist demands. Research on the inclusion of a feminist agenda in institutional programs across Latin America suggests that new state policies have progressively transformed the feminist political goal of increasing the enforcement of women's rights into a series of technical activities reflected in the design, implementation, and evaluation of public policies, processes that Veronica Schild (2013) refers to as the appropriation and mainstreaming of feminism. Transformative components of feminist demands are emptied since such programs fail to question the relationships of structural inequality and since the accumulative effects of capital tend to deepen the tendency to feminize poverty (Schild 2000). Although Oportunidades claims to empower women living in extreme poverty, it in fact fails to address either the conditions of social inequality in which they live or their demands for gender equality.

If Oportunidades fails to respond to the demands either of indigenous people and peasant farmers or of different feminist strands, then what does it actually represent? The answer may be found when considering the gendered effects of the first wave of neoliberal policies on women's spheres. As mentioned earlier, the gradual removal of state social services during the 1980s and 1990s implied that women—particularly those living in poverty—would take on responsibility for maintaining the household economy and for managing the resources necessary for subsistence, together with those activities relating to care work. In this regard, much of the "political stability" reached during the neoliberal reordering of the economy rested and depended on the administrative and reproductive capacities of women, especially those living in conditions of racialized marginalization. In the institutional spheres that design and evaluate gender policies and policies for combating poverty, the phrase that synthesizes this tendency is "women at the service of the state" (Molyneux 2007, 35).

In October 2007, Mexico City played host to the International Seminar on Gender and Poverty: Scope and Limitations to Its Measurement, in which a range of multilateral institutions took part, including United Nations Women and the United Nations Development Programme, together with Mexican national bodies such as the Instituto Nacional de las Mujeres (National Institute for Women) and the Consejo Nacional de Evaluación de Política de Desarrollo Social (National Council for the Evaluation of Social Development Policy). The participants spoke of the impact of policies pursued during the 1980s and 1990s in terms of converting poor women into the backbone of the neoliberal state. In her contribution, Gina Sens, a professor at the Center for Public Policy of the Indian Institute of Management, emphasized that neoliberal policies of the new millennium are not the same as those of decades past. Sens argued that it is no longer possible to continue implementing policies that hide the additional pressures to which poor women are subject, above all peasant or indigenous women, those from the Dalit caste in India, or other women treated as racially inferior. It became necessary to introduce women's domestic tasks into public policies targeting highly impoverished sectors of the population. The new social programs cannot grant monetary transfers without first establishing conditions and demanding that the counterpart—in this case the woman beneficiary—meet her responsibilities. The argument justifies the state's entry into the "private sphere" to regulate domestic tasks. I suggest that if the social and political "stability" of a neoliberal state rests in part on the capacity of women to reproduce domestic activities, then this sphere acquires greater significance for effective governance.

In the 1980s and early 1990s, during the first phase of neoliberal policies, the state relied on a masculinized logic rendering female work invisible while at the same time basing itself on the "traditional" role played by women in moments of crisis. However, by the end of the 1990s, neoliberal policies entered a second phase defined by the so-called Santiago Consensus (by contrast with the Washington Consensus), which shifted the priority of governance to a reorganization of social life and the microregulation of individuals. Public policies during this period focused on targeted social spending, efficiency, and shared responsibility. Schild argues that "heteronormative families have been the explicit object of social regulation. . . . The neoliberalized state, in its ameliorative form, relies heavily on the public extension of women's practices and emotional investments in care" (2013, 212, 217). Public policies thus incorporate new perspectives in the design of social programs; in particular, the domestic sphere is transformed into a key territory through which operates racialized neoliberal governance.

Regulating Racialized Cultural and Corporal "Degeneration"

Following her research on the program to combat conditions of extreme poverty for women in Chile, Programa Puente (Bridge Program), Schild identifies a mainstreaming of the feminist movement's contributions, teaching logics, and expertise. The program responds to the female beneficiaries as legal subjects by offering personalized psychosocial support, family food vouchers, guaranteed monetary subsidies, and preferential access to programs for social improvement, employment, and social security (Schild 2013, 219). I would suggest that, in contrast to the Chilean state's enabling change, the Mexican neoliberal state fosters a reactivation of racialized tropes that reproduce underlying inequalities through Oportunidades.

Oportunidades aims to regulate those spheres related to health and education by means of altering cultural habits. A racialized and gendered framework of analysis invites us to ask: what role have these spheres historically played in the production of racialized subjectivities in Mexico? In different moments of the country's history, beginning with the Porfiriato, at the height of the estate economies, state projects used the lack of education or hygiene—as an indicator of inadequate health conditions—to explain why the indigenous population continued to live in conditions of socioeconomic marginalization. In response, social-engineering programs during the postrevolutionary period based themselves on Latin American eugenicist theories to promote cultural improvements of citizen-subjects in these very spheres. In her book *"The Hour of Eugenics": Race, Gender, and Nation in Latin America*, Nancy Leys Stepan (1996) contrasts the history of eugenics in Latin America with that in the United States and Europe. The author recalls that social Darwinism identifies poverty, criminality, and other forms of "degeneration" as genetically predetermined in ways that parallel the attitudes of estate owners toward their peons, as I described in chapter 3. In Latin America, such arguments open the possibility of social progress through direct forms of state intervention. The engine driving this social engineering operates on the assumption that genetic attributes shape the population's culture, which can then be modified through the transformation of habits and behaviors. Constructing social problems on the basis of cultural and biological "degeneration" justifies the active role of the state in cultivating *mestizo* citizens, principally through hygiene, education, sports, care, and reproductive-health programs.

My interest in bringing forth this history is to illustrate the continuity of social-eugenics ideologies embodied in the underlying assumptions driving Oportunidades. To begin with, the program focuses on altering habits in those spheres historically targeted as embodying the cultural "degeneracy" of indigenous populations and of other populations living in conditions of racialized poverty. A second focus, which is a logical consequence of the first, on achieving proper hygiene and health conditions — particularly in relation to reproductive health — figures prominently given that changes in these spheres function as indicators of cultural improvement or of cultural regeneration. This is reflected in the visits made by health officials to the homes of the beneficiaries to evaluate conditions of personal hygiene and to ensure that the women are maintaining certain standards of cleanliness in the home, boiling water for drinking, and maintaining latrines in proper conditions, as well as verifying that they are implementing what the health workshops teach them. With these home visits, the state enters the domestic sphere to regulate and monitor tasks of social reproduction. The same assumptions operate in the medical checkups, such as annual visits to the gynecologist and participation of beneficiaries in reproductive-health workshops.

As the representative of the Oportunidades program interviewed in San Cristóbal explained, if the women who are beneficiaries do not comply with their side of the co-responsibility agreement, they lose the fellowships provided for their children along with the opportunity to better their families. Government documents on the outcomes of the Oportunidades program, together with explanations offered by state representatives interviewed, suggest that the obligatory checkups are exclusively a public-health matter. Despite the fact that cervical cancer rates in Mexico are the highest in the continent, few women in rural or semirural areas get their annual checkups.[2] Without denying the alarming nature of these figures, we cannot rely wholly on a public-health justification, but — following the initiative of Stepan — we need to read the effects of Oportunidades in the light of historical, racial, and gender processes. In this regard, we may note that the activities monitored by the state — medical examinations, school attendance, standards of household hygiene — belong to the liberal-constructed private sphere, in contrast to the public sphere, which has historically been subject to state scrutiny. However, for women in conditions of racialized poverty, along with their families, this division becomes blurred, as the "private" forms part of the "public" sphere to the degree it is subject to state forms of surveillance. "We do our part and so do they, as long as they attend their medical checkups, take their children to school, go to the health workshops," Dávalos told me in my interview. "I see this as a way of improving the country because the indigenous people are also a part of our culture. They can *improve* themselves through education and better health."

Research conducted by African American women in the United States sheds light on how Oportunidades operates through gendered forms of racialization. Dorothy Roberts, in *Killing the Black Body: Race, Reproduction, and the Meaning of Liberty* (1998), writes about the public policies and legal system of the United States to demonstrate how the stereotype of "welfare queens" was constructed. She refers to mostly African American and Latina women accused of living off state welfare programs, of being lazy, feckless, and prone to reproducing irresponsibly. Starting with the neoliberal period of President Ronald Reagan in the 1980s, public policies began to represent impoverished populations—above all, African Americans and Latinos—as poor because of these cultural "defects." They were accused of lacking sufficient human capital to emerge from their condition of poverty, and as a result, these "defects" justified the incursion of the state into their homes. Based on conditions of joint responsibility that find echoes in Oportunidades, female welfare recipients were granted monthly checks on the condition that they accept home visits from representatives of the state programs, that they use birth-control methods, and that they make efforts to change the habits and attitudes that trap them in a situation of high socioeconomic marginalization (Roberts 1998).

Continuing with this parallel, Mexican state representatives construct the "problem" of populations living in extreme poverty as resulting from cultural defects and corporal "degeneration," primarily through poor hygiene and reproductive-health habits (such as having too many children). The underlying assumption assigns responsibility for these "defects" to poor—mostly indigenous—women, who are then invited to alter their cultural habits. It is the women who are obliged to adapt new practices so as to improve their children's future opportunities, while simultaneously they are blamed for their inability to improve their family's living conditions, as Dávalos noted in my interview.

So far we have analyzed the racialized and gendered logics of governance of the Mexican state through social-development programs in regions of high marginalization, such as the valleys of the Lacandon Jungle. However, the state materializes through the articulation of multiple forms of power in specific locations (Hart 2002; Joseph and Nugent 1994). In the case of the states of Chiapas, Guerrero, and Oaxaca, we cannot address state formation during the past twenty years without addressing the militarization of everyday life that emerges in response to the politically organized indigenous populations. This task obliges us to analyze the articulation of social-development policies to state security policies, processes that scholars such as Lars Buur, Jensen Steffen, and Fina Stepputat (2007) describe as the "security-development nexus." The authors indicate that although there is nothing new about this connection, as the nexus figured prominently during colonial periods and during the Cold War, it takes on new nuances and meanings following the fall of the Berlin Wall and again as part of the post-9/11 world. They propose a review of the relationship between these two pillars of state formation, not as complementary "soft" and "hard" sides but rather as mutually constitutive and interdependent. The Zapatista women of Diecisiete de Noviembre offer a similar theorization through their interpretations of lived experiences.

The Fragmentation of Social Reproduction and the Militarization of the Everyday

We were returning from the forest along a narrow path after gathering firewood for the household when Alfonsina nodded toward a group of women from Morelia. "Look, there go the *priistas*, I think they're arriving back from Altamirano after collecting their opportunities," she said sarcastically.

She was referring to a dozen non-Zapatista women descending from an overloaded bus. They were carrying bags stuffed with clothes, household articles, backpacks, and school materials for their children. Some had stayed behind in Altamirano, waiting for their husbands while they celebrated the funds by heading to the town's cantina. Later that evening the village would bear witness to drunken men (and a few women) stumbling down the street, shouting incoherently and fighting each other for unknown motives. From where we stood, we observed that some of them were already inebriated, though the majority bid each other good-bye and quietly headed for their homes. I asked Alfonsina her opinion of the program. "Well, it's just part of the government's war. They want to control women. The way I see it, it's about getting a few crumbs in exchange for doing whatever the government tells you to do."

We had just been talking about how the economic situation was so difficult that when a family decides to withdraw from "the organization," they often enroll in the program to obtain a source of income. I was interested in learning more about why Alfonsina linked Oportunidades to "the government's war." She answered,

> It is a way of living our lives as they want us to. They don't want us to organize ourselves, or to have responsibilities. It is so that the women and their families abandon the struggle. And when they leave the struggle the government tells them what to do anyway. That's why it's all part of the same thing.

Alfonsina drew attention to the ways that this "war" waged by the federal and state governments against the Zapatista support bases seeks to regulate and impose control over their lives, pressuring them to accept the terms of obedience. In the previous section I described the different ways in which Oportunidades regulates the social-reproduction activities of female beneficiaries and generates a particular type of woman-subject. Where does the militarization of everyday life overlap with development programs like Oportunidades? In what way does this correlation lead us to understand the logics of gender implicit in the formation of the neoliberal racialized state in militarized zones? How is this connected to Alfonsina's statement that they are one and the same because both seek to exercise control over women's lives? The answers to these questions lie in the *testimonios* of the women I interviewed in Diecisiete de Noviembre, above all in their reflections on the effects of a comprehensive war of attrition, as social psychologists from San Cristóbal refer to counterinsurgency mechanisms in operation after 1994 (Santiago 2011).

During these interviews, the women referred to the period of the heaviest militarization of the territory under EZLN influence, over the first five years after the uprising, between 1994 and 1999, when the army patrolled forest paths, set up camp on the riverbanks where the women washed their clothes, and overflew the communities — especially when the men were away in the fields — as well as threatened to launch operations and enter the villages. Faced with these daily occurrences, the women felt deep anxiety about their potential inability to properly harvest crops, prepare food, gather firewood, or collect water, in addition to having to care for the sick when they were "sick with nerves" or when they "felt sadness in their hearts." Martina, from Zapata, observed that "people often get sick because they are sad. As a woman you cannot afford to get sick, however, because you have to look after the kids, and prepare the food, even when your head hurts, your stomach hurts, your heart aches."

Taken together, these *testimonios* center on care work and the domestic sphere. These women's anxieties, understood as the outcome of a comprehensive war of attrition, heightened the pressures brought about by the privatization of social services, cuts to public spending, and the reduction of social institutions. At the same time, the "armed withdrawal" of the neoliberal state—a term I borrow from Lesley Gill (2000, 16), who uses it to refer to the Bolivian state in El Alto prior to the administration of Evo Morales—intensified how indigenous Zapatista women experienced a war of attrition. According to studies and testimonials produced by feminist academics, counterinsurgency tactics sought to dismantle the family production base (Olivera Bustamante 1998). These studies point to state tactics such as burning the harvests of rebel communities, destroying crops, stealing cattle, and restricting the movement of people, especially to limit access to their *milpas* and coffee plants. The fragmentation of a productive base creates additional pressures on women's social-reproductive tasks. They then need to develop strategies to continue to manage household needs, primarily activities that allow for subsistence, even under progressively precarious conditions. Women like Juana, a health promoter for Ocho de Marzo, described the anguish they felt in fulfilling their daily activities. Juana said,

> With the presence of the army, sadness enters the heart, people feel stressed and fall sick. I see how this sadness leads men not to respect their women. It was all about nervous breakdowns in those years, and when there's another red alert [as in 2006], it is like the body remembers the anxiety and the number of people falling sick rises again. It is always worse for the women: how are they going to feed their children?

Through the systematization of a series of training workshops held over several years with health promoters from Caracol V, in the northern zone, Ximena Antillón Najlis describes additional kinds of impact, particularly the fragmentation of political and solidarity alliances across families and between family members. The Zapatista health promoters Antillón interviewed similarly point to how government assistance programs not only attempt to control the population, but also threaten the food sovereignty of communities. The combined sets of pressures generate health issues and diseases ranging from diarrhea and gastritis to fevers, depression, insomnia, and alcoholism (Antillón Najlis 2011).

It was not only the militarization of everyday life that fractured the capacity of women to carry out their tasks, but the acts of physical violence the soldiers inflicted on their bodies. In armed conflicts, the bodies of indigenous women become a territory over which state forces exercise mechanisms of disciplinary and violent control over biological reproduction. Sexual torture and other acts of violence directed at their bodies are the most horrific expressions of this logic. In conversations, female Zapatista members would point to these military actions as a continuation of the sexual violence their grandmothers suffered on the estates.[3] The best-known cases include those of the three González sisters, who were raped at a military checkpoint in the town of Altamirano in July 1994; the three nurses from the Health Department who were raped and beaten in San Andrés Larráinzar in October 1995; and the case of femicide during paramilitary actions in the northern zone of the state in 1997 (CDHFBC 1998b). Between 1994 and 1998, the group Women of San Cristóbal recorded fifty cases of rape linked to political conflict in the areas under Zapatista influence (Hernández Castillo 1998).

Hortensia from Nueva Revolución made the following observation about the physical violence: "They attack us because they see that we are already involved [politically]. We go on marches, we run collectives, and we defend our villages from the army. The resistance couldn't exist without us. That is why the men have to value us, but it is also why the government wants to control us."

Several feminist academics suggest that the mutilation of bodies and sexual torture used as an element of repression in conflict zones is aimed at decreasing women's participation in organized processes; it is using their bodies as a battlefield to demonstrate the weakness of the enemy in terms of its inability to protect "its women" (Denich 1994). The accounts gathered shortly after the Acteal massacre in Chiapas in 1997 describe how paramilitary soldiers cut open the bellies of those murdered women who were pregnant and declared that this was "to kill the seed" (Hernández Castillo 1998). Andrea Smith considers such acts genocide because, as conquest controls territory, so this controls those bodies that condition the possibility of future generations of the indigenous population. "Native people have become marked as inherently violable through a process of sexual colonization. By extension, their lands and territories have become marked as violable as well" (Smith 2005, 55). The relationship between sexual violence and control over land is evident in the actions as well as the threats of the owner of the Yaxolob ranch, as described by members of Nueva Revolución in chapter 3.

Celia González, one of the three Tseltal sisters raped at a military checkpoint in Altamirano in 1994—a case reviewed by the Inter-American Commission on Human Rights, which issued a report in 2001—provided testimony of the long-term impact of these acts of sexual violence against support bases. González appeared as a witness at the Permanent Court of the Peoples, an ethical court that in March 2012 held a pre-hearing session on femicides and gender violence. This was the first time she presented her testimony in public. While other female victims opted to speak from behind a screen to maintain their privacy, González declared that she had spent her whole life in silence and had decided that it was finally the moment to speak openly. I was seated on the stage, as part of the jury, where I noticed how her legs trembled behind the podium while her voice and hand gestures maintained a level of control that bore testimony to her deep inner strength. She repeated over and over that she came to speak the truth: she and her two sisters were raped by members of the military. Speaking in Tseltal (which was translated into Spanish by an interpreter and then into English here), González declared, "This happened seventeen years ago, and while they didn't kill me, they did break my heart. I want to tell you that I was filled with fear, yet I am fighting against injustice, against the government, not only here, but in all Mexico. I demand that the army leave indigenous lands, because we are suffering rape and torture."

State security policies direct attempts to fragment the biological- and social-reproduction capacities of indigenous populations so as to "neutralize" a rebel army like the EZLN. They reflect the ideological normalization of acts of dehumanization and exploitation of the vulnerability to premature death of populations racialized as inferior, as the sociologist Ruth Gilmore (2007, 28) so aptly defines racism. State mechanisms operating in spheres of social and biological reproduction simultaneously regulate and fragment, discipline and mutilate, interrupt and reconfigure. In their articulation they reflect the processes of (dis)integration of a racialized state that simultaneously requires and discards as inferior the figure of the indigenous woman. Under the historical conditions framed by its neoliberal "armed withdrawal," the state simultaneously relies on the figure of the indigenous woman to maintain a particular social stability as part of the process of neoliberal restructuring and systematically interrupts her activities with the mechanisms of low-intensity warfare.

In highlighting these parallels, I recognize that there is a marked difference between how an act of violence against the body is experienced and how the body is disciplined and regulated. In no sense am I arguing that they are the same; to do so would be to diminish the impact of the act of sexual violence. What I do wish to emphasize is that they form part of accumulated violences, or what I refer to as a continuum of violences. The combined effect intensifies how indigenous women in militarized zones experience states of war, both as a condition of being and as an effect of sovereign power. They witness the fusion of military tactics with social programs, including the militarization of the police force, and the use of social-welfare tasks as an excuse for the army to become involved in the everyday life of the general population. Dismantling social-reproduction activities acts as a guiding thread between these mechanisms of a comprehensive war of attrition and turns social reproduction into a matter of state security.

Conclusion

In this chapter, I demonstrated how the characteristic ambiguities of a racialized and gendered state operate on a highly politicized terrain. Using a framework that analyzed Oportunidades alongside militarized counterinsurgency forces, I described the ways in which the neoliberal logics of governance generate the progressive devaluation of indigenous lives. Such mechanisms operate through a double effect that simultaneously conceals race while activating explicit racialized tropes, particularly those of cultural degeneracy that originated in the Porfiriato. At the same time, counterinsurgency tactics have the racialized effect of controlling indigenous territory by attempting to dominate indigenous women's lives and their bodies. Both the explicit invisibility of race and its hypervisibility sustain extreme acts of gendered racial violence (Kyungwon Hong and Ferguson 2011).

This chapter established a biopolitical framework focused on social-reproduction activities to argue that indigenous female praxis in autonomy profoundly destabilizes and alters the category of indigenous woman, on which these aspects of Mexican state formation rest. Firstly, the processes of collective self-reflection that identify and seek to transform the power relations connected to "traditions" and to broad structures of social inequality serve to destabilize a number of symbolic roles associated with indigenous women. I argued that these political assertions influence the meanings ascribed to autonomy and modify its everyday dynamics. Secondly, the politicization of everyday life linked to domestic tasks points to *kuxlejal* politics in autonomy as a collective drive to define the terms of social and biological reproduction. This has major implications for decolonization processes driven by the Zapatistas, as it highlights the immanence of politics in the social life of people who have historically suffered the loss of their territories, their bodies, and their knowledge. In the next chapter, I analyze how these aspects of *kuxlejal* politics influence governing practices in Diecisiete de Noviembre as part of *mandar obedeciendo*.

SIX

Mandar Obedeciendo; or, Pedagogy and the Art of Governing

January 1, 2008. Throughout the night, hundreds of people arrived at the administrative center of Diecisiete de Noviembre on open-backed trucks to celebrate the anniversary of the creation of the autonomous municipality. Suspended lights, easy to confuse with stars in the thick fog, illuminated the area surrounding the auditorium. Not long before dawn, a volley of fireworks interrupted the elders' morning prayers. The distant beat of maracas and the slow, melancholy melody of a harp merged with the aroma of the pine needles spread over the floor of the building to mark the ceremonial nature of the event. The handover of the *bastones de mando*, the "staffs of authority," to the new members of the autonomous council would take place that day.

At nine o'clock that morning, the six representatives of the new council, wearing pressed white cotton shirts and pants and with red bandanas draped around their necks, awaited the commencement of the ceremony in one of the secondary school classrooms. The representatives of the outgoing council stood nearby. A line of people acted as a bridge uniting the two groups as the elders played their drums and flutes. An elder, Ernestino, spoke in Tseltal, combining prayers and words of advice with stories of times past. Standing beside me, Teodoro, from Siete de Enero, visibly moved, summarized the speech for me: "Since long ago, before the arrival of the Spanish, indigenous people already knew how to govern. They had

Figure 6.1. Zapatista leadership taking notes on what Zapatista sympathizers are saying during a meeting of the Other Campaign, La Garrucha, Caracol III, 2006; photo by author

their own authorities and knew how to order and to obey. Then the Spanish came and they told us that we don't know how to govern, that only the *kaxlanes*, the *ajvalil*, are authorities."

Seven kilometers away, in the state municipal office in Altamirano, the new official local government was holding its own inauguration ceremony. Months earlier, the local residents had elected as president a teacher, an Institutional Revolutionary Party candidate whose husband had governed the municipality a few years earlier. Members of the Party of the Democratic Revolution and the Green Ecological Party, together with independent citizens' groups, expressed their disagreement with the election results. They accused the teacher of buying votes, engaging in influence peddling, and expressing racist attitudes toward the local population. A driver who belonged to a citizens' organization in Altamirano claimed that he had heard the teacher say that the "Indians" were only good for being the slaves and laborers of the *mestizos*.

Shortly before Christmas, the dissidents occupied the municipal administrative building to demand that, in place of a president, the state government set up a council made up of representatives of all the political parties, as residents of the municipality of Ocosingo had successfully done in 1995.[1] The civil resistance lasted only a few days and ended with the local police force removing those who had set up camp in the central park. By January first, representatives of the opposition parties threatened to chase the police from the same spot. The streets of Altamirano filled with tension and police vehicles.

Events in Altamirano and in the autonomous school in Diecisiete de Noviembre, rather than representing opposite poles, frame a highly politicized terrain, where the investiture of the new autonomous councils reflects a dispute not only over the exercise of power, but over its ascribed meaning, as Ernestino highlighted as his speech continued:

> When you are a council member it is necessary to *hold* authority, not to *be* an authority. And in order to hold authority you must possess patience, respect, and a desire to listen and to learn. It is not your choice to become an authority; it is because the people have chosen you. The people must be respected and not be taken for granted. God, which is also the land, and the people, chose you. There are no authorities without people, and without people there is no life. That is why to govern is to obey.

With his words, Ernestino emphatically reminded those listening that divine powers, including those that connect a people to their land, hold the authority that the new council members needed to emanate as well as respect. To obey while governing implies complying with the needs communicated by these divine powers, the earth as well as those who inhabit it. After emphasizing that the chosen members' new role depends on maintaining a tightly woven relationship with the communities, Ernestino, along with the other elders, then accompanied the outgoing autonomous government representatives, who slowly walked forward before coming to a halt at the front of the classroom so as to respectfully face the incoming authorities and address all of those present. Mauricio, whose *cargo* was now ending, avoided establishing eye contact with anyone. I saw that his eyes brimmed with tears which he vainly to contain. The people close to him maintained tight control over their expressions, and they held their bodies rigidly upright as a sign of respect for the solemnity of the event. The brief seconds of heavy silence were shattered when slogans burst from the line of Zapatista sympathizers: "*Viva* the councils! *Viva* autonomy! *Viva* the EZLN, the new authorities, the *sup*! [in reference to Subcomandante Insurgente Marcos]."

The members of the outgoing council walked to the foot of the stage, where each of the men stood holding a *bastón de mando* that the elders had given him. A few steps behind, the female council members stood together alongside members of the land and territory and the honor and justice commissions. Juan Miguel rose to read the following text written by way of a farewell:

> *Compañeros*, today we are happy to leave our *cargos* as we know that it brings to a close three years of serving the people. . . . We know that we made errors in our work, but it is through errors that we learn. We feel sad and beg your forgiveness for not being able to do enough. You all saw the good work and the bad work we did. We give you our thanks for the trust you placed in us as authorities. We learned a lot from you. The best teachers are you, the people.

Juan Miguel, Mauricio, and the rest of the outgoing authorities handed over the staffs to their counterparts and accompanied them to the stage to formally cede their responsibilities to them. Then the party began. Ignacio, the council's new president, is also the lead singer of the regional group Los Quetzales. Wearing a cowboy hat, he sang verses from the most popular *cumbia* and *música de banda* songs of the moment: "El zancudo loco" (The crazy mosquito), "Cómo matar al gusano" (How to kill the worm), "Cacerola," (Saucepan), and "El gato y el ratón" (The cat and the mouse). At one point he left his place at center stage to speak briefly with the new representatives of the council and the honor and justice commission, handing the microphone to his brother, who carried on singing "Mi bizcochito" (My honeybun). Half an hour later he continued the show as lead singer in the festivities. At some point, Ignacio switched once again to his role as authority, pausing to affirm what Ernestino had stated earlier:

> With this *bastón* and this intention as council we show that as indigenous people we are capable of walking, we are capable of fighting, that we are capable of governing in our own way. We are new to this task, and we are going to learn about the problems and needs, and learn how to hold authority. The people will tell us how

This chapter addresses the collective affirmation of self-governing by Tseltal and Tojolabal Zapatistas as reiterated in the speeches held throughout this ceremony. My interest is to illustrate the ways in which Zapatista community members attempt to subvert a naturalized fixed location for indigenous people when the local population is divided into those who are born to govern and those who are born to obey, as the comment by the candidate for the Altamirano municipal presidency suggested. The words of Ernestino, along with those of Mauricio and Ignacio, serve as an invitation to reflect on the different meanings associated with being a "good government" versus a "bad government," through the lens of indigenous peoples historically and systematically denied not only spaces of political power but their own knowledge base that references other ways of understanding that power. In the following pages, I return to the emphasis that Ernestino placed on *having* authority over and above *being* the authority, as part of the exercise of self-government. In turn, I take as a starting point Ignacio's reference to *having authority by learning to be the authority*, that is, when those temporarily in positions of power seek to listen to the guidance and instructions of those they represent, which he highlights by saying that the people will guide the leaders, and which Juan Miguel signals by thanking his teachers, the people he represented when holding the *cargo* of the autonomous council. Opening one's heart to learn to *be* an authority, as that which *grants* an individual authority, forms part of a Tseltal and Tojolabal political ethic inscribed in the concept of *mandar obedeciendo*, a term that encapsulates a series of principles, coherences, and strengths of the praxis of liberation particular to the Zapatistas (Dussel 2006), first described in a communiqué dated February 26, 1994:

> It is the will and reason of good men and women to seek and discover the best way of governing themselves. What is for the good of the greater number is good for all. . . . This has always been our path: that the will of the majority become one in the heart of men and women leaders. The will of the majority is the path that must be followed by the one who governs. If this path of the people's reason is abandoned, then the heart who governs should be changed for another that obeys. Thus was born our power in the mountains: the one who governs obeys if it be true; the one who obeys governs by the common heart of all true men and women. (EZLN 1994a)

Ernestino referred to governing by obeying during the handover ceremony when he explained that authorities are responsible for implementing these decisions reached by consensus in the assemblies, rather than taking decisions in the name of the people. He established the capacity to listen, what Zapatista community members express as "opening your heart" to learn, as one of the principles of *mandar obedeciendo*. The significance of this political philosophy must be understood as situated in a disputed political terrain, where these Tseltal and Tojolabal communities' experiences with government officials, with local *mestizo* estate owners, and with other figures of authority are permeated by racialized airs of superiority that not only seek to reproduce the message that indigenous people are born to obey but undermine their collective capacities to enact decisions for the well-being of the collective.

Since the 1994 uprising, scholars who have written extensively about the principle of governing by obeying have singled out the concept as a fundamental contribution of indigenous peoples to political philosophy, particularly the concept of democracy (González Casanova 2005), as moving beyond the limits of electoral politics (Street 1996) and as a more profound understanding of the effects of constitutive power (Speed 2008; Speed and Reyes 2002).[2] In turn, authors describe the concept as engendering a new collective political subject, a praxis that unravels the power of the sovereign entity, in contrast with the political aim of Marxist vanguard movements that aspire to take power (Reyes and Kaufman 2011). I offer in this chapter a contribution to these earlier academic studies by focusing on how governing by obeying dismantles the racialized fixed location of indigenous people as those destined to receive orders. I center my arguments on three aspects that emerge from the daily practices in Diecisiete de Noviembre. First, I refer to the shared practice of establishing a consensus agreement, which is not reduced to the spaces of the assemblies that previous studies highlight but rather extends decision-making capacities to a vast range of community spheres and daily activities. I suggest that the set of cultural practices render inseparable political action and the collective actor. In relation to the argument of chapter 5, I suggest that although this tendency is condensed in the activities of the women's collectives, it extends through the different decision-making spheres in the autonomous municipality.

Second, governing by obeying opens the possibility of governing by learning to govern. In the space between *ser* (being) and *aprendiendo a hacer* (learning to do), a juxtaposition of terms that could be translated as "learning to be by doing," emerges a praxis of knowledge production grounded in an embodied knowledge that makes it possible to transcend the boundaries of racialized neoliberal relations. I suggest that such practices encapsulate cultural politics linking pedagogy to the art of governing. Finally, I reflect on the implications of both effects—the pedagogical aspects of governing and the diffuse distribution of decision making—for transforming power relations with the Mexican state.

In developing these arguments, I set out in the first part of the chapter a genealogy of local cultural practices that converge in what is now understood as *mandar obedeciendo*. The following section describes the various ways in which governing by obeying inverts the logic of command-obedience that we find in classic Westernized political theory and in the comments of individuals, such as racist labeling of indigenous people by the newly elected Institutional Revolutionary Party municipal president in 2008. The third section describes the pedagogical impulse of governing by learning to govern. Finally, I address the effects of these political practices in interactions with state officials.

Autonomous Government, Obeying Collective Governing

Members of the autonomous council commit to coordinating the activities of the Zapatista municipal government for a three-year period, a responsibility assigned to them by the communities who nominate candidates during an assembly; they are subsequently named through consensus. Council members facilitate and oversee activities undertaken by the different municipal commissions and administrative bodies responsible for the implementation of the various programs and activities associated with the principal spheres of autonomy, including agricultural production, education, health, the implementation of justice, civil registry, and the use of appropriate technology, such as ecological latrines and fuel-saving stoves. Promoters, such as the education promoters in the communities, then carry out the activities in each of these spheres. The administrative responsibilities of the autonomous governments differ by region. Even within a single *caracol* there are variations. For example, Alejandro Cerda (2011) notes that the autonomous municipality Vicente Guerrero (in Caracol IV) has a women's commission and a commission of elders, while, as I observed, these committees existed only briefly in the adjacent municipality of Diecisiete de Noviembre.

Since 2003, the autonomous councils for each municipality of Caracol IV (during the time this research was conducted, there were seven) have coordinated to form the *juntas de buen gobierno*. Caracol IV, "Whirlwind of Our Words," refers to its *junta* as the Rainbow of Hope. Outside its office, the following words are written with bright splashes of color in Spanish, Tseltal, Tojolabal, and Tsotsil:

> Oficina de la Junta de Buen Gobierno
> Yot'an xojobil yu'un smali yel lequil cuxlejal
> Yo'onton me'qu'inibal yu'un ti smalaele
> Ja yalzil ja k'intumi aytik smajlajel
> (Radiant heart seeking a dignified life)

The *junta* represents a new layer within the administrative demarcations of autonomy as well as an expanded sphere made up of authorities from the various municipalities. It groups together the representatives of each of the autonomous councils in the *caracol*. Roughly twelve individuals serve at a time; these authorities rotate weekly and return to their communities and to their responsibilities in their respective municipalities. Every month they return to take their turn as a member of this collective governing body. Just as Ignacio, the new council president, switched back and forth between his role as authority and as a singer in the celebrations throughout the night of the ceremony in Diecisiete de Noviembre, all the other autonomous governing authorities maintain multiple roles that keep them grounded in community life. The constant movement between community activities and *junta* responsibilities requires a difficult balance between overseeing the needs of the entire *caracol*, of their municipality, and of their daily family lives, including caring for their corn, beans, coffee plants, and other crops.

The *junta* reviews matters that have not been resolved at a lower level, and if it fails to reach a resolution, the issue then reaches the *caracol*'s highest collective authority, the *caracol* assembly. The agrarian cases I described in chapter 4 represent the type of politically delicate cases that require the debate and subsequent decision of the *caracol* assembly. The *junta* similarly ensures the distribution of the *caracol*'s resources, to prevent any one municipality from taking more than its share. This priority resulted in part after communities in Caracol IV accused the communities of Morelia and Siete de Enero of concentrating municipal resources during the first years of the autonomous project. At the same time, the different council members that make up the *junta*, along with representatives and members of the different commissions, prepare proposals for discussion, approval, reformulation, or rejection by the *caracol* assembly. For example, if the agricultural production commission wishes to propose a way to continue improving crop production without the use of fertilizers, the members present their ideas to the assembly so as to initiate a process of collective discussion and debate.

Not long before the handover ceremony for the autonomous council in Diecisiete de Noviembre, I interviewed Zapatista authorities on the practices and responsibilities of the *junta*. My interests centered on understanding the importance of rotating the members of the council and the relationship between the various spheres of authority. Santiago explained,

> The councils rotate because the idea is that we are all governing among ourselves, so it is not only a few who are in charge. We don't want a fixed *junta*

because we don't want a government like the state government. If everyone governs then they can see the needs of the people with their own eyes. . . . The duty of the *junta* is to be a great tree with many branches. It is the trunk that has to observe everything that happens and to ensure it is functioning properly. The trunk does not propel the work, but rather [that is the task of] the commissions, which are the branches, and the leaves are the delegates along with the rest of the people.

Mauricio and Santiago both emphasized the importance of rotating authorities to avoid a concentration of power, while at the same time, the *junta* provides certain cohesion and purpose to this fluidity. The resulting tension requires a balance between avoiding the reduction of decision-making capacities to a few people and at the same time holding authorities accountable for their actions as well as maintaining communication among the numerous representatives who constantly move through the offices of the *junta*. During fieldwork, I would periodically meet with the rotating *junta* members to inform them of the progress of my research or to ask questions regarding future interviews. Often this communication involved meeting with the *junta* one week and then returning one or two weeks later to inquire if they had an answer to my question. It was always a guess whether the next week's representatives would have the accurate information I communicated to those representatives with whom I originally met or whether I would have to repeat all the information again. Despite *junta* representatives' keeping a notebook recording the questions and claims of each person who entered their office, ensuring effective communication from one week to the next proved a challenge, yet it was that communication that was required for decisions to be enacted as a collective body.

At the same time, decision-making practices are distributed among the commission members, delegates, other authorities, and the rest of the population of the *caracol*. The sum of all these parts is the exercise of self-government. Taken as a whole, they reflect cultural practices linked to self-determination initiatives in Mexico, as demonstrated by the studies conducted on the Community Police—Regional Coordinator of Community Authorities, which since 1995 has operated in the Mountain and Costa Chica regions of Guerrero (Sierra 2013), together with studies on the *keris*, the authorities of the indigenous Purépecha municipality of Cherán, Michoacán (Aragón 2013). Though the rotating system of *cargos* and decision-making practices in assemblies maintains similarities across these organizations, in the case of the autonomous municipalities, they are unique because of the particularity of the *junta* rotation dynamics and because they reject funds and projects from government agencies along with the presence of public officials.

Through the responsibilities of the autonomous councils and other commissions, the women and men of Diecisiete de Noviembre exercise their rights to autonomy and self-determination as stated in the San Andrés Accords of 1996: "The state should promote the recognition, as a constitutional guarantee, of the right to free determination of indigenous peoples. . . . They may, in consequence, decide their form of internal government and their modes of organizing themselves politically, socially, economically, and culturally" (CEP/FOCA n.d., 4).[3]

The definition of indigenous rights written into the San Andrés Accords reflects the framing of rights as established in international treaties signed by the Mexican government, including Convention 169 of the United Nations International Labor Organization and the United Nations Declaration on the Rights of Indigenous Peoples. Although the Zapatista support bases, via communiqués and public discourses, refer to such treaties to legitimize their actions, the meanings of autonomy and self-determination are not reducible to these but rather emerge from their own use of rights regimes. A naturalized narrative that reproduces state legitimacy emphasizes that all rights are necessarily linked to nation-state projects, when in fact rights regimes have historically existed, and continue to exist, in semiautonomous fashion vis-à-vis the state.[4] As part of the latter, indigenous Zapatista autonomy and self-determination reflect initiatives taken up by numerous indigenous and Afrodescendant peoples throughout the continent that exercise and inject with meaning their rights through what Boaventura de Sousa Santos and César Rodríguez-Garavito refer to as the "critical use of rights from below" (2005, 1). As I will illustrate, such an autonomous praxis of rights rests on particular epistemological genealogies of Tseltal and Tojolabal ways of being in these communities.

As mentioned at the outset of this chapter, at the center of Zapatista political praxis lies the concept of governing by obeying, as that which establishes the terms of engagement between those temporarily in positions of authority and the remaining inhabitants of Zapatista-aligned communities. In the group interviews, it struck me that instead of focusing solely on the inversion of the relationship between governing and obeying, men and women emphasized a multidirectional relationship between the two poles. For example, a group of a dozen men in the new settlement of Pancho Villa pointed to a productive friction inherent in the notion of governing by obeying, which they explained in a phrase in Tojolabal as "ja jas oj yali oj k'uultik sok ja jas kaltik oj sk'uuk." The explanation they offered in Spanish was not a literal translation, but was expressed thus after I translated to English:

> The authority governs without giving orders, because it has to obey the citizens. What the authority says, the citizens also have to obey. But if what the authority orders is bad in some way, then we will remove them, because their work is no good. The one who governs has to obey, and what the authority says to the citizens also has to be obeyed.

It should be emphasized that the support bases position governing by obeying in direct contrast to a classic liberal model in which the governed delegate their decision-making capacities to their representatives, who in turn acquire an irresolvable contradiction as figures who must simultaneously represent the interests of those they represent as well as those of a sovereign power. In contrast to the fetishization of power when it "orders by governing," Enrique Dussel (2007, 502) argues that governing by obeying inverts the definition of power under conditions marked by the continued permanence of colonial forms of knowledge. Here I stress that these dominant forms of racialized ideas rest on the trope that indigenous people are born only to obey.

With regard to the origins of the concept, linguist Carlos Lenkersdorf (2000) identifies governing by obeying as an intrinsic aspect of Tseltal and Tojolabal forms of internal government, characterized by the exercise of communal power among assembly participants. Ramón Grosfoguel (2007) argues that governing by obeying reflects _____ belonging to the Tojolabal democratic tradition. In this chapter, rather than treating governing by obeying as a preestablished cultural form, I deconstruct the very notion of tradition so as to highlight the active processes of transmission, selection, and reappropriation of practices and concepts as part of collective political actions. Thus, in the following section I set out elements of a genealogy that weave together different processes that converge in the Zapatista cultural practice of *mandar obedeciendo* in the Caracol IV region.

A (Partial) Genealogy of *Mandar Obedeciendo*

Mauricio, as a member of the autonomous council, reviewed with me the content of the most recent interviews I had conducted in the region's communities. After talking in general terms for a while, our discussion gravitated toward the ways in which the support bases refer to the concept of governing by obeying. Based on our reading of the transcriptions, Mauricio and I identified three central qualities that community members associate with the expression. First, we noted that the elders tend to contrast the use of power expressed in *mandar obedeciendo* with the authority figure referred to in Tseltal as the *ajvalil*, which means an authority that can simultaneously be a government representative and a *patrón* (master). Mauricio noted that community members interviewed referred to the image of this master-governor as granting orders while seated in an elevated chair, as he who "ascends to his throne and thereby assumes power." Those interviewed contrasted such figures with those in positions of power exercised collectively in the autonomous municipalities.

Second, we noticed that those interviewed relate governing by obeying to the construction of a collective learning process associated with the affirmation of "doing [*hacer*] and being [*ser*] in accordance with our history and our own thoughts." Mauricio enjoys the use of metaphors to make his points, which on this occasion he used to refer to colonial times in ways that parallel the words of the elders in the handover ceremony described at the beginning of the chapter: "When the Spaniards came, they planted weeds inside our heads and in our hearts. We started to believe that those ideas would help us grow. But now, through autonomy, we are pulling out those weeds to plant our own ideas and our own history."

Third, we identified that the members of the municipality describe the practice of governing by obeying as part of the affirmation of an indigenous identity, as that which allows the Tseltales and Tojolabales to act and think "based on our strengths, and not ask the government for handouts." In this section I take these three elements as key aspects injecting meaning into *mandar obedeciendo*.

It is also worth noting that the interviewees generally displayed greater interest in identifying the social transformations represented by governing by obeying than in identifying the precise roots of the concept. Indeed, no one stated with any certainty its origins. When I asked the men of the Zapata community where the term came from, they confessed their ignorance, while emphasizing that it expresses the changes that have taken

Figure 6.2. Second-generation Zapatistas during a public event, Oventic, Caracol II, 2015; photo by Francisco Vazquez

place over recent years, particularly with regard to the participation of women in the assemblies and their inclusion in community, municipality, and *caracol* positions of responsibility. Aurelio mentioned that governing by obeying reflects the fact that "traditions have changed. Before, there was a lot of discrimination toward Tojolabales [by the Tseltales], but we realized that we are all the same indigenous people, and that discrimination serves no purpose."

The focus on the transformations brought about by the praxis of governing by obeying, in this case a political identity built upon a common notion of indigeneity uniting Tseltal and Tojolabal communities, reflects the fact that both the EZLN and its support bases make selective use of preexisting cultural practices, assigning them new meanings and directing them toward particular ends (Baronnet 2010). If we take the elements Mauricio and I identified as a starting point, these new meanings rest on the reappropriation of a collective history and knowledge base as part of that which rejects paternalistic relationships to the state or to the local *ajvalil*. It is the capacity to facilitate such reappropriations and to affirm the collective capacity to enact decisions for the well-being of the collective, as indigenous peoples, that permits one in power to hold authority, as opposed to simply being an authority.

Based on my conversations and formal interviews in Diecisiete de Noviembre, I identify particular reference points that establish a local genealogy connected to present-day forms of *mandar obedeciendo*, beginning with the figure embodying the idea of bad government, which Ernestino referred to in his speech during the ceremony at the beginning of this chapter, the *ajvalil*. In fact, as Mauricio noted in our revision of the transcribed interviews, *ajvalil* was the word used most frequently by support bases to refer to the relationship between the people and the authorities as part of racialized civilizing projects. As noted by Mauricio, men and women tend to describe the *ajvalil* through the image of a man (yes, always a man) sitting on a chair from which he observes the comings and goings of other people and gives orders. The constant reference that Zapatista community members made to a *kaxlan* sitting on a chair as *the* image of he who governs by ordering led me to search for other, complementary images in local history of he who commands by sitting above the rest. I found those images through descriptions of how estate owners used indigenous males literally as beasts of burden to transport *kaxlan* individuals.

The deep isolation and steep geography of the Lacandon Jungle valleys of Chiapas meant that from the colonial period well into the second half of the twentieth century there were limited transportation routes to commercial centers, such as the city of Comitán, where estate owners sold their tobacco, coffee, sugar, lard, cheese, and other products. The two transportation options they chose were either mules and other beasts or their indigenous *mozos*. Accounts of *kaxlanes* traveling *a lomo de indio*, "on the back of an Indian," or sending their products to be sold in the New Spain markets this way exist in fact as early as the mid-eighteenth century (Viqueira and Ruz 2004). Similarly, documentation by other scholars identifies that into the postrevolutionary period of the 1920s and 1930s, the cost to transport products on the backs of mules or humans was virtually the same, on average three pesos per ton per kilometer distance (Reyes Ramos 1992).

One of the most detailed narrative accounts of travel *a lomo de indio* appears in Jan de Vos's 2003 book *Viajes al desierto de la soledad: Un retrato hablado de la Selva Lacandona* (Journeys to the solitary desert: A spoken description of the Lacandon Jungle). De Vos reprints excerpts of the travel diaries of John Lloyd Stephens, an American lawyer who traveled to Chiapas to see the archeological site of Palenque in 1839 and 1840. Stephens describes how he traveled through the Lacandon Jungle with

Figure 6.3. Three *mestizo* children being carried in chairs by Tsotsil men in the highlands of Chiapas, 1956; photo by Juan Guzmán, from the Juan Guzmán Archive, used by permission of the Fundación Televisa

the contracted help of indigenous guides, who not only carried his belongings on mules but themselves carried a chair so that he could rest as they advanced along the steep, winding trails. The lawyer described how he sat on a chair placed on the ground that was then elevated onto the back of the person who would carry him by two other indigenous people. A thick cord tied the chair to the person's back and was then harnessed across his forehead, with a soft pillow placed on his skin so as to "lessen" the pressure on the head. Stephens describes how he could feel his carrier's "every movement, even the elevations of his chest as he breathed" (in de Vos 2002, 6n).

While Stephens briefly describes the person carrying him, photographic images of this form of travel, taken much later, tend to highlight the bodies of those being carried, as is the case of one of the most widely circulated images, taken by Juan Guzmán in 1955 in the highlands of Chiapas (see figure 6.3). The photograph focuses on the expressions of three *mestizo* children as they quietly travel on the backs of three Tsotsil men from Chamula. The two young boys in the photograph are dressed in newly pressed cotton pants and shirts, one with a bandana draped around his neck and a tightly woven straw hat on his head. The only aspect of his attire that betrays the image of absolute cleanliness is the mud splashed across the front of his boots. The girl has her hair neatly drawn behind her ears and a shawl draped across her shoulders. The hands of the three children are elegantly pressed together as if they are attending church, while their faces contemplate the scenery in a saintly way. So as to protect the children from the weather and separate their bodies from those of the men on whose backs they travel, the seats form part of upright rectangular boxes draped in white fabric, the top of which can be unrolled so as to avoid direct sunlight or rainfall. In contrast with these visible details associated with the children traveling, of the three Chamula men carrying them we can see only the ends of their respective *chuj*, the wool ponchos covering them to their knees, and their calves tightened with the effort required to walk up a hillside.

The dehumanizing conditions this photograph portrays are grounded in the social memories narrated by elders in Diecisiete de Noviembre who opened deep collective wounds when describing how their fathers or grandfathers carried estate owners and their family members from the Tzaconejá River valley to Comitán or transported cheese and molasses on journeys lasting two or three days. Some even described how the *kaxlanes* treated them with such disrespect that the men traveling would urinate from their chairs rather than stopping to walk discreetly a few meters away. Situated historically, the metaphorical image of a *kaxlan* seated in a chair governing parallels this actual use of indigenous male bodies as beasts of burden. Both images of *kaxlanes* seated on chairs above other individuals reinforce the idea that it is they who were born to govern while indigenous people were born to obey by carrying, sometimes literally, the weight of an *ajvalil* on their backs. In this sense, past descriptions of estate owners riding *a lomo de indio* converge in the narratives of more recent interactions with government authorities prior to 1994 that describe the attitudes and actions embodying the figure of the *ajvalil*.

In the community of Nueva Revolución, the women offered such descriptions of the *ajvalil* in the *ejido* Lázaro Cárdenas during the 1980s. They explained that because so many residents suffered a lack of access to a nearby spring or river, a request for a reliable water source was evidently the main petition presented to each municipal president that entered office. They laughed in embarrassment as they described how they would welcome the government representative when he visited the village to hear the petitions. Hortensia explained that they treated him "as if he were a saint. All night we prepared his chicken soup and his bread, just the way he liked it. The women then surrounded him and greeted him with flowers." She then went on to describe how the women would follow him in a procession as he surveyed the land and would then offer him food and beverages as he listened to the petitions presented by male community members.

Santos reminds us that the "social contract embodies the founding metaphor of the social and political rationality of Western modernity" and the criteria that legitimize the terms of inclusion and exclusion (2005, 9). Santos invites us to inquire into the effects of the social contract under the figure of the *ajvalil* as that which controls the terms of relative inclusion by excluding the figure of the *mozo*. The *mozo*, as a social category, embodies the ways in which the racialized liberal social contract operates through the negation of the other while at the same time extending the false promise of *mestizaje* ideology that extends the possibility of integration into society through paternalistic tutelage relations. As the women from Nueva Revolución described, the denial of their existence operated in relation to the actions of the *ajvalil*, actions that alternated between infantilization and dehumanization, with the most extreme form of dehumanization narrated through experiences of being treated as a beast of burden and through acts of sexual violence. In turn, such colonial relations of power internalize a sense of inferiority, as described by the same women who now ironically interpret how they used to treat local *kaxlan* authorities as if they were sanctifying the master-governor when he arrived to their village.

The permanence of the embodied figure of the *ajvalil* establishes a reference point that both feeds into and reproduces the racialized tropes concentrated in the master-*mozo* relations on the estates. Here I wish to remind the reader that although the local figure of the *mozo* lies in the past, the racialized relations grounded on the institution of the estate on which *ajvalil-mozo* interactions continue to shape current neocolonial forms of domination. Autonomy, as a series of practices attempting to unearth the continued resiliency of colonial institutions in the present day, locates the *ajvalil* as the primary counterpoint to the figure of authority that emerges from the practices of *mandar obedeciendo*. The *ajvalil* represents the image that community members reject when accepting positions of authority, while at the same time it is a powerful figure that entices and even seduces with its potential to abuse power. Though I never heard any Zapatista community member criticize a representative of the autonomous council for acting like an *ajvalil*, I did register several criticisms of Tseltal or Tojolabal individuals who became government employees in the official municipal administration for acting as if they were now *kaxlanes*. As Orlando, of San Pedro Guerrero, stated during an interview, "Before, in the official municipality, it was only *kaxlanes*, only ranchers [in office]. Now it has changed a bit. Now it is peasants and indigenous people, too, but slowly they start to become *kaxlanes* in their way of thinking. [They act like *kaxlanes*] when it is only for individual interest, when they are not with the people."

Faced with the daunting task of engendering alternative relations between the authority and the collective that do not reproduce the image of the *ajvalil* but rather seek to govern by holding authority, members of the Zapatista communities draw from four reference points: their experiences in the *cargo* systems in their communities; communal work; the *ejido* assemblies, as described in chapter 4; and inter-*ejido* organizations such as the Union of Unions. The *cargo* system acts as a first grounding point in this alternative political map as it is a system of authority and of responsibility that existed throughout the colonial period in Tseltal and Tojolabal communities. Studies in the early twentieth century of the *cargo* systems in the Tseltal communities of Cancun and Oxchuc describe how the responsibilities for the religious festivities were divided among stewards, captains, and lieutenants. The captains, or principals, elected two *baj kawilto* (leaders), who presided in positions of authority for four years, primarily in religious matters. In terms of the church stewardships, studies refer to the first mayor, second mayor, first alderman, and second alderman (Pitarch 1996). In turn, the political *cargos* were divided among the governor, mayor, and aldermen (Romano 2002).

In the course of a conversation I held with Anselmo, an elder of the Diez de Abril community, he recalled that "in the past those who lit the candles were the stewards, captains, and the president of the *principales* [the respected elders in positions of moral authority]. Above all, it was the president who was responsible for this." He emphasized the fact that these *cargos* underwent substantial change after 1994. "With the organization, the custom changed. The stewards and captains are no longer nominated. Instead all of us elders are in charge of the ceremonies." While before 1994 a small group of males were *principales*, in the newly created autonomous municipality the assembly decided to expand the role to include all elders, who are primarily male. During ceremonial events in Diecisiete de Noviembre, such as the handover ceremony described at the beginning of this chapter, the elders are responsible for lighting the candles, placing the offering, and leading the prayers that ensure that the gods and spirits of the ancestors take care of those participating in the festivities and that the heart of the collective remains in a state of tranquility. Anselmo related this shift to the expansion of the decision-making capacity in all spheres of community and intercommunity life.

A second grounding point in the alternative political map emerged in the 1970s in communities inspired by the "Indian theology" of the Diocese of San Cristóbal, the Word of God, wherein priests promoted communal work in the *ejidos*. *Ejidatarios*, who had spent a large part of their lives working on the estates and were largely unfamiliar with communal work, reflected on the meaning of group activities as well as asked themselves who benefits from these efforts. Such concerns are condensed in the book *El diario de un tojolabal* (Lenkersdorf 2001), based on the notes of Javier Aguilar Moreno, a young Tojolabal from the community of Puebla Vieja who adopted the name Sak K'inal Tajalki and tragically died from acute leukemia in 1976. In 2001, Carlos Lenkersdorf published this book of Tajalki's diverse personal reflections on the events between 1974 and 1976. These writings have largely been ignored in scholarship on the Zapatista movement.

Throughout his journal, Tajalki expresses a constant concern for understanding the logics of oppression that locate the indigenous population in conditions of exploitation. He makes lists to describe the oppressor in relation to the oppressed. At the same time, his concern for locating structural conditions appears parallel to interspersed thoughts on how these are then internalized. Under the heading "Problems in the *Ejido* Puebla Nueva," he observes, "We say many things that are copies of other thoughts but that don't come from our own hearts; we hide our problems with other things: alcohol, clothes, games, radio, parties with women; we don't respect someone who is our compañero and says things we don't yet understand. Only if he is a non-Indian do we respect him ..." (in Lenkersdorf 2001, 69).

Tajalki then seeks to locate community actions that enhance the organized ability to transcend prevailing social conditions and in particular turns to the possibilities embodied in the act of communal work. For Tajalki, the transformative potential of collective activities marks a distinction from what until then had been carried out in communities of former *mozos*, where collective work tended to benefit the *cacique* (local bossman), who "governed the people, who organized and dictated, and then sometimes grew even greater in power" (ibid., 145). In other Tseltal regions, such as San Juan Cancuc, the local *caciques* were referred to as the *tatil lum* (fathers of the people), especially those who maintained close ties with the leading public officials of the Institutional Revolutionary Party (Pitarch 1996). In contrast, Tajalki reflects on the need to establish new cultural practices based on collective labor that benefit the community as a whole, not the *cacique*, the *tatil lum*, or the *kaxlan*.

As part of these preoccupations, Tajalki insists on the need to establish new relationships between community authority figures and the people. In essence, without stating the term *mandar obedeciendo*, he proposes dynamics where the authority remains integrated in the community, is held accountable by the collective, and thus does not rise above others. In his fifth notebook, he lists ten points that the general assembly in the *ejido* needs to respect, from which he proposes an ethics for indigenous authorities more generally. The last three points center on defining the relationship between *ejido* authorities and the rest of the population:

> The authorities need to govern according to the accords reached in the assembly; the assembly will monitor if the authorities govern based on the accords reached in the assembly; if in the authority meeting [prior to the assembly] they don't reach an agreement on what to propose to the assembly, the assembly needs to make the proposals that the authorities have to respect. (in Lenkersdorf 2001, 101)

During my research in Diecisiete de Noviembre, I had the opportunity to speak at great length with Tajalki's younger brother, Estacio, who was just three years old when his sibling died. In our conversations he emphasized that his older brother's thoughts contributed significant political ideas to the region, above all with regard to establishing different decision-making practices that benefit the entire community rather than just the *cacique*. In the decades after his death, his critical ideas influenced collective decision-making practices and agricultural production activities, all of which laid the foundations for understanding concepts that we now associate with the notion of *mandar obedeciendo*. In fact, Estacio explained that as part of his responsibilities in the municipality and in the *caracol*, he frequently returns to the ideas of his brother for inspiration and guidance. One central concern is how to spark reflection on the past that helps inform the production of new ideas to solve problems in the present and what are the most effective roles those in temporary positions of authority must enact so as to ensure that such possibilities unfold.

A third reference point for the new political system has to do with the *ejido* assemblies, where male heads of household once enacted all decisions. In chapter 4, I described how prior to the 1992 official government reforms, only male members of the *ejido* were officially authorized to take part in the assembly, hence excluding women and *avecindados*. At these assemblies, the *ejidatarios* selected the *ejido* commissioner and the members of the oversight committee. In turn, the assembly either accepted or rejected the proposals of the commissioner in regard to the internal operation of the *ejido*. In this sense, the general assembly of *ejidatarios* was—in principle—a basic nucleus of male-centered democracy, although in practice it largely functioned otherwise. As I noted in chapter 4, the members of the agricultural production and the land and territory commissions indicated that power concentrated in the figure of the commissioner, and tended to satisfy the political interests of public officials rather than the collective interest of the *ejido*. Despite these limitations, the model of the *ejido* assembly forms another grounding point for collective decision-making practices in Caracol IV.

Finally, members of Diecisiete de Noviembre referred to their long experience with intercommunity organizations that have operated in the region since the 1970s, including the Unión de Uniones Ejidales, particularly the Unión de Ejidos Quiptic Ta Lecubtesel. According to documents gathered by Xochitl Leyva and Gabriel Ascencio, the Quiptic quickly grew from 18 *ejidos* in 1975 to 50 a few years later, and eventually to more than 150 *ejidos* by its tenth anniversary. The members of the Quiptic designated regional representatives of the *ejido* unions, who in turn formed regional councils and sent delegates to a general assembly (Leyva and Ascencio 1996). I considered that this form of regional representation and inter-*ejido* assembly resembles to an extent how the *caracoles* operate, and I asked Pánfilo, a member of the municipal agricultural production commission, if he agreed with the parallel I observed. He replied to the contrary, stating that though the inter-*ejido* assemblies are clearly important to the people's political formation as Zapatistas, in his opinion the Union of Unions' external advisors guided the discussions and presented their ideas at the assemblies. According to his interpretation, "The ideas came from outside, from far away. They were discussed, but they were the ideas of certain people who came to say what ideas should be discussed. Meanwhile, here it is a single idea that emerges from everyone. That's why it is autonomy, we get the ideas from everyone in order to build with them."

Though I would suggest that such a clear-cut separation between internal and external ideas is much messier in practice, I relate his words to specific decisions implemented by the autonomous assemblies that limit the participation of external actors or even go so far as to expel them for intruding too much in internal affairs. At least twice since 1996, the autonomous municipalities expelled members of NGOs and other solidarity activists for introducing ideas without respecting the terms of engagement as established by the assembly. While NGOs offered workshops on all sorts of issues in the *caracol*—human rights, appropriate technology, agro-forestry, etc.—between 2010 and the time when this book went to press, the role of external actors had been reduced to a trickle as the autonomous communities placed progressively greater emphasis on internal processes involving the evaluation, redesign, and implementation of the different spheres of autonomy.

How do these cultural practices frame meanings ascribed to *mandar obedeciendo*? In what ways do they influence broader cultural politics in Diecisiete de Noviembre, specifically "holding authority, rather than being authority"? How do they affect the dynamics established between these Tseltal and Tojolabal communities and state institutions? The following sections aim to point toward responses to these questions.

Being-Making Authority

Vans and pickups packed the dirt road leading to the entrance of the *caracol* compound. At the gate, groups of people waited to discuss their issues with the council of Diecisiete de Noviembre and with the *junta*. A *mestizo* woman from Comitán parked her vehicle alongside those of a group of Tseltal men from a nearby village. Members of Payasos sin Fronteras (Clowns without Borders) arrived to ask the education commission and the health commission if they could offer sex education classes in the schools through the use of puppets, marionettes, and other figures. It was the weekend in which the *caracol* assembly, made up of more than a hundred representatives of the seven municipalities, was to debate these as well as numerous other matters. I entered the *caracol* compound and walked across the esplanade until I reached the basketball court, where everyone was immersed in discussion. Following a lengthy plenary session, they agreed upon a series of questions to debate and then split up into small groups to discuss particular issues in greater detail. The matter at hand involved ensuring that the autonomous education system included females, both girls and adult women, who wish to learn to read and write. Community members had been complaining that sometimes women were not participating in the collectives or holding *cargos* because they are illiterate, and others noted that the girls of some families sometimes miss school when their mothers keep them home to help take care of their younger siblings or to do household tasks.

To discuss these matters, the authorities coordinating the assembly sent groups to different corners of the compound; some pulled together chairs in the auditorium, others sat in the shade of the dormitory building, and still others remained seated on boulders beside the basketball court. Though I was eager to listen to what they said, I remained respectful of their internal dynamic and limited my presence to observing from a distance. In the small groups, a combined set of interactions unfolded. During some aspects of the discussion those involved remained seated as they spoke, while in other moments, one person would stand to speak in a stance that reminded me of the use of *testimonio* during the collective interviews I conducted in the communities. I interpreted the corporal performance as a form of relaying personal experiences so as to state an opinion on the issue at hand. The small groups' discussions lasted several hours, until no one else stood up from their seat to speak.

Those present eventually returned to the plenary so that each group could set out their principal conclusions and begin once again the broader assembly discussion that would converge in agreements. In total, the assembly lasted all day Friday and Saturday and late into the night on the second day. One of the members of the council later explained to me that once the agreements are made, the representatives return to each of their municipal assemblies to confirm the decisions, and, if necessary, make required adjustments. In this case, the *caracol* assembly agreed to invite the women in the production collectives to incorporate literacy classes, to be taught by Diecisiete de Noviembre's educational promoters. Given that the agreement remained on a voluntary basis, many ~~...~~ ~~were not~~ ~~convinced of how effective~~ it would be since learning to read and write requires vast amounts of time, on top of that required for household duties and multiple community responsibilities. The second decision was labeled as mandatory: all girls were required to attend school, it was forbidden that they stay at home to help their mothers take care of siblings.

This scene of collective discussions and debates illustrates a key aspect of the concept of governing by obeying, when daily life experiences become political matters to the degree that embodied knowledge is a point of departure to enact decisions in benefit of the collective. In her ethnography *We Are the Face of Oaxaca: Testimony and Social Movements*, Lynn

Stephen (2013) focuses on the 2006 dissident teachers' movement and the Asamblea Popular de los Pueblos de Oaxaca (APPO, Popular Assembly of Oaxacan Peoples), which organized in demand of improved teaching conditions as well as against the corruption of the state governor in Oaxaca at the time. Stephen suggests that testimony serves as a powerful practice of cultural politics shared not only by the organizations grouped under APPO but by many indigenous and peasant organizations throughout Mexico more generally. The format of the testimony forms part of the production of political identities and acts as an initial impulse promoting alternative democratic practices. Through a description of an *ejido* assembly in the Zapotec community of Teotitlán del Valle, Stephen describes the ways community assemblies enact the genre of the testimony both to convey and to analyze community issues so as to come to problem-solving decisions. Stephen draws parallels to the ways women and men involved in the movement used community radio stations as testimonial spaces connecting individuals spread out in different localities to a shared sense of political purpose.

I observed a similar emphasis placed on testimony as a point of departure for collective decision-making practices in Diecisiete de Noviembre. For the sake of the arguments elaborated in this chapter, I would like to highlight that the relationship between daily life experiences and the way these are interpreted to mobilize political decisions is not reduced to the public sphere of assemblies, such as the one described above, but rather extends to broader and diffuse collective undertakings. In chapter 5, I focused on women's production collectives, where the exchange of reflections based on personal and collective events in the home, in family affairs, and in the broader community fuels a sense of identity as Zapatista Tseltal and Tojolabal women and sparks group demands as part of autonomous initiatives in the municipality. We can understand the women's collectives as situated at one end of the spectrum, with the *caracol* assemblies at the other extreme. In between the two spaces, however, lie a broad range of decision-making spheres, including the male production collectives, such as the municipal fair-trade coffee cooperative; the religious spaces of reflection on the Word of God; the discussions and debates by education, health, and appropriate-technology promoters; the activities of the different autonomous commissions; the community and municipal assemblies; and the *juntas de buen gobierno*.

In this section, I would like to examine the effects of this diffuse exercise of power—which includes decision making, the implementation of agreements, the elaboration of new proposals, and critical reflection on their implementation—through daily activities in the Zapatista communities, in the municipalities, and at the *caracol* level. I suggest that when the praxis of autonomy emerges from the sum of all these spaces, it intensifies the politicization of daily life, discussed in the previous chapter. Beginning in 1996, though more visible since the *juntas de buen gobierno* were founded in 2003, the frequent rotation of positions of authority, the number of political *cargos* in Diecisiete de Noviembre, the relationship between the various assemblies and the representatives of the autonomous government, and the involvement of all generations in governing aimed to increase collective participation in decision making. These aspects reflect an impulse toward such an extended and extensive exercise of collective power.

As highlighted in my description of the ceremony held in January, the municipal council representatives rotate every three years. And each of the seven municipalities names six representatives to its respective council, making a total of forty-two representatives who take weekly turns making up the *junta*. The oversight committee, in turn, responsible for monitoring the activities of the *junta*, is made up of support bases who also take weekly turns keeping track of each visit and matter presented to the *junta* offices. The commissions are the bodies that administer the information and activities; if the autonomous communities approve of the work carried out by the members of the commissions, the incumbents can remain in their posts for an indefinite period.

Another aspect of the Zapatista drive toward collective power is the distribution of responsibilities among community members through the proliferation of *cargos* connected to the autonomy project, including the positions of community representative, educational and health promoter, and member of the numerous autonomous commissions, as well as representative of the different production collectives. During fieldwork, it drew my attention that in the communities I visited with a population of between twenty and twenty-five families, almost all the adults held positions of authority of some kind, either at the community level (for example, as a community representative or head of a collective), at the municipal level (for example, on one of the commissions), or at the *caracol* level (for example, as a member of the technical committee for education). Of the communities with a population larger than twenty-five families, more than two-thirds of the inhabitants held such a *cargo*. It also struck me that the most "politically relevant" *cargos*, such as the autonomous councils or the municipal commissions, were not concentrated in those communities identified as holding the most political weight in Diecisiete de Noviembre—such as Morelia or Siete de Enero—but that even the settlements most distant from the *caracol* center, with fewer years in "the organization" and with fewer historical cadres, were home to individuals who held significant responsibilities.

The assemblies form part of an additional cultural practice that links the representatives with those they represent and expands political participation. With the exception of the community assemblies, where all community members participate, the others—the municipal and *caracol* assemblies—are made up of representatives. Community representatives participate in the municipal assembly, and, in turn, representatives of each municipality participate in the *caracol* assembly, along with the members of the various commissions. The *caracol* assembly is the highest decision-making body.

The last aspect I wish to highlight is the intergenerational makeup of authorities, who include the elders, the adults who joined the peasant organizations in the 1980s, and those who received their political upbringing within the Zapatista movement. I will examine this aspect in greater depth in the following section, but the point of interest here is that at any given moment the authorities are not all from a single generation. It might be expected that those who underwent clandestine political formation and played an active role in the uprising would dominate as the leading political cadres of the Zapatista autonomous municipalities, but in fact those in civilian positions of authority are filled by people from several generations, including young people whose first position of responsibility is as education delegate and whose second is as a member of the municipal council.

This does not mean, however, that decision making proceeds in a harmonious manner or that there do not exist tensions, power struggles, or lack of accountability for responsibilities. In fact, I suggest that *mandar obedeciendo* as a Tseltal and Tojolabal political ethic in Diecisiete de Noviembre engenders new forms of knowledge production and political practices precisely because it hinges upon friction-filled terms of engagement, friction that inevitably exists when collective decisions are made in so many spheres. Tensions, for example, occur between the different generations involved, both in the temporary positions of authority and in assemblies or spaces of collective discussion. I refer to intergenerational frictions in terms of the different interests, ways of understanding au-

Figure 6.4. A woman and some men harnessing cattle for vaccination, Cinco de Mayo, Diecisiete de Noviembre, 2007; photo by author

tonomy, or emphasis placed on issues that exist primarily between the generation of those involved in the clandestine work of the EZLN and the generation that grew up within Zapatismo.

One such tension is related to the increased tendency by the younger generations to migrate for extended periods of time to the United States or to the Caribbean. At the same time that the *juntas* were formed, global political-economic pressures combined with new generational desires sparked waves of migration by the generation of Zapatistas educated within the project of autonomy. One of the first responses by Zapatista authorities was to prohibit semipermanent migration, such as going to the United States in search of employment. However, young men, primarily those of a post-1994 generation, paid little heed and continued to seek work elsewhere. Faced with the dilemma of either forcing these men to stay or potentially losing them as members of the autonomous communities, Caracol IV authorities were obliged to open up assembly discussions on the matter. The assembly in Diecisiete de Noviembre came up with a proposal designed to increase the possibility of generating local sources of income by increasing cattle production. As one Zapatista member once explained, despite the contradiction that cattle constituted the commodity on which many estates reproduced their existence, "it is our Zapatista bank." The assembly agreed to set aside a large tract of communal land for cattle grazing in order to strengthen a local form of economic investment and provide incentives for young men to stay. This idea was proposed by an older generation of Zapatista community members. However, they had to make concessions and accept that the *caracol* extends permission for those who need to migrate for several months at a time to earn much-needed income.

During the series of interviews I conducted in Nueva Revolución, the topic of women's participation in the community assembly figured as central. It was not a topic I proposed, but rather one they placed as part of the group discussions on the advances and limits of the previous ten years of autonomy. A few women began speaking about why women do not want to participate, despite the fact that the autonomous municipality clearly says that women have the right to do so. This group of women placed the blame on themselves: "It is women who block their own path. The men gave us our rights and we are free, but we don't want to get involved [in community or municipal affairs]." Other women interjected to debate this opinion by describing concrete cases of domestic violence or male jealousy that prevent women from leaving their homes to participate in the political affairs of the community or taking on positions of authority. Other women contributed to the reflections by drawing attention to the subtle ways in which women are silenced when they attempt to take part in the assembly. It is not only the more apparent cases of violence in the home or husbands who accuse their wives of participating in municipal affairs so as to be able to leave the house and find a lover, these women stated, but the little acts that sometimes are difficult to see. To elaborate on this point, Silvia, in her midtwenties and one of the few women in Nueva Revolución that affirms a Tseltal identity, drew from the way she registers her emotional state of mind before speaking publicly: "I feel like my head isn't going to work properly when I go to the assembly. I have an idea of what I want to say, but when I have to stand up [to speak], I forget it, so I hardly participate." Her narrative apparently sparked reflections in Rosa, who then interpreted assembly dynamics by drawing from the following example: "The men mock us when the women say something. They don't want to listen. They pretend to be deaf. When they don't like the proposal we make, they all start to talk at once or they make faces like they are bored. After that the women lose interest [in participating]."

I draw from the debates by the women in Nueva Revolución to highlight that it is the differing viewpoints that have the potential to spark critical collective self-reflection so as to generate social analysis of a specific community issue and then elaborate strategies to push forward a particular agenda, such as women's participation in spaces where their roles tend to be devalued by some men. The combined use of embodied knowledge through the cultural practice of giving testimony with the wide range of autonomous spheres that require collective decision making has the effect of inverting the relationship between the government and the governed and spurring *mandar obedeciendo*. At the same time, the politicization of life via the distribution of decision-making abilities is linked to the second effect I wish to highlight: governing by learning to govern and pedagogy as part of the art of governing. We shall now turn to this second aspect.

Pedagogical Practices and the Art of Governing

In Diecisiete de Noviembre, the implementation of an autonomous education project finally started in 1999; military threats and the fear of counterinsurgency actions by government officials had frustrated countless previous attempts. At the onset of the autonomous project, the frequently increased level of risk led support bases to cancel meetings, training sessions, and other initiatives. During the early years of the autonomous municipalities, the support bases took part in education workshops with NGOs and named education leaders. However, the political instability rendered it impossible to consolidate an organized body that could develop autonomous education in a systematic fashion. When suitable conditions finally arose, one of the first tasks of the assembly was to design the curriculum for the autonomous primary schools.

The education commission, together with the representatives of the autonomous council, set themselves the task of visiting all the Zapatista settlements in the municipality. In each community they convoked an assembly to discuss the priorities for education and to reflect upon personal experiences with the official education system prior to 1994. On these occasions, family members would take turns standing up to address those gathered and narrate how they as children or the children of other family members had gone through public schooling. One woman described with pain in her voice how a village schoolmaster obliged one of his female students to work for him, cleaning and washing clothes, as if she were his maid. A man spoke with anger about teachers who simply did not turn up for classes. His children learned next to nothing, he complained, yet the absent teacher granted his students passing grades that allowed them to move up to the next level even though they were still basically unable to read and write. An elder confessed that he had felt torn when he decided to send his children to school, given that what little they learned in the classroom had nothing to do with what he and his wife were teaching them at home and with what community authorities stressed as important for a communal identity. Yet, if he had not taken them to school, they would not have learned Spanish or the ways of the *kaxlanes*, knowledge that was key in enabling his children to defend themselves. The most obvious sign of this split, the elder continued to explain, was the language used, with Spanish in the classroom and Tseltal in the rest of the child's daily spheres. "It made my children learn to be ashamed of their language and of being indigenous people," he concluded.

Without using the word "racism," his narration sparked other *testimonios* that attested to the multiple ways in which the public education system negated the community members' identity as Mayan people and made children feel inferior for being Tseltal or Tojolabal. The imposition of knowledge alien to what the children learned at home led to an internalized sense of inferiority. "Look what happens in Nueva Revolución," another woman stated. "There they feel superior because they say they aren't indigenous, they feel *kaxlan* because they only speak Spanish." The women accused members of the new Zapatista settlement, which was populated primarily by previous residents of the *ejido* Lázaro Cárdenas, of negating their identity as Tojolabales and Tseltales to the point that some families there refuse to allow their children to marry someone from a family whose members still wear an *enagua* (long skirt) or a *traje* (traditional dress), since they believe it means they would be marrying into being an "Indian." She used the example to argue for the need of a school system that foments a sense of pride in being indigenous and that has as its core teachings their own *saberes*, or knowledges and ways of being. "But what if our children only learn Tseltal and Tojolabal?" another person inquired. "Then they will only be able to speak to their own people and won't be able to defend themselves from the *kaxlanes*. They will keep getting taken advantage of, just like our parents were taken advantage of in the *fincas*."

The diverse narratives and exchanges described above engendered new interpretations of past collective experiences so that the people in the assembly could then come to decisions for the implementation of the new, autonomous educational system. These were the aspects highlighted by Antonio of the community San Pedro Guerrero when I asked him about the relationship between autonomy, decision making, and knowledge production. He explained that the elementary school curriculum offered something concrete to discuss and to agree upon in the municipality. To prepare the course materials, they first had to discuss the content, which then sparked critical reflection on lived experience. Linda Martín Alcoff (2010) refers to experience-based theory founded on embodied knowledge shared among a group of people, in contrast with a process whereby an external figure imposes an idea or thought. It was in this sense that Antonio recalled the discussion processes as being just as significant as the materials that the education commission eventually prepared.

> Among ourselves we discussed what we wanted for the education of our children. This had never happened before. Prior to this decision, it was simply imposed on us. But the way we are making decisions lets us know we are constructing autonomy. Agreement about what our education should be emerged in the discussions in the assemblies, as it is about granting people power, not taking it away. The ideas emerged from the heads of all of us, the proposals couldn't have come from a single head.

Antonio set out the points of agreement reached after months of assembly debates. First, learning at school should go hand in hand with what is being learned at home, in the forest, and in the fields. For this reason, the children should not be shut up all day in the classroom, but should be involved in contexts where they may learn from everyday life and from the practices of autonomy. Second, the group agreed that children are not empty vessels to be filled with information from adults in order to learn to act in the world. Rather, children are subjects of rights in autonomy and may take decisions about the education system in which they are being taught. This includes their participation in the assemblies, where they, too, can voice their opinions. Finally, one of the central agreements was that education begins in the mother tongue, and other languages, including Spanish, are subsequently incorporated.

After assembling these principles and processing all the information into a series of agreements, the autonomous government authorities at the time (before the *juntas de buen gobierno* were created) drew up a proposal to be debated and approved by the intermunicipal assembly. Once collective approval had been obtained, the agreements were then verified by each municipal and community assembly in order for each group to approve the final version of the curriculum. The entire process stretched across more than a year and produced two outcomes: the content of the teaching materials for the elementary schools and a body of knowledge based on specific sets of experiences designed to nourish a collective awareness of the structures of oppression experienced by Tseltal and To-jolabal communities in the realm of education. Although each Zapatista municipality and *caracol* has its own dynamics, and thus it is impossible to generalize, scholars document the democratization of education practices in other regions, such as Caracol III, centered in La Garrucha, as "the confluence of the logics of community organization (uses and customs) and of the community organizations (regional political militancy)" such that "the citizen consultation and mobilization process in the Zapatista education sector demands the involvement not only of parents but of the entire community" (Baronnet 2010, 251).

The relationship between governing and collective discussions similarly became evident in the process of this research. In the second chapter, I described how the support bases subjected the research study to the decision-making practices of autonomy. I described how my proposal was sent to the *junta* only to later be discussed at the *caracol* assembly by representatives of all the municipalities (independently of any other parallel approval process conducted by the political and military structure of the EZLN, of which I am unaware). After it was agreed upon in the highest decision-making body, the *caracol* assembly, the matter was debated again at the municipal assembly with the representatives of the thirty-five communities that at the time formed Diecisiete de Noviembre. In every village where I conducted interviews, the entire community—not only the local representatives—had been informed of my fieldwork and most had read my list of questions prior to the assembly. The municipal assembly delegated to the autonomous council the responsibility for ensuring that I conducted the research as planned and according to the agreements established. In turn—and this is important to emphasize—they allowed enough flexibility for each community to enact its own decisions regarding the format, methods, and any changes to the questions posed.

The obligation to discuss whether to accept a proposal to gather historical information gives rise to discussions about the importance of local history, including what aspects of the past hold meaning in the present, particularly their relation to current political struggle. The assemblies in the villages I visited lasted at least two hours. Although not all community members attended, the discussions to determine the format of the interviews invariably led those present to reflect on the role social memory plays in engendering autonomy. Not only did some people choose to narrate memories of past moments of regional political history, but others put to discussion the best methods to be used to ensure that those memories are shared among other community members. For that reason, the communities opted for collective interviews. Participants in the assembly remarked that if the interviews remained individual, this would inhibit critical reflection that would be sparked in a group setting. Older community members highlighted their interest in having younger generations learn about and reflect upon the era of the estates and in general agreed that an intergenerational meeting would promote the circulation of regional history within the community. Without this active participation by the support bases, the research project would not have been effective for these parallel processes of political education that I described in chapter 2, nor would the critical reflections on life on the estates have emerged, leading to discussions of broader structures of power. Throughout the research, the pedagogical logics of governing by obeying made it possible to open up spaces for the dissemination of memories as part of the development of a collective political consciousness and as part of the collective theory based on what Alcoff (2010) describes as embodied experience.

This is not to say that all decisions taken involve such dual effects, nor that every single one of the support bases participates in and understands the process in the same way. For other issues, discussions have not involved the same level of participation or debate. Indeed, when asked about the activities carried out by the autonomous government, some interviewed simply replied that they had little information, given that "those are matters for our government; they are looking after it." Nor are all aspects of autonomy discussed in the assemblies, and nor do they require the same level of discussion. However, I would emphasize that the distribution of decision-making practices and the inversion of roles through governing by obeying opens up the exercise of power to a greater production of knowledge *about* autonomy as part of the daily work *within* autonomy.

Self-defined Third World feminists such as Jacqui Alexander and Chandra Mohanty theorize on the collective production of knowledge as part of social transformation in postcolonial settings. In their book *Feminist Genealogies, Colonial Legacies, Democratic Futures* (1997), Alexander and Mohanty critically reflect on the role of the political cadres who led national liberation struggles in Africa and South Asia at the end of World War II in an attempt to understand why proposals for radical social transformation were only partially realized or became sidetracked. They point not only to the continuity of neocolonial relations and to the physical, epistemological, and symbolic violence that defines them but also, and above all, to internal social processes of colonized peoples, hence acknowledging their agency and thus their responsibility in the complex equation that creates both the possibilities as well as the challenges of emancipation.

More than half a century ago, the postcolonial intellectual Frantz Fanon posed a similar question in his book *Black Skin, White Masks* (1967). Fanon analyzed the ways in which former colonized peoples in different countries in Africa repeated the cultural practices of their former rulers in newly independent nation-states. A native bourgeoisie emerged that embarked on a type of colonial political and psychological mimicry. By putting on these "masks," colonized peoples reproduced significant aspects of the colonial habitus (Bourdieu 1984), hence the partial nature of radical social transformation. Alexander and Mohanty undertake a feminist reading of the theoretical and political contributions of the revolutionary psychoanalyst Fanon so as to offer a detailed analysis of postcolonial processes in varying corners of the globe. The authors conclude that the limitations of many of the national liberation projects are due to an absence of action and reflection needed to produce new forms of knowledge from below so as to move beyond the binary of colonizer/native. One aspect limiting knowledge production in postcolonial settings involves masculinized politics that set up monolithic blocks of knowledge to confront the ruler, which in turn erases the microdynamics of power and prevents a broader participation of subaltern actors. Alexander and Mohanty argue that in these processes of social struggle, male leaders tend to create counter-meta-narratives in opposition to the monolithic version of history as written by the victors, relegating other acts of social transformation to silence and to the margins (Mora 2014).

To provide an alternative political response, Alexander and Mohanty lay out an initial map traversed by individual, collective, and organizational processes that rest primarily in everyday praxis. They emphasize the need for people to undertake critical collective self-reflection to enable themselves to act on the basis of the interconnected forms of oppression experienced by (neo)colonized peoples, where struggles are fought not only against what is located "out there" but also within organizational contexts of social transformation. Alexander and Mohanty argue that these give rise to collective decolonization processes since the production of a communal praxis focused on critical self-reflection drives the possibility of new conditions in all spheres of social life.

The multiple spaces for collective discussion and decision-making practices as part of the autonomous municipality partly respond to the call to attention and invitation made by Alexander and Mohanty. At the same time, such pedagogical processes linked to decision making locate the role of autonomous authorities as "reflections from the rear-guard," where "theory is a servile obedience," as opposed to the location of the vanguard (Dussel 2012). Pánfilo, a member of the agricultural production commission, explained it thus one day when we spoke just after he returned from sowing the fields and before heading to a preparatory meeting for the municipal assembly:

> Before each assembly, we meet to discuss the points we want to work on and to make proposals for the work in progress. This was something we learned along the way. We realized that if we just turned up at the assembly, and no ideas emerge, then we make no progress. On the other hand, if we have proposals, we can put them forward, if no one else has ideas to bring up, we put them up for discussion. If there are ideas coming out of the assembly, then we don't say anything. So there are two parts working together, the support bases and those of us who have *cargos*.

For his part, Ramón Grosfoguel describes the dialogical exercise of Zapatismo as a fundamental aspect of decoloniality reflected in the political action of "walking by asking" (2007, 76). To this dialogical impetus, I would like to add a pedagogical aspect: *to walk by learning*. During the time they are in positions of authority, the support bases learn as they govern, they learn to be and to do government, while remaining support bases and part of the broader community. In this sense, they represent an exercise in leadership that is more open, fluid, and rotational, and that has a greater possibility of generating new knowledge. As a result, this learning to govern while governing enables a collective praxis surpassing the limits imposed by the conditions of the present. I also refer to the pedagogical because the support bases, in their temporary roles of authority, are not the wise elders of the village. By "wise," I refer to the notion of authority as defined both by classic political philosophy since Rousseau in the eighteenth century—where the person with the greatest experience and ability to lead is designated the authority (Rousseau 1967; Sartori 2001)—and by the role traditionally played by elders in communities in these regions. Neither the elders nor the best-prepared individuals are the authorities there now, but rather those who make an ethical commitment based on the principle of holding authority and learning to govern by governing. In the next section I reflect on these implications as they affect the autonomous communities' relationship to the local Mexican state.

Governing by Obeying and the Ambiguous Relationship to the Sovereign State

One day in March 2005, I arrived very early to the offices of the autonomous council of Diecisiete de Noviembre with the expectation of being one of the first in line to talk to the authorities. To my misfortune, many individuals were already there and I ended up number nine on the list. I sat on a wooden plank to wait for my turn, an activity I became accustomed to throughout the course of my fieldwork. The door remained open during each meeting, making it impossible for those outside not to overhear the content of the cases under discussion. Residents of the *ejido* Venustiano Carranza arrived at the autonomous council office to inquire whether the ecological regulations permitted them to cut down a number of trees close to the road. Later, two communities entered the offices to resolve a dispute over the boundary separating their respective lands. The procession of cases was interrupted when those responsible to oversee the water system arrived to inquire about the possibility of extending a piped water system that served only the secondary school and the community of Zapata so that it would reach the *ejido* Morelia. Though this is an issue that takes on greater significance each year during the dry season, in this case its relevance was increased more than usual due to an unannounced visit to the region by Luis H. Álvarez, the federal government's coordinator of the dialogues for peace in Chiapas, who offered to lay seventeen kilometers of water pipeline from a spring to Morelia and thus ensure a sufficient supply for the *ejido*. Such deceivingly apolitical proposals to build infrastructure projects, such as a water system, were among the continual efforts by the federal and state governments to undermine the project of autonomy and to fragment local political alliances with the Zapatistas.

Following the emergency meeting to discuss the water issue, a dozen Tojolabal inhabitants from two Zapatista communities entered the offices to deal with a divorce.[5] The village where the couple originally lived prohibited the man from having two wives and two homes. His current wife sought a divorce, and their community representatives demanded that he move to another village, while she chose to return to her community of origin. The discussion lasted more than an hour, and although the woman was present, she offered few contributions to the debate, given that these took place in Spanish but she only spoke Tojolabal. Finally, one of the council members addressed the husband:

> We are not going to instigate proceedings for the separation since you both are agreed to divorce, but it remains to be seen what to do with the livestock and five children. Your community does not want you to stay there because they do not want you to live with two women. Your wife is an education delegate of this municipality and you mistreated her. The other village does not want you there either, since your former wife is going to live there. You will be sent to another community.

The husband replied, "I accept. The people govern, and if this is the people's will, then I accept it and I will leave. But I want my children to come with me."

A member of the council responded: "Well, we cannot prepare the resolution order because your children are not here and they have to decide where they want to go. Without them, we cannot complete the decision. Bring them here next Monday and we will deal with it." A council member then asked them how much they had spent on traveling to the office and gave them 120 pesos (12 US dollars) to cover all their fares.

These myriad conflicts and administrative decisions are among the obligations of the local and state government offices. In this sense, one could say that Diecisiete de Noviembre usurps the functions of the state. Although the cases described above were resolved in the autonomous offices, such cases exist in constant competition, and indeed frequent interaction, with official institutions. In this section I am interested in analyzing the effects of the practices of *mandar obedeciendo* as the local exercise of autonomous power vis-à-vis local government institutions. My argument is that the collective decision-making processes in autonomy slip between the ambivalences of state regulatory logics to unravel attempts to contain the Zapatista project as well as the production of particular racialized subjectivities.

A review of the relations between both local and state governments and the autonomous municipalities over almost two decades bears testimony to their mutable and ambiguous interactions. To begin with, the official municipality of Altamirano has the peculiarity of being the only one where the rebel organization succeeded in negotiating with the Party of the Democratic Revolution to elect a Zapatista sympathizer to the municipal presidency. From 1995 to 1997, many of the activities of the official municipality were directed toward strengthening the priorities of Dieci-siete de Noviembre, by providing logistical support, infrastructure, and political coverage. Subsequently, between 1998 and 2000, the relationship between the official and the autonomous municipality passed through a period of great tension, many disputes, and increased police and military surveillance, including threats of intervention by federal security forces to dismantle the rebel municipality. This period coincided with the repressive policies of Chiapas governor Roberto Albores Guillén and the political lockdown of President Ernesto Zedillo. The following state governor, Pablo Salazar (2000–2006), chose to implement a policy of nonintervention with regard to the processes of Zapatista indigenous autonomy, while maintaining strict surveillance on the activities of the communities.

Following the founding of the *juntas de buen gobierno* in 2003, implicit state acceptance and nonintervention moved up a notch, reaching even de facto recognition. Several cases bear testimony to this. In 2003, in the autonomous municipality of Miguel Hidalgo, in Caracol IV, the police detained support bases for felling trees in violation of state ecology laws. However, the judge freed those arrested on the basis of evidence, which included a permit granted by the *junta*. In most Zapatista regions, the federal transit police accepted vehicle registration licenses granted by the *juntas* to taxis and other public-transport vehicles. Members of the *junta* in Caracol IV described that on a number of occasions, representatives from the Secretariat of the Environment and Natural Resources and the Secretariat of Agrarian Reform and other institutions approached them to ask permission to enter the communities and then respected their decisions afterward; they would leave the Zapatista communities if the *junta* denied their requests, as was generally the case.

As for the municipal office of Altamirano, its Department of Works and Services maintained frequent contact with the *caracol* between 2005 and 2008. In a 2006 interview, the department head explained that the people of Altamirano believed that Zapatista communities suffered poor living conditions because the local government did not want to help them. He argued that in reality they did not want to be "helped." In his view, they lacked decent housing because they refused to accept the local assistance programs or the federal program Oportunidades, meaning they effectively marginalized themselves. He said that the official municipality respected their decisions and did not enter the communities uninvited. However, the situation was different for the Department of Works and Services since improving the local roads benefits all communities in the municipality regardless of their political affiliation. This required constant negotiation with the autonomous council of Diecisiete de Noviembre and the *junta*, he said. The government official, a light-skinned *mestizo* in his mid-forties with an undergraduate degree in engineering, explained,

> If we are planning road improvements that affect their lands, we have to pay them a right-of-way fee. Sometimes, instead of giving them money we do work for them. If we are working in the area they consider their territory or their lands, they demand a fee. In general, it is 10 percent of the road improvement budget. That is what their laws say. Of course, that is impossible. We have to negotiate to reach a reasonable compromise, which is generally around 3 percent to 5 percent of the budget, depending on the size of the work.

He described that sometimes the negotiation involves repairing or opening up roads that lead to the Zapatista communities, for example, spreading gravel on the dirt road that leads to the autonomous secondary school. In other cases, paying 10 percent of the budget for a public project would mean giving the Zapatistas a sum of around 30,000 pesos (3,000 US dollars at the time), so the municipality offers the alternative of an in-kind payment, with materials such as a generator. "In 2005, we carried out five infrastructure projects in the region covering both the official municipality of Altamirano and the autonomous one of Diecisiete de Noviembre," the head of the public works department said, explaining that in these cases, agreements were reached with the Zapatistas. The agreements take place between two bodies of authority, one official and one autonomous, concerning a single geographic area under political dispute.

In a different arena, both the municipal president's office and the public prosecutor's office attempted to compete with the autonomous council and the *caracol junta*, principally when it came to social-development, infrastructure, and economic support projects, while at the same time, police forces and military networks maintained strict surveillance. As a last resort, both state and federal institutions maintained the option of open acts of repression. Military operations to arrest the EZLN leadership on February 9, 1995, and to dismantle the autonomous municipalities in 1998 served as stark reminders of this possibility. State forms of engagement thus emerged from the ambivalent militarized promises of indigenous rights recognition and the tolerant respect for cultural differences mixed with latent racism.

A commonsense view of the state is that it is a rational actor formed from a set of rules, laws, administrative systems, and bureaucratic structures, in contrast with the actions of public officials and state representatives, which are arbitrary, indecipherable, and hard to predict. However, studies on the state that focus on its margins direct their analysis to both those regulations existing on paper and concrete practices that fluctuate between rational and "magical" modes (Das and Poole 2004). Exclusion, ambiguity, and indecipherability figure as central components of state formation and operate as constitutive elements. Ambivalences and indecipherable elements contain mechanisms of control, as they introduce the state to different spheres of community life through multiple levels of exception.

However, the same ambiguities serve alternative political purposes, particularly those of rebel organizations acting against regulatory state effects. Subaltern political actors move within state cracks and fissures to advance their own transformative potentials. Thus the political and cultural practices of governing by obeying operate in flexible, malleable spaces that exist within the frictions created by the different roles taken on by the state. It is between these ambivalences that the decision-making activities of the autonomous government alter the conditions in which the state government interacts with the Zapatista indigenous communities as well as with non-Zapatista-aligned peasant and indigenous actors.

During the Salazar gubernatorial administration (2000–2006), the politicization of the Zapatista justice system served to divert the regulatory discourses and practices of the state, thereby avoiding social isolation and fragmentation at the local level. In Diecisiete de Noviembre, the justice system dealt above all with non-Zapatista individuals and organizations. During the Salazar administration, when regulatory policies spurred divisions between peasant and indigenous organizations allied with the Zapatistas and those who supported state institutional change, the spaces for conflict resolution figured prominently so as to establish new dialogues with other political actors and rebuild social legitimacy for those who had rejected Zapatismo. I observed that this trend toward restoration of social alliances, although not political alliances, occurred in three principal arenas of conflict resolution: agrarian conflicts, cases of divorce or domestic violence, and the monitoring and oversight of the public prosecutors' offices.

The effects of Zapatista autonomy, in particular the implementation of justice, were visible not only in undermining state attempts to isolate and contain the autonomous municipalities but also at the level of the production of subjectivities that contrasted with the ideal type that upheld the figure of the *ajvalil*. This could be seen in specific events associated with the arena of justice. I will focus on the monitoring of how the public prosecutor's office investigated and resolved minor offenses. In these cases, the autonomous government acted as an oversight body to ensure that state officials fulfilled their assigned responsibilities, including in the event of a false accusation or attempted act of corruption (demanding money, making threats, etc.). In these situations, the representatives of the autonomous government defended the accused and exerted pressure to ensure that justice was delivered in accordance with the law.

Though she had held her post for only three months when we spoke, Marisa of the honor and justice commission had already gone to the public prosecutor's office at least four times to denounce acts of corruption, extortion, and abuse of power. One of the cases arose because a man affiliated with the Institutional Revolutionary Party was accused of theft. The prosecutor stated that the man forced entry into the house of a couple that arrived home to find him stealing their belongings. Though the thief used a knife and chain to attack them, the man managed to wrest the weapons from him. The former then accused the latter of battery and filed charges with the public prosecutor's office, arguing that he had suffered physical injury. The prosecutor accepted the case in order to demand a bribe to resolve in favor of the accused. As Marisa narrated the events,

> We went to sort out the situation. We defended the accused and he didn't have to pay anything. I got really angry with the public prosecutor. They are *kaxlanes*. The first time I was scared, because he is an educated man and I have hardly been to school. I was frightened to speak out. But I was angry and he had to listen to me. We sorted it out and he had to accept the word [the decision] of the *caracol*.

I asked Marisa how she feels when the *kaxlanes* come to ask for permission or to resolve conflicts in her municipality and when she has to enter into discussion with public officials such as those from the public prosecutor's office. She answered, "There has been a real change. Before it was all, 'Damn Indian! You're an Indian! Indians are dumb, they know nothing! You're dirty!' They treated us real bad. Now we find a bit more respect. Things have changed. They have to show respect because they come here to ask us permission and to resolve the problems."

I will close this section by underlining the implications of Marisa's remarks in relation to the authority figure of the *ajvalil*, who remains in power through a dynamic that both upholds and feeds on indigenous inferiority. The exercise of the type of authority created in autonomy along with the production of indigenous political identities interrupts the relation of command-obedience that requires the authority of the *ajvalil*.

Conclusion

This chapter traced a local genealogy of political influences that converged after 1994 in the cultural practice of *mandar obedeciendo*, as a Tseltal and Tojolabal ethic shaping the relationship between the governed and the governing in Diecisiete de Noviembre. I have argued for the need to extend the gaze beyond the assemblies in Zapatista regions so as to locate how *mandar obedeciendo* forms part of the politicization of social life in diverse daily spheres, spurred by the act of *governing by learning to govern*, as there are pedagogical elements implicit in the practices of autonomy. This is central to the production of *kuxlejal* politics. In turn, I have described how the everyday exercise of the autonomous government not only inverts the command-obey relationship of a sovereign entity but seeks to break free from a particular type of authority figure, that of the master-governor embodied in the image of the *ajvalil*. Over time, these practices of governing by obeying became reference points that influenced the exercise of power, as well as the definitions of power, in other social movements and indigenous organizations struggling for liberation (Nahuelpan 2013).

The Zapatista political ethic of *mandar obedeciendo* fissures the racialized trope of indigenous peoples as born to obey and those in positions of racial economic privilege as born to govern. Such interventions complicated the well-oiled engine behind consolidated power in a historical moment, during the Vicente Fox and Felipe Calderón administrations, focused on demonstrating greater democratic aperture in the Mexican political system. At the federal level, the shift toward democracy was largely expressed through political parties, electoral politics, legal reforms, opinion surveys, and the greater representation of women and indigenous peoples in predetermined political spheres. It was on the basis of this limited definition of the political arena that a democratic transition was proclaimed in the year 2000, when the National Action Party candidate, Fox, defeated the Institutional Revolutionary Party candidate, Francisco Labastida, after that party's seventy-one years in power. It was thanks to the same hobbled democratic exercise that the Institutional Revolutionary Party returned to power twelve years later. And it is for this reason that the reconfiguration of the Mexican state may be said to have taken a double turn, simultaneously promoting greater participation of the population and limiting the spaces and the sectors of society that set the terms through which the democratic transitions are defined. In this context, Zapatista autonomy interrupts the repetition of color-blind neoliberal forces by demonstrating that the state political terrain continues to rest on gendered and racialized hierarchies that reinscribe the role of command-obedience, render invisible alternative forms of engaging in the political, and largely eliminate pushes toward resource redistribution. This interruption simultaneously spurs the production of knowledge from which emerges *kuxlejal* politics as a daily struggle toward a decolonizing horizon.

Conclusion

Zapatismo as the Struggle to Live within the *Lekil Kuxlejal* Tradition of Autonomy

In August 2013, I returned to Morelia for the festivities marking the tenth anniversary of the creation of the *caracoles* and the *juntas de buen gobierno*, almost twenty years after the Zapatista uprising and forty years after the founding of the National Liberation Forces (see Yañez Muñoz 2003). Though each *caracol* organized its own celebration, I went to Morelia alongside about forty people from other parts of Mexico and from other countries to be with several thousand Zapatista members from all over Caracol IV.

Since completing fieldwork for this book, I have returned on a yearly basis to Morelia, but I had not had the opportunity to be present at a large public event there. In contrast to the communiqué issued ten years earlier, during the founding of the *juntas* and the transformation of the *aguascalientes* into *caracoles*, when Subcomandante Insurgente Marcos stated that research was welcome as long as it was at the service of the communities, on this occasion the EZLN issued a communiqué prior to the festivities announcing the opposite: "We ask for your understanding, for us it is not the time for caravans, or projects, or interviews, or exchanges of experiences or such things" (EZLN 2013b). In a similar vein, regional internal agreements from this point no longer allowed external actors to visit individual families in the communities, but rather restricted visits to the physical space of the *caracol* center itself and to meetings with the autonomous council or the various commissions. All of these changes shifted priorities inward, as had occurred during most of the Felipe Cal-

Figure 7.1. Students in an autonomous classroom in the remains of the estate house, Ocho de Marzo, Diecisiete de Noviembre, 2006; photo by author

derón administration (2006–2012) and even more so after the return of the Institutional Revolutionary Party to power, under Enrique Peña Nieto (2012–2018).

During the celebration, I could not help but compare and contrast it with the national and international events that over the course of almost two decades I had witnessed in the same space. I particularly recalled the Intercontinental Meeting for Humanity and against Neoliberalism in 1996 as the first time support bases from then Aguascalientes IV organized a massive global gathering. In fact, as I sat on the benches outside the cafeteria building, located at the top of the slight incline where the esplanade surrounding the *caracol* buildings merges with the slopes of the hills, I watched all the activities taking place below and shared my reflections with Teodoro, whom I have known since that time. I remarked on how different this celebration felt in relation to the Zapatista events in the immediate years following the uprising. Teodoro commented that at the time they had literally built the *aguascalientes* compound out of nothing, without knowing where their efforts would lead. Yet building the space of the *aguascalientes* compound with their hands, with the wooden planks cut from local trees, and with the creativity that propels the beginning of any significant endeavor sparked activities previously unimaginable to him. He then contrasted how he and others had felt and what things had been like seventeen years earlier to the now well-rehearsed political practices as well as to how the new generations, who never knew what the Tzaconejá valley was like under the estate economy, experience daily life. Teodoro closed his thoughts with the reflection, "Yes, at that time, in 1996, we had the task of inventing the tradition [of autonomy], and now the new generations live in that tradition."

His explanation of *living in the tradition of autonomy* as part of a way of doing politics made it something so everyday, so inseparable from the act of daily life, that it made me feel that the energy surrounding the tenth anniversary of the *caracoles* had little air of a celebration outside the bounds of the ordinary. The hundreds of families present, who had arrived from the different communities in the *caracol*, ate broth with the meat of eight cattle that Zapatista authorities donated for the occasion. More than a dozen makeshift food vendors selling *quesadillas*, *tamales*, chicken with *mole*, beans and eggs, homemade bread, and coffee provided additional meals. The entrance to the *caracol* compound was transformed into a massive public parking lot. Basketball and soccer tournaments filled three entire days of activities. At night, students from the Zapatista primary and secondary schools provided cultural performances—poetry readings, theater productions, guessing games—which culminated in dancing to *cumbia* music until well past midnight.

The role of those who were being honored by the celebrations—the members of the *junta*, the autonomous councils, and the commissions— was limited to the largely invisible task of resolving logistical matters. Their brief appearances on stage were to announce information like the time lunch would be served, the beginning and ending times of the dance, and the hour at which everyone would return to their communities in the transportation provided by the *caracol*. "The music will last four hours. Wake-up time is at 5 a.m., so we can all clean the *caracol* [compound] and pick up trash. Prepare to pack your belongings to leave by 9 a.m.," instructed one of the council members over the loudspeaker. There was no formal ceremony, much less an official speech made by the autonomous authorities to seal the importance of the event. The three days in fact represented an ordinary party. Yes, it was a special event to the degree that the anniversary brought together thousands of people, but, at the same time, it was simply a celebration of what it represents to live in Zapatista communities.

This book has been about what it signifies to walk through and grant meaning to daily life within the tradition forged by Zapatista indigenous autonomy in Diecisiete de Noviembre. Throughout its chapters, I have described the multiple ways in which this way of doing politics forms part of a daily lived aspiration for *lekil kuxlejal*, manifested through ways of collective being in relation to the land, to the exercise of power, and to the production of shared knowledge. In these pages I have described how such ways of doing politics emerge when resistance stretches beyond temporal constraints to that which expands beyond a parenthesis. Resistance, rather than a suspended moment liberated when transformation arrives, so that the collective can rest, or lower their guard, is itself a form of living that reaches out to the apparently unattainable possibility of the horizon of social justice, along with the everyday efforts required to live life in another manner and to collectively reflect on its implications. In this sense, *kuxlejal* politics reflects the struggle for a dignified life, through a claimed power to be, *poder ser* (López Intzín 2013), in opposition to the civilizing crisis of Westernized relations of rule (Santos 2009a).

In this book, I have been careful to point out that under Zapatismo, politics is not *reduced* to daily life, or, as certain feminist circles claim, to the phrase "the personal is political," and much less to individual everyday endeavors of neoliberal self-improvement. Rather, for Tseltal, Tsotsil, Tojolabal, and Ch'ol Zapatistas, as for other indigenous and Afrodescendant peoples in the Americas subjected to historical acts of dispossession, genocide, racism, and exploitation as part of neocolonial relations of rule, the act of living, of maintaining, stretching, modifying, and engendering social life as a perpetual act of resistance, and of collectively recognizing oneself in such a struggle, holds the radical potential for social transformation. Thus, transformation in autonomy represents not so much the alteration of social composition but rather the stretching, expansion, reaffirmation, and materialized reimagination of the present (Gutiérrez Aguilar and Salazar 2015).

Through the *kuxlejal* politics of autonomy, the act of resisting fuses with the practices of daily life so as to subvert and unearth power relations expressed in the economy of racialized and gendered forms of domination. In these chapters, I have pointed to the multiple forms in which this way of doing politics under Zapatismo becomes a perpetual act of negating particular imposed ways of being—including the racist and paternalistic government social-development programs, the dehumanization of bodies encapsulated in the niche of the peon as economically exploitable and culturally degenerated, and the vertical power relations reproduced by the *mestizo ajvalil*. At the same time, Zapatista autonomy represents the ability to shift the collective gaze toward alternative paths so as to continue walking.

The *Escuelita* and the Pedagogical Act of the Political

During the festivities in Caracol IV in August 2013, I observed that an entirely new generation was now represented in the governing bodies. In the multiple conversations I had over the course of the three-day celebration, the priority placed upon political training and leadership by those generations raised under Zapatismo was evident, with those who participated in the uprising and in the design of the autonomous government playing advisory roles. This does not mean that key local figures had retired. Pánfilo, from the agricultural production commission, continued to oversee the implementation of agro-ecology techniques in the region. Macario still worked closely with the education commission, while Audalia still played a prominent role as a midwife and Ernestina continued to hold exceptional moral authority. While men who were part of the autonomous council during my fieldwork, such as Mauricio, were focusing on the tasks associated with being grandparents at the ripe age of fifty-five or so, their children had stepped up to serve on the autonomous council and the commissions. That is, an intergenerational presence continued alongside the transfer of the exercise of power.

In these intergenerational dynamics, governing by learning, as that which locates pedagogical practices of critical self-reflection at its heart, continues to form a central component of Zapatista daily practices. I locate the relationship between politics and the pedagogical particularly in the autonomous educational system, as that which Arjun Appadurai (2004) describes as an investment in aspirational capacities, or the collective possibility of a future, in contrast to the overwhelming tendency to divest from such priorities as a result of neoliberal reforms. In 2010, Caracol IV operated one secondary school; three years later, four secondary schools were providing education to students in the region. Upon receiving their diplomas, the young adults have the option to then become schoolteachers in the primary or secondary schools or to integrate themselves into the various commissions that form part of the autonomous government. The two options represent comparable pedagogical spheres.

Figure 7.2. Young Zapatista health promoters at an event honoring Galeano, a Zapatista community member assassinated in 2014, La Realidad, Caracol I, 2015; photo by Francisco Vazquez

During a conversation held in the midst of the festivities, the son of Teodoro explained to me that "instead of going to high school or to university, the *cargos* are the university, that is where we continue to learn."

During the festivities, I held several conversations with youth from these secondary schools, who shared that in terms of local history, the time of the *fincas* is highlighted in their courses. It drew my attention that not only did they go into detail on the names of the estates and narrate some of the stories recorded by the elders, but they did so not simply to repeat a history lesson but as part of critically engaged reflection on local relations of domination. I was left wondering if these social memories will continue to resonate with new generations so as to interpret racialized relations of rule or if other social memories will be added into the shared political toolbox: if so, what will these be?

The folding of politics into the pedagogical similarly formed part of the Zapatista project through the *escuelita* (little school), which took place immediately following the anniversary. In early 2013, the EZLN issued a communiqué announcing a series of new activities in their autonomous municipalities. Though many expected a grandiose event or a forceful political action, the leadership of the rebel army announced that the *escue-*

lita would take place and that it would be an educational event for those who desired to participate to be held over the course of five days in the *caracoles*:

> After the anniversary of the *caracoles*, we will start our little school, where our leaders, that is to say, the Zapatista support bases, will give classes on their thoughts and actions related to how in Zapatismo we understand liberty, along with the lessons, errors, problems, and solutions, the progress we have made, where we are stuck, and what remains to be done, because what remains to be done is what always remains to be done. (EZLN 2013a)

The communiqué goes on to state that the students would be required to diligently study subject matter in four courses: Autonomous Government I, Autonomous Government II, the Participation of Women in the Autonomous Government, and Resistance. Each course included its own textbook, which the students were to pick up at the enrollment center in San Cristóbal. After the anniversary festivities ended, those designated as the "teachers" remained at the *caracol* center to prepare for the arrival of their students. During the following days, I observed as Zapatista community members named to be teachers in the *escuelita* prepared for their roles in small groups, writing down and discussing the topics they wished to address and emphasize during their week-long classes.

Once back in San Cristóbal, I spoke to several friends who were to participate as students; they were curious to know what the methods would be. Most assumed that they would learn in a classroom setting and study from their textbooks. However, upon arriving at the designated *caracol*, each student was introduced to her or his *votán*, which in Mayan means "guardian-heart of the community." A prior communiqué explained that the *votán* would be the backbone of the *escuelita*, "the method, study plan, the teacher, the school, the classroom, the blackboard, the notebook, pencil, desk, exam, graduation ceremony and gown" (EZLN 2013b). For five days, student participants went to the cornfields, walked in the mountains, learned to cook on an open-fire stove in the home, and participated in the daily tasks that sustain, in all senses of the word, the daily practices of autonomy.

The lesson could not be clearer: knowledge production emerges not by extracting the student from daily life into a classroom setting but rather as the body moves through and acts within daily life. It is in the cornfield, the mountains, in the small conversations over coffee in the kitchen with the *votán* host where learning takes place. It is this same low-volume experience that then holds the possibility for initiating substantial social change. As I have argued throughout this book, it is in these apparently low-decibel moments that the pillars of Zapatista praxis surface and from which specific key political and theoretical contributions emerge.

In 2003, the Mexican sociologist Pablo González Casanova wrote on a particular method of thought associated with Zapatismo as a decolonial multicultural action, which he explained as "a type of common sense through which there emerge different forms of thinking, expressing, acting, with the understanding that a necessary dialogue clarifies affinities and differences, allowing for more expansive common languages and consensus capable of multicultural actions for an alternative world." Collective common sense forged through such exchanges, such as between the *votán* and his or her student in the *escuelita*, requires decisions to be implemented and commitments to be made. It is the spaces merging politics with the pedagogical that this book has highlighted as central to generating knowledge beyond the limits framed by current historical conditions.

Final Reflections: Autonomy and Collective Grammars against the Machinery of Death

As my work on this book came to a close, twenty years after hundreds of thousands of Zapatista sympathizers took to the streets in support of the EZLN after the uprising and against state repression, Mexico witnessed marches of the same magnitude, not in demand of indigenous rights or autonomy and self-determination but in demand of justice and truth in the case of the three assassinated and forty-three disappeared indigenous and peasant students from the Raúl Isidro Burgos Normal School in Ayotzinapa, Guerrero. On September 26, 2014, the students collected funds and negotiated the use of public buses in the city of Iguala, Guerrero, so as to participate in the events commemorating the 1968 Tlatelolco Plaza student massacre in Mexico City. As the five buses on which the students were traveling headed toward the town center, police surrounded them and fired their weapons directly at them. They forcefully pulled the youths from the vehicles before pushing them into patrol cars. Two years after the heinous acts, their whereabouts were still unknown.

The case sparked a level of collective outrage not seen in years. For more than four months following the tragic event, thousands upon thousands of people took to the streets in Mexico City, in the Guerrero state capital of Chilpancingo, and in hundreds of cities in Mexico and around the world. The case of the forced disappearance of the Ayotzinapa students resonated strongly with the assassinations of African Americans, such as Mike Brown and Eric Garner, by the police in the United States, fueling political actions across national boundaries and social actors (Morris 2015). Public demands for justice and solidarity with the mothers of the disappeared as well as the students from Ayotzinapa stretch from Ferguson, Missouri, to as far away as India and into refugee camps in Palestine.

The case of Ayotzinapa both crystallized a humanitarian disaster in the country and caused its overflow. The following numbers provide a sense of the magnitude of the crisis. Since the beginning of the Calderón administration in 2006, more than 100,000 people have been assassinated in events associated with the "war against organized crime" and more than 25,000 have been disappeared, almost 45 percent of these disappearances taking place during the first two years of the Peña Nieto administration, 2012–2014. Of the cases presented to the Office of the General Prosecutor, 98 percent remain unresolved (Antillón Najlis 2014). The magnitude and tragedy of such figures are reflected in the words of individuals during the massive public gatherings in 2014: "The necro-politics of the narco state. Enough!" read one sign held up during a march in Mexico City in October of that year.

The context was one unimaginable twenty years prior, or even a little more than a decade before, when the EZLN announced the creation of the *juntas* and the *caracoles* as part of indigenous autonomy and self-determination. To the historical legacies of land dispossession and territorial plunder, we must now add violent actions by (il)legal actors who operate with near impunity, along with the diversification and decentralization of all sorts of contraband economic activity, from narcotics smuggling to human trafficking. Twenty years after the uprising, those taking to the streets faced not only the challenges brought on by national liberation struggles that invited collective political actors to reimagine the nation–state, but the challenge of survival in times of genocide. Though undoubtedly inspired by the Zapatista autonomous municipalities, key indigenous political actors in Mexico, including the *keris*, or Purépecha indigenous authorities in the municipality of Cherán, Michoacán, and the Na saví, Nahua, and Me'phaa Community Police along with their Regional Coordinating Body of Community Authorities in Guerrero, lay claims to meanings of self-determination that involve community defense, collective security, and the implementation of justice (Aragón 2013; Sierra 2013). The disappearance of the indigenous and peasant students of Ayotzinapa is a stark reminder that in place of the brief multicultural era, subsequent Mexican state formation linked racism to de facto criminalization, both of which justify the removal of dehumanized bodies and the dispossession of their geographic regions, rendering particular social lives utterly disposable.

In this new context, the Zapatista movement held an important ethical political role in fueling collective social struggle. Subcomandante Insurgente Marcos, retired from public gaze since May 2014, was replaced by Subcomandante Insurgente Moisés, a Tojolabal EZLN leader from the Lacandon Jungle valley of Las Margaritas. The new subcomandante announced the activities of the Festival of World Resistance and Rebellion against Capitalism held at the end of 2014 in the *caracoles*. Though not originally a part of the plans for the festival, the tragic events in Iguala only three months before led the EZLN to invite the families of the disappeared along with student survivors from Ayotzinapa to attend. The festival took place between the Christmas and New Year celebrations, a time when the mothers and fathers of the Ayotzinapa students were emotionally devastated and particularly vulnerable to acts of state repression. Their participation in the events in Zapatista territory was political in nature as it represented a deeply affective expression of solidarity. Though the families of the disappeared protested that they did not deserve such honors, the EZLN leadership ceded the rooms usually reserved for themselves to the families and ensured that the family members were the first to eat meals as well as being granted all necessary attention. All these small acts represented the efforts of hosts insisting upon the dignity and humanity of their guests, in direct opposition to their neglect and humiliation by the government authorities overseeing the investigations.

During the speech marking the twenty-first anniversary of the EZLN uprising, Subcomandante Insurgente Moisés directed his words to the Ayotzinapa family members, recognizing in their pain a familiarity experienced by those whose lives are deemed worthless to the state and whose constructed racialized inferiority strips them of their humanity:

> We the Zapatistas say that we live in a society where we are exploited, kept down, disregarded, deprived, and robbed by centuries of *patrones* and leaders. . . . They have tried to fool us, saying that they, those who are above, are better than us, and we are worthless. We are stupid, they tell us. We don't know how to think, imagine, create, and we are only their wageworkers. To hell with that! we said in 1994. . . . And then your pain and your rage

appeared in us. That is why we asked that you be present these days with us. (EZLN 2015)

Subcomandante Insurgente Moisés requested that members of the National Indigenous Congress, who were present at the event, then offer forty-six embraces to the families, forty-three for their children disappeared and three more for those sons assassinated by the police on September 26. The political priorities expressed in the act led by Moisés demonstrate that after twenty years, those aspects I have repeated throughout this book as central contributions of the Zapatista movement to decolonial struggles continue to permeate social relations. The events held in honor of the Ayotzinapa students highlight that the political exists in apparently mundane acts and in expressions of affect as thinking-feeling-acting through the heart. The act of embracing the families was the culmination of an enactment of solidarity that exists only with the understanding that radical social transformation is possible when you are able to touch the pain of the other and to allow their pain to resonate with that of your own people so that the shared encounter can convert collective trauma into something else. After the event, I heard several people question the significance of this act as not being important enough or as not responding quickly enough to the urgencies required of the moment. Yet the elements of Zapatismo political praxis I have highlighted throughout this book, such as the group discussions of the pain and suffering lived on the estates, point to the contrary: that decolonial social justice is possible only through acts that stretch out to, and recognize, in the profound pain of the other, her and his negated humanity.

The current "necropolitics" (Mbembe 2003) of the Mexican state makes such political acts all the more urgent. How should people listen to the contributions of Zapatista autonomy more than twenty years after the EZLN uprising, and in a context shaped by the forced disappearances in Iguala? To what extent can the lessons learned from Zapatismo provide the political grammars necessary to name and act against a possible new racialized project in this era of violence and criminalization? How do they allow for a disordering of the racialized tropes sustaining the apparently color-blind Mexican state? In what ways can the politicization of daily life and the constant reactivation of memory as part of *kuxlejal* praxis play critical roles against acts of (il)legal organized crime linked to current expressions of the Mexican state? What decolonial imaginaries in the broader cognitive map can we draw on so as to relocate the potential for a politics of refusal at the margins of the state? What is the role of politically committed academic research in this context?

This book ends with these difficult yet urgent questions. My task in this book has not been to set out prescriptive answers. Rather it is my hope that the descriptions and arguments traced throughout its chapters contribute to the necessary dialogues and critical reflections required to locate new exit doors through which to escape a terrain of destruction in order to forge horizons for decolonial politics of being in the present, as that which resides alongside those historical legacies rendering possible their very existence.

Notes

Introduction

1. I use pseudonyms for all members of the Zapatista communities except for public figures such as the EZLN *comandantes*.

2. All transcriptions of interviews that I conducted in Chiapas and during my research elsewhere are in my possession, as are all my field notes.

3. Maldonado-Torres (2008) provides a theoretical description of the way these three realms—knowledge production, ways of being, and power—form decolonial struggles.

4. The other three planned rounds of the peace talks were never held. They were to be on democracy and justice, development and well-being, and the rights of women.

5. During the crisis of 1982, the country formally entered into profound economic restructuring, which focused on opening the economy to international investment by way of an export-oriented industrialization strategy, the privatization of more than two-thirds of national companies, and the deregulation of wages. It was not until 1988, during the beginning of the Carlos Salinas de Gortari administration, that the opening of the agrarian sector figured prominently (Otero 1996).

6. The terms "Spaniard," *criollo*, *ladino*, *mestizo*, and *kaxlan* are each injected with particular meanings depending on specific historical and geographical contexts, but I use the terms the way Zapatista community members use them: to identify nonindigenous people of European descent in positions of relative privilege.

7. At the beginning of the Calderón administration, public policies targeting indigenous people began to be categorized as programs for "vulnerable groups," a term used in the administration's National Development Plan in 2007.

8. My framework draws from Jennifer Goett's (2011) proposal that to understand the political implications of multiculturalism it is necessary to extend the gaze beyond multicultural initiatives so as to analyze other state spheres that implicate multicultural subjects. For a detailed analysis of how multicultural policies can in fact have an adverse effect and lead to a failure to deter racism, see Ambikaipaker 2015.

9. Emerging during the dictatorship of Porfirio Díaz at the end of the nineteenth century, a period known as the Porfiriato, *mestizaje* ideology refers to the cultural and biological amalgamation of European and indigenous people and the belief that it leads to progress and modern civilizing traits. Though African presence in Mexico figured prominently during the first hundred years of colonial rule and African blood-

lines played a central role in caste social hierarchies of the seventeenth and eighteenth centuries, by the time of the Porfiriato, African presence had been eliminated from the ideological equation.

10. Focusing on ethnicity privileges the perception that social hierarchies are due both to class differences and to the inability to engage in a positive manner across cultural differences (Saldivar 2014). The category fails to account for the continued inferiorization of indigenous peoples and communities and of those read as closer to indigenous on a social-evolutionary scale. It inhibits locating the varying ways in which markers of inferiority attached to bodies operate in part by displacing particular tropes to a historical past, such as biological racism to the colonial period, divorcing them from present-day conditions.

11. In fact, one of the first public documents by the EZLN *comandancia* that explicitly refers to racism was written by Subcomandante Insurgente Moisés in November 2016, when he wrote of specific left intellectual elites in Mexico, calling them "racists" and referring to the "burlas, sus desprecios, su racismo que ya no pueden esconderlo" (jokes, contempt, and racism that they can no longer hide) (EZLN 2016).

12. Frantz Fanon's theorization helps render visible how Zapatista members repeatedly highlight forms of dehumanization as effects of racism activated by assemblages linked to state making (McKittrick 2015; Weheliye 2014). Colonial subjects, according to Fanon, occupy a "zone of non-being, an extraordinarily sterile and arid region, an utterly naked declivity where an authentic upheaval can be born" (1967, 8). Colonized subjects exist not just as objects but as subhuman, as dehumanized, as not quite human enough. The posited inferiority acts as the motor behind racialized violence, exploitation, and genocide.

13. Community members shared that encouraging reflection on the conditions of exploitation and racialized inferiorization during the time of the *fincas* was among the EZLN's clandestine methods of organization in the region. In this sense, the continued emphasis on that time period forms part of a long-term trajectory of Zapatista political formation.

14. Depictions of indigenous people as childlike, innocent, and inherently vulnerable are common throughout Latin America. Such representations form part of social evolutionary ideologies that locate indigenous people on the primitive scale and more "mature" populations at the civilized end of the spectrum.

15. For parallel discussions of the concept of "living well" versus the "good life" that are similarly used by Aymara and Quechua indigenous organizations in Bolivia and Ecuador, see Schavelzon 2015.

16. Antonio Paolí (2001) refers to *lekil kuxlejal* as a Tseltal ideal of peace, where nature and society are integrated so as to engender the ability to live well. I emphasize the way Zapatista community members refer to the term as a site of struggle, rather than only an ideal.

Chapter 1: A Brief Overview of the First Years of the Zapatista Autonomous Municipalities (1996–2003)

1. To avoid confusing the administrative matters of Diecisiete de Noviembre with the rest of Caracol IV, the center of Diecisiete de Noviembre was moved to another location in the *ejido* Morelia in 2007.

2. The rebel army maintains its political and military structure while relying on its support bases, who are individuals from civilian communities. Although in the first few years of the movement the two structures were intermingled, over time and especially after 2003, authorities made attempts to separate the two spheres and thus to avoid the involvement of the political-military structure in civil affairs that are under the jurisdiction of the autonomous governments.

3. See EZLN 2003 and the discussions held at the first plenary session of la Otra Campaña (the Other Campaign) in August 2005 (EZLN 2005a).

4. Tzotz Choj means "jaguar bat man." It reprises the name of the last king of Toniná, which is now an archeological site ten kilometers from Ocosingo and thirty from Morelia. During the latter half of the Classic Mayan era, his kingdom controlled this area, which is now under Zapatista influence. According to archeological studies, it was an empire so powerful that it conquered the Lords of Palenque.

5. At the time there were four municipalities; in 2007 there were seven municipalities and four autonomous regions that were not formally called municipalities.

6. The municipal authorities were mainly men in this age range and mainly Tseltal, something that on occasion generated frictions with the Tojolabales, who are the minority in the region. According to national census figures for 1940, 43 percent of the population of the official municipality of Altamirano (which became Diecisiete de Noviembre under the Zapatistas) were Tojolabal, while 39 percent were Tseltal. In 1980, 40 percent were Tojolabal and 59 percent Tseltal. By 1990, the proportions were 45 percent Tojolabal and 53 percent Tseltal. In the early years of the autonomous municipality, Diecisiete de Noviembre covered the entirety of the municipality of Altamirano and part of the municipality of Chanal. However, in 1999 the Tojolabales from the region of San Miguel Chiptic decided to form their own municipality, which they call Vicente Guerrero. The decision to divide the municipality was due in part to the fact that the Tojolabales "did not feel they were being listened to." (See Cerda 2011: Van der Haar 2004.)

7. According to investigations carried out by the Centro de Derechos Humanos Fray Bartolomé de las Casas (CDHFBC, Fray Bartolomé de las Casas Center for Human Rights), anti-Zapatista indigenous groups from Los Altos were provided weapons and military training by the Mexican Army and members of the police forces in order to attack Zapatista sympathizers.

8. Flinchum (1998) and Speed (2003) both provide summaries of these events.

9. Fobaproa was a government fund set up to solve the 1995 economic crisis, which was not unlike the savings and loan scandal in the United States in the 1980s. The Party of the Democratic Revolution held a plebiscite in response to the unilateral decision by the Zedillo government to go ahead with the bank-rescue package.

Chapter 2: The Production of Knowledge on the Terrain of Autonomy

1. Besides independent initiatives, there were also attempts to modify the role of the INI within its governmental institutions. At the beginning of the 1970s, Mercedes Olivera Bustamante became the director of the INI School of Development in San Cristóbal. Shortly thereafter, she drew from Marxism and popular-education methods to attempt to create a bilingual and bicultural curriculum for students from the Ch'ol indigenous region. Aguirre Beltrán fired her and accused her of "inciting an indigenous movement similar to the black movement [Black Panthers] in the United States" (Mercedes Olivera Bustamante, interview by author, January 2007).

2. This is particularly important in the case of research involving shared political visions and the space necessary to create them. Anzaldúa and Keating (2004) and Mohanty (2003) all discuss the concepts of "bridgework" and the "politics of solidarity."

3. The same practices occur in other spaces in Chiapas, such as during Bible lectures after mass on Sunday and in NGO popular-education workshops. In this sense, the dynamics used for the interview have historical trajectories that are similar to cultural practices in the region dating to the late 1960s.

Chapter 3: Social Memories of Struggle and Racialized (E)states

1. This local understanding of social struggle contrasts sharply with dominant representations, which tend to eliminate the agency of the subjects themselves. In the case of Chiapas, studies ascribe this active role to a range of political actors viewed as external to the local communities, including the Diocese of San Cristóbal, under the guidance of Bishop Samuel Ruiz García; the various Maoist and Marxist-Leninist groups that went to the jungle to "organize" the indigenous people; and the various government agencies in connection with the local elite (Legorreta Díaz 1998; Estrada Saavedra 2007; Tello Díaz 1995; Viqueira 2004).

2. I borrow from Robin D. G. Kelley's *Freedom Dreams: The Black Radical Imagination* (2002). Kelley narrates diverse social struggles central to African American political imaginaries, which served to foster the revolutionary vision within the African American community and the African diaspora in general across the twentieth century. Kelley argues that the imagination does not exist simply at the level of a metaphysical abstraction but rather takes form in concrete practices that entail an analysis of the multiple expressions of oppression. Assembling these cognitive maps, along with their history of advances and frustrations, creates the possibility of generating alternative forms of knowledge.

3. The historical archives at the Diocese of San Cristóbal de las Casas, which I used in my research, refer to the colonial political-administrative region known as the Tzendal Province, a vast region that now encompasses the official municipalities of San Juan Cancuc, Chanal, Oxchuc, Tenejapa, Altamirano, Sitalá, Socoltenango, Yajalón, Chilón, and Ocosingo. Caracol IV partially overlaps with a small section of that colonial jurisdiction.

4. See folder 2864, file 1, Diocese of San Cristóbal Historical Archive. The document

includes a letter granting the *mozos* of the Chiptic estate permission to attend mass in the local church.

5. Manuel Ruiz to Bishop, January 2, 1806, folder 2844, file 1, Diocese of San Cristóbal Historical Archive.

6. Notary certification by Guzman, February 22, 1806, folder 2844, file 1, Diocese of San Cristóbal Historical Archive. By 1809, Nacaxlan had 739 inhabitants (folder 3008, file 8).

7. Letter dated November 1806, folder 2844, file 1, Diocese of San Cristóbal Historical Archive.

8. See census report in folder 3008, file 10, Diocese of San Cristóbal Historical Archive. In 1815, Ocosingo had 525 families of "natives" plus 124 single men or women and 135 *ladino* families. San Carlos Nacaxlan had 309 Indian families plus 40 single people and 2 *ladino* families. The estates named in the census report are Santo Tomás, San Antonio, San Vicente, Santa Rita, Dolores, San José, El Rosario, Suchil, and Rancho Marco.

9. Letter by Mariano Guzman, November 23, 1816, folder 2844, file 1, Diocese of San Cristóbal Historical Archive.

10. The 1817 church census shows a total of 361 *yndio* families in San Carlos and 13 *ladino* families (folder 2861, file 4, Diocese of San Cristóbal Historical Archive).

11. Letter by Mariano Ramírez de Paramo, folder 2971, file 2, Diocese of San Cristóbal Historical Archive.

12. Letter dated June 30, 1848, folder 3547, file 1, Diocese of San Cristóbal Historical Archive.

13. A letter written in 1912 by inhabitants of San Carlos to Bishop Francisco Orozco y Jimenes to establish a parish in the town justifies the need based in part on the number of estates that exist in the region, which the writers state is thirty-seven. The estates identified in this letter, spelled as they appear in it, are La Laguna, Palma Real, Santiago, Vergel, San Francisco, Chiptic, Carmen Lomán, Cafetal Santa Elena, La Soledad, Livingstone, San Marcos, Gran Poder, Porvenir, Palmira, Yacholob, San José la Unión, Buenavista, Cruz San Martin, Santo Tomás Tzaconejá, Corrachén, Sibaquil, La Codicia, Jamanavil, Rancho Mateo, San Juan Chochilá, Santa Elena Mait, Suchilá, Tulipán, La Reforma Mendoza, Zaragoza, San Ysidro, La Soledad, El Triunfo, Puerto Rico, La Aurora, Guayaquil, and El Amolar. See folder 3540, file 7, Diocese of San Cristóbal Historical Archive.

14. *Nixtamal* is corn that has been prepared for human consumption by being cooked and soaked in limewater.

15. According to Bobrow-Strain (2007, 63), the debts the *mozos* accrued in the *tienda de raya* could be quite substantial, accounting for up to a third of all their assets.

16. Before peasant farmers could become eligible to receive loans and economic support, the federal development programs required them to legally constitute themselves as a union of *ejidos*, a union of unions of *ejidos*, or a rural association of collective interest. Thus the state reorganized rural Mexico, which opened up spheres of local participation even in the regions where freedom of association did not exist beyond the community (Martínez-Torres 2006).

Chapter 4: Zapatista Agrarian Reform within the Racialized Fields of Chiapas

1. According to data I gathered in the Diecisiete de Noviembre communities where I conducted interviews, before 2005, between 10 percent and 20 percent of the young people in these communities were living elsewhere. The emigrants were earning between 800 and 1,800 pesos a week. Most of what they saved was spent on construction materials, family medical costs, or purchasing corn and beans after a harvest affected by drought.

2. According to the 2005 population census conducted by the National Institute of Statistics and Geography (INEGI), more than 55 percent of the population in the state of Quintana Roo was originally from other parts of the country, including 28,000 people from Chiapas. Of the almost 500,000 people who had migrated to Quintana Roo by 2005, 60 percent came in search of a better source of employment (cited in Martoccia 2006).

3. The exact quantity of land is disputed. According to the historian Antonio García de León (2002, 247), shortly after the armed uprising, indigenous peasants, including members of the EZLN, took over almost 97,000 hectares. Other sources record that about 16,000 hectares were taken over when more than 4,000 properties were confiscated by indigenous peasants (Secretaría de la Reforma Agraria 1998). Daniel Villafuerte Solís (1999, 23) estimates the number to be between these two figures, calculating that in total the Zapatistas took over more than 55,000 hectares.

4. Such disputes persist despite the fact that these peasant organizations successfully appropriated lands after 1994. Between 1994 and 1998, the agrarian accords signed between the state, peasant organizations, and individuals resolved more than 2,100 demands for agrarian land (García de León 2002, 286).

5. The changes wrought were closely linked to the policy recommendations promoted by experts from multilateral institutions such as the World Bank. Despite the fact that few substantive differences exist between the agricultural output of *ejidos* and that of private small landowners, the World Bank prompted market-dictated agrarian reforms, in contrast to earlier policies that gave the state a greater role (De Janvry, Sadoulet, and Wolford 1997; Deininger 2003).

6. Specific data for Altamirano varies slightly depending on the source. According to INEGI (2006), twenty-four *ejidos* exist in Altamirano, of which algunos concluded the first phase of delineating their lands, with the resulting cartographies of *ejido* lands presented to the community members.

7. I held this interview jointly with Richard Stahler-Sholk.

8. In 2000 there were at least 14,000 agrarian conflicts in Chiapas, and a year later almost 700 non-Zapatista peasant organizations demanded the right to purchase more than 71,000 hectares of land, 22 percent of which these groups had already settled (Villafuerte Solís and García Aguilar 2006, 108). Between 2001 and 2003, the state government registered 617 agrarian disputes, which included land invasions and conflicts over limits (Gobierno del Estado de Chiapas 2003).

9. Calva, Encinas, and Meneses (1991) make similar arguments about other regions of the state.

10. These were the conclusions emerging from the National Indigenous Congress and the peasant marches against NAFTA in January 2008.

11. Jan Rus (2012) identifies in the highlands a contradiction that existed in the 1970s between a collective narrative among Tsotsiles in Chamula of being self-sufficient indigenous farmers who subsisted with what their *milpas* provided and the fact that a large percentage of community members traveled as laborers to coffee plantations to generate the income necessary to ensure household social reproduction.

12. *Ejidos* situated in those municipalities that concentrate indigenous populations also have the tendency to concentrate communal lands rather than divide those lands into family parcels. In the 803 municipalities in Mexico with more than 30 percent indigenous population, 71 percent of the *ejido* lands are collective (Robles Berlanga 2000, 127).

13. A similar sense of political identity emerged on the Atlantic coast of Nicaragua (see Gurdián, Hale, and Gordon 2004).

14. According to the INEGI, in 2005 almost 106,000 people migrated from Chiapas. The state they most migrated to was Quintana Roo, where 20 percent of the total went (INEGI 2016). While internal migration reflects a fairly consistent pattern since the 1970s (Collier 1994), migration to the United States until 2000 did not figure prominently in Chiapas. However, according to the National Population Council, the tendency to migrate accelerated in a short time frame. While in 2000 Chiapas accounted for a very low level of migration to the United States, in just four years, the state had surpassed states like Zacatecas that for decades had expelled population to the other side of the border (Villafuerte Solís and García Aguilar 2006, 119). In 2006, the Encuesta sobre Migración en la Frontera (Study on Migration in the Northern Border) identified 118,510 Chiapanecans attempting to cross the border, an almost 5,000 percent increase compared to the same data collected in 1995 (Martínez Velasco 2014, 369). In her fieldwork in the valley of La Realidad, Aquino documents migration patterns from Zapatista communities to the United States beginning in 2004, though the first migration of non-Zapatista-aligned men from the region occurred in 2000, almost ten years after individuals from other parts of the state had begun to head north in search of work.

Chapter 5: Women's Collectives and the Politicized (Re)production of Social Life

1. The direct beneficiaries are the women who receive the checks; the indirect beneficiaries are members of their families.

2. Cervical cancer is the second leading cause of premature death of women in Mexico (Secretaría de Salud 2015).

3. For a similar discussion of the ways that physical acts of violence on the estates inform how indigenous women make sense of current forms of violence, see Cervone and Cucurí 2017.

Chapter 6: *Mandar Obedeciendo*

1. A plural council of representatives from different political parties and peasant organizations governed the municipality of Ocosingo from 1995 to 1998 (see Burguete Cal y Mayor 2000).

2. In her book *Rights in Rebellion: Indigenous Struggle and Human Rights in Chiapas* (2008), Shannon Speed establishes this argument, that *mandar obedeciendo* is a more profound understanding of the effects of constitutive power, through an analysis of the de facto exercise of rights in autonomous communities. She draws from two concepts of power in Spinoza: *Potestas*, Power with a capital P, and *potencia*, power in lowercase. According to Antonio Negri, *Potestas* refers to a central command-obedience authority, while *potencia* is the creative authority or constitutive force. Both expressions of power reflect not only different potentialities and subjectivities but different forms of authority and organization (Negri 1993, 318). Speed argues that the Zapatista support bases not only struggle through *Potestas*, but also in *potencia*, as a power that constitutes itself without becoming a sovereign entity, hence generating an alternative logic.

3. For an analysis of the San Andrés Accords, the juridical reforms posed and the actual implementation of the right to autonomy, see Mattiace, Hernández, and Rus 2002.

4. Regarding my use of the word "semiautonomous," I am drawing from Latin American critical legal studies that point to the relatively autonomous nature of the law in relation to the state. That is, not all juridical frameworks are necessarily linked to the state (Santos 1987, 2002).

5. For additional descriptions of the Zapatista justice system, see Fernández 2014.

Bibliography

Aguilera, Manuel. 1969. *La reforma agraria en el desarrollo económico de México*. Mexico City: Instituto Mexicano de Investigaciones Económicas.

Alarcón Lavín, Roberto Rafael. 2010. "La biopiratería de los recursos de la medicina indígena tradicional en el estado de Chiapas, México—El caso ICBG-MAYA." *Revista Pueblos y Fronteras Digital* 6 (10): 151–180.

Alcoff, Linda Martín. 2010. "Sotomayor's Reasoning." *Southern Journal of Philosophy* 48 (March): 122–138.

Alexander, Jacqui, and Chandra Mohanty. 1997. *Feminist Genealogies, Colonial Legacies, Democratic Futures*. New York: Routledge.

Ambikaipaker, Mohan. 2015. "Liberal Exceptions: Violent Racism and Routine Anti-Racist Failure in Britain." *Ethnic and Racial Studies* 38 (12): 2055–2070.

Antillón Najlis, Ximena. 2011. "El territorio del alma: Una experiencia de acompañamiento psicosocial en la zona norte de Chiapas." In *Luchas "muy otras": Zapatismo y autonomía en las comunidades indígenas de Chiapas*, edited by Bruno Baronnet, Mariana Mora Bayo, and Richard Stahler-Sholk, 299–316. Mexico City: UAM, CIESAS, UNACH.

———. 2014. "Más allá de las cifras de personas desaparecidas." SinEmbargo. September 1. http://www.sinembargo.mx/opinion/01-09-2014/26850.

Anzaldúa, Gloria. 1987. *Borderlands/La Frontera: The New Mestiza*. San Francisco: Aunt Lute Books.

Anzaldúa, Gloria, and AnaLouise Keating, eds. 2004. *This Bridge We Call Home: Radical Visions for Transformation*. New York: Routledge.

Appadurai, Arjun. 2004. "Capacity to Aspire: Culture and the Terms of Recognition." In *Culture and Public Action*, edited by Vijayendra Rao and Michael Walton, 59–84. Stanford, CA: Stanford University Press.

Aquino, Alejandra. 2011. "Entre el sueño zapatista y el sueño americano." In *Luchas "muy otras": Zapatismo y autonomía en las comunidades indígenas de Chiapas*, edited by Bruno Baronnet, Mariana Mora Bayo, and Richard Stahler-Sholk, 447–488. Mexico City: UAM, CIESAS, UNACH.

———. 2012. "La migración de jóvenes zapatistas a Estados Unidos como desplazamiento geográfico, político y subjetivo." *European Review of Latin American and Caribbean Studies (CEDLA)* 92:3–22.

Aragón, Orlando. 2013. "El derecho en insurrección: El uso contra-hegemónico del derecho en el movimiento purépecha de Cherán." *Revista de Estudos e Pesquisas sobre las Américas* (Universidade de Brasilia) 7 (2): 37–69.

Asad, Talal. 1973. *Anthropology and the Colonial Encounter*. London: Ithaca.

Aubry, Andrés. 1984. *Estrategia popular e investigación científica*. Doc. 025-VIII-84. San Cristóbal de las Casas, Mexico: INAREMAC.

———. 1985. *10 años de labores de INAREMAC: Sus instrumentos de desarrollo alternativo*. Doc. 028-029-VI-85. San Cristóbal de las Casas, Mexico: INAREMAC.

———. 2011. "Otro modo de hacer ciencia: Miseria y rebeldía de las ciencias sociales (1927–2007)." In *Luchas "muy otras": Zapatismo y autonomía en las comunidades indígenas de Chiapas*, edited by Bruno Baronnet, Mariana Mora Bayo, and Richard Stahler-Sholk, 59–78. Mexico City: UAM, CIESAS, UNACH.

Avendaño, Amalia. 2005. "Victoria pírrica de ganaderos." *Contralínea*, June, 12–17. http://www.chiapas.contralinea.com.mx/archivo/2005/junio/html/victoria.htm.

Baronnet, Bruno. 2010. "Zapatismo y educación autónoma: De la rebelión a la dignidad indígena." *Sociedade e Cultura* 13 (July–December): 247–258.

Baronnet, Bruno, Mariana Mora Bayo, and Richard Stahler-Sholk, eds. 2011. *Luchas "muy otras": Zapatismo y autonomía en las comunidades indígenas de Chiapas*. Mexico City: UAM, CIESAS, UNACH.

Barot, Rohit, and John Bird. 2001. "Racialization: The Genealogy and Critique of a Concept." *Ethnic and Racial Studies* 24 (4): 601–618.

Bartra, Armando. 1996. *El México bárbaro: Plantaciones y monterías del sureste durante el porfiriato*. Mexico City: El Atajo.

Behar, Ruth. 1993. *Translated Woman: Crossing the Border with Esperanza's Story*. Boston: Beacon.

Beverley, John. 2004. *Testimonio: On the Politics of Truth*. Minneapolis: University of Minnesota Press.

Bizberg, Ilán. 2003. "Estado, organizaciones corporativas y democracia." In *México al inicio del siglo XXI: Democracia, ciudadanía y desarrollo*, edited by Alberto Aziz Nassif, 183–229. Mexico City: CIESAS.

Blackwell, Maylei. 2007. "Desde Estados Unidos, las mujeres indígenas ante la violencia sexual." *La Jornada*, May 21, *Ojarasca* (supplement on indigenous affairs). http://www.jornada.unam.mx/2007/05/21/oja121-mujereviolencia.html.

———. 2012. "The Practice of Autonomy in the Age of Neoliberalism: Strategies from Indigenous Women's Organising in Mexico." *Journal of Latin American Studies* 44: 703–782.

Bobrow-Strain, Aaron. 2007. *Intimate Enemies: Landowners, Power, and Violence in Chiapas*. Durham, NC: Duke University Press.

Bonilla-Silva, Eduardo. 2010. *Racism without Racists: Color-Blind Racism and the Persistence of Racial Inequality in the United States*. Lanham, MD: Rowman and Littlefield.

Bourdieu, Pierre. 1984. *Distinction: A Social Critique of the Judgement of Taste*. London: Routledge.

Burguete Cal y Mayor, Araceli. 2000. *Indigenous Autonomy in Mexico*. Copenhagen: IWGIA.

Buur, Lars, Jensen Steffen, and Fina Stepputat. 2007. *The Security-Development Nexus: Expressions of Sovereignty and Securitization in Southern Africa*. Capetown, South Africa: HSRC.

Buzan, Barry, Ole Waever, and Jaap de Wilde. 1998. *Security: A New Framework for Analysis*. Boulder, CO: Lynne Rienner.

Calva, José Luis. 1991. *El ejido en México: Crisis y modernización*. Mexico City: Fundación Friedrich Ebert.

Campos García, Alejandro. 2012. "Racialización, racialismo y racismo: Un discernimiento necesario." *Revista de la Universidad de la Habana*, no. 273: 184–199.

Cancian, Frank. 1977. *Economía y prestigio en una comunidad maya*. Mexico City: SEP-INI.

Castillejo Cuellar, Alejandro. 2009. *Los archivos del dolor: Ensayos sobre la violencia y el recuerdo en la Sudáfrica contemporánea*. Bogotá: Universidad de los Andes, Facultad de Ciencias Sociales, Centro de Estudios Socioculturales. CESO, Ediciones Uniandes.

Castro-Gómez, Santiago. 2010. *Historia de la gubernamentalidad: Razón de estado, liberalismo y neoliberalismo en Michel Foucault*. Bogotá: Pontificia Universidad Javeriana, Siglo del Hombre.

CDHFBC (Centro de Derechos Humanos Fray Bartlolomé de las Casas). 1998a. *La guerra que quieren ocultar*. San Cristóbal de las Casas: CDHFBC.

———. 1998b. *Ni paz ni justicia: Informe general y amplio acerca de la guerra civil que sufren los ch´oles en la Zona Norte de Chiapas*. San Cristóbal de las Casas: CDHFBC.

CDI (Comisión Nacional para el Desarrollo de los Pueblos Indígenas). 2011. "Acciones de gobierno para el Desarrollo Integral de los Pueblos Indígenas, informe 2011." Mexico City: Gobierno Federal, Comisión Nacional para el Desarrollo de los Pueblos Indígenas.

CDMC (Centro de Derechos de la Mujer en Chiapas). 2015. "Las mujeres y nuestro derecho a la tierra." San Cristóbal de las Casas: CDMC.

CEP/FOCA. N.d. "Acuerdos de San Andrés: Material formativo de apoyo a la consulta convocada por el EZLN sobre la ley elaborada por la COCOPA en materia de derechos y cultura indígena." Pamphlet 2. San Cristóbal de las Casas: CEP/FOCA.

Cerda, Alejandro. 2011. *Imaginando zapatismo: Multiculturalidad y autonomía indígena en Chiapas desde un municipios autónomo*. Mexico City: UAM Xochimilco.

Cervone, Emma, and Cristina Cucurí. 2017. "Gender Inequality, Indigenous Justice, and the Intercultural State: The Case of Chimborazo, Ecuador." In *Demanding Justice and Security: Indigenous Women and Legal Pluralities in Latin America*, edited by Rachel Sieder, 120–149. New York: Rutgers University Press.

Césaire, Aimé. 2000. *Discourse on Colo̶ni̶a̶li̶s̶m̶.* Ne̶w̶ ̶Y̶o̶r̶k̶:̶ Monthly Review.

CIZ (Centro de Información Zapatista). 2001. *La Marcha del color de la tierra, comunicados, cartas y mensajes del Ejército Zapatista de Liberación Nacional del 2 de diciembre 2000 al 2 de abril 2001*. Mexico City: Editorial Rizoma, Causa Ciudadana.

CODIMUJ (Coordinación Diocesana de Mujeres). 1999. *Con mirada, mente y corazón de mujer*. San Cristóbal de las Casas, Mexico: CODIMUJ.

Collier, George. 1994. *Basta!: Land and the Zapatista Rebellion in Chiapas*. Oakland, CA: Institute for Food and Development Policy.

Comandante Esther. 2001. "Mensaje central del EZLN ante el Congreso de la Unión." *Debate Feminista* 24 (October): 337–348.

Comas, Juan. 1945. "La discriminación racial en América. Primera parte." *América Indígena* 5 (January): 73–89.

Comisión de Reforma Agraria. 2004. "Boletín informativo." July 5.

Cumes, Aura. 2009. "Cuando las otras hablan: Mujeres indígenas y legitimidad en la construcción del conocimiento." In *Mujeres, ciencia e investigación: Miradas críticas*, edited by Ana Silvia Monzón, 21–42. Guatemala City: USAC, Ministerio de Educación.

———. 2014. "La 'india' como 'sirvienta': Servidumbre doméstica, colonialismo y patriarcado en Guatemala." PhD diss., CIESAS, Mexico City.

Das, Veena. 1995. *Critical Events: An Anthropological Perspective on Contemporary India.* New Delhi: Oxford University Press.

———. 2007. "Commentary: Trauma and Testimony: Between Law and Discipline." *Ethos* 35 (3): 330–335.

Das, Veena, and Deborah Poole. 2004. *Anthropology at the Margins of the State.* Santa Fe, NM: School for Advanced Research Press.

Deininger, K. 2003. *Land Policies for Growth and Poverty Reduction: A World Bank Policy Research Report.* Oxford: Oxford University Press/World Bank.

De Janvry, Alain, E. Sadoulet, and W. Wolford. 1997. "The Changing Role of the State in Latin American Land Reform." In *Access to Land, Rural Property and Public Action*, edited by Alain De Janvry, G. Gordillo, J. P. Plateau, and E. Sadoulet, 279–303. Oxford: Oxford University Press.

Denich, B. 1994. "Dismembering Yugoslavia: Nationalist Ideologies and the Symbolic Revival of Genocide." *American Ethnologist* 21 (2): 367–390.

Denzin, Norman. 2002. "Confronting Anthropology's Crisis of Representation." *Journal of Contemporary Ethnography* 31 (4): 478–516.

De Vos, Jan. 2003. *Viajes al desierto de la soledad: Un retrato hablado de la Selva Lacandona.* Mexico City: CIESAS.

Dias Martins, Mónica. 2006. "Learning to Participate: The MST Experience." In *Promised Land: Competing Visions of Agrarian Reform*, edited by Peter Rosset, Patel Raj, and Michael Courville, 265–276. Mexico City: Fundación Friederich Ebert, Institute for Food and Development Policy.

Diócesis de San Cristóbal. 1980. *Caminante* 23 (January).

———. 1983. *Caminante* 31 (February).

Dulfano, Isabel, ed. 2015. *Indigenous Feminist Narratives: I/We: Wo(men) of an(Other) Way.* Basingstoke, UK: Palgrave Macmillan.

Dussel, Enrique. 2006. *20 tesis políticas.* Mexico City. CREFAL/Siglo XXI Editores.

———. 2007. *Política de la liberación: Historia mundial y crítica.* Colección Estructuras y Procesos, Serie Filosofía. Madrid: Trotta.

———. 2012. "A manera de prólogo." In *Asedios a la totalidad: Poder y política en la modernidad desde un encare de-colonial*, 7–16. Mexico City: CEIICH-UNAM/Anthropos (Pensamiento crítico/Pensamiento utópico).

Eber, Christine. 2012. *The Journey of a Tzotzil-Maya Woman of Chiapas, Mexico: Pass Well over the Earth.* Austin: University of Texas Press.

ECLAC (Economic Commission for Latin America and the Caribbean). 2007. "The Equity Gap: A Second Assessment." LC/G.2096, Economic Commission for Latin America and the Caribbean, United Nations, Santiago.

Escobar, Arturo. 2007. *La invención del tercer mundo: Construcción y deconstrucción del desarrollo.* Caracas: Fundación Editorial el Perro y la Rana.

Escobar, Arturo, and Sonia E. Alvarez. 1992. *The Making of Social Movements in Latin America: Identity, Strategy, and Democracy.* Boulder, CO: Westview.

Espinosa Damián, Gisela. 2009. *Cuatro vertientes del feminismo en México.* Mexico City: UAM.

Espinosa Damián, Gisela, Libni Iracema Dircio Chautla, and Martha Sánchez Néstor, eds. 2010. *La coordinadora guerrerense de mujeres indígenas.* Mexico City: UAM.

Estrada Saavedra, Marco. 2007. *La comunidad armada rebelde y el EZLN.* Mexico City: Colegio de México.

EZLN (Ejército Zapatista de Liberación Nacional). 1993a. "Ley Agraria Revolucionaria." *El Despertador Mexicano*, December. Enlace Zapatista. http://enlacezapatista.ezln .org.mx/1993/12/31/ley-agraria-revolucionaria/.

———. 1993b. "Primera Declaración de la Selva Lacandona." *El Despertador Mexicano*, December 31. Enlace Zapatista. http://enlacezapatista.ezln.org.mx/1994/01/01 /primera-declaracion-de-la-selva-lacandona/.

———. 1994a. "Al pueblo de México, hablaron los hombres verdaderos, los sin rostro. Mandar obedeciendo." Communiqué. February 26. http://palabra.ezln.org.mx /comunicados/1994/1994_02_26_a.htm.

———. 1994b. "Creación de municipios autónomos." Communiqué. December 19. Enlace Zapatista. http://enlacezapatista.ezln.org.mx/1994/12/19/creacion-de-muni cipios-autonomos/.

———. 1994c. "Las demandas del EZLN." Communiqué. March 1. http://palabra.ezln .org.mx/comunicados/1994/1994_03_01_a.htm.

———. 2003. "Chiapas: La treceava estela." Communiqué. 7 pts. July. http://palabra .ezln.org.mx/comunicados/2003/2003_07_c.htm.

———. 2005a. "Palabras de inicio en la primera reunión preparatoria." Enlace Zapatista. August 6. http://enlacezapatista.ezln.org.mx/2005/08/06/comienza-la-otra -campana/.

———. 2005b. "Sexta Declaración de la Selva Lacandona." Communiqué. Enlace Zapatista. June. http://enlacezapatista.ezln.org.mx/sdsl-es/.

———. 2013a. "Fechas y otras cosas para la escuelita zapatista." Enlace Zapatista. March 17. http://enlacezapatista.ezln.org.mx/2013/03/17/fechas-y-otras-cosas -para-la-escuelita-zapatista /

———. 2013b. "Votán II: L@s guardian@s." Enlace Zapatista. July. http://enlacezapa tista.ezln.org.mx/2013/07/30/votan-ii-ls-guardians/.

———. 2015. "Palabras del EZLN en el 21 aniversario del inicio de la guerra contra el olvido. Subcomandante Insurgente Moisés." Enlace Zapatista. January 1. http:// enlacezapatista.ezln.org.mx/2015/01/01/palabras-del-ezln-en-el-21-aniversario -del-inicio-de-la-guerra-contra-el-olvido/.

———. 2016. "No es decisión de una persona." Subcomandante Insurgente Moisés. Enlace Zapatista. November 11. http://enlacezapatista.ezln.org.mx/2016/11/11 /no-es-decision-de-una-persona/.

Fals Borda, Orlando. 1986. *Conocimiento y poder popular: Lecciones con campesinos en Nicaragua.* Bogotá: Siglo XXI.

———. 2008. "Origenes universales y retos actuales de la IAP (Investigación Acción Participativa)." *Peripecias*, August, 1–14.

Fanon, Frantz. 1967. *Black Skin, White Masks*. New York: Grove.

Favre, Henri. 1973. *Cambio y continuidad entre los mayas de México*. Mexico City: Siglo XXI.

Federici, Silvia. 2013. *Revolución en punto cero: Trabajo doméstico, reproducción y luchas feministas*. Madrid: Traficante de Sueños.

Fernández, Paulina. 2014. *Justicia autónoma zapatista: Zona selva tzeltal*. Mexico City: Estampa/Ediciones Autónom@s.

Flores, Richard. 2002. *Remembering the Alamo*. Austin: University of Texas Press.

Forbis, Melissa. 2006. "Autonomy and a Handful of Herbs: Contesting Gender and Ethnic Identities through Healing." In *Dissident Women: Gender and Cultural Politics in Chiapas*, edited by Shannon Speed, Rosalva Aída Hernández Castillo, and Lynn Stephen, 176–202. Austin: University of Texas Press.

Foucault, Michel. 2003. *Society Must Be Defended: Lectures at the Collège de France, 1975–1976*. New York: Picador.

Freire, Paulo. 1970. *Pedagogy of the Oppressed*. New York: Continuum.

Gall, Olivia. 2003. *Guerra interétnica y racismo en la historia de Chiapas: Ladinos e indios, miedos y odio*. Mexico City: UNAM.

García de León, Antonio. 1985. *Resistencia y utopía: Memorial de agravios y crónicas de revueltas y profecías acaecidas en la Provincia de Chiapas durante los últimos quinientos años de su historia*. Mexico City: Ediciones Era.

———. 2002. *Fronteras interiores. Chiapas: Una modernidad particular*. Mexico City: Oceano.

Géliga Vargas, Jocelyn, and Inés Canabal. 2013. "Las rupturas de la investigación cola-borativa: Historias de testimonios afropuertorriqueños." In *Otros Saberes: Collaborative Research on Indigenous and Afro-Descendant Cultural Politics*, edited by Charles Hale and Lynn Stephen, 154–179. Santa Fe, NM: School for Advanced Research Press, Latin American Studies Association.

Gill, Lesley. 2000. *Teetering on the Rim: Global Restructuring, Daily Life, and the Armed Retreat of the Bolivian State*. New York: Columbia University Press.

Gilmore, Ruth. 2007. *Golden Gulag: Prisons, Surplus, Crisis, and Opposition in Globalizing. Berkeley:* University of California Press.

Gobierno del Estado de Chiapas. 2003. "Tercer informe de gobierno: A la mitad de un buen camino." Tuxtla Gutiérrez, Chiapas. No longer available at http://www.planeacion.chiapas.gob.mx.

Goett, Jennifer. 2011. "Citizens or Anticitizens? Afro-Descendants and Counternar-cotics Policing in Multicultural Nicaragua." *Journal of Latin American and Caribbean Anthropology* 16 (2): 354–379.

Goldberg, David Theo. 2002. *The Racial State*. Malden, MA: Blackwell.

Gómez, Magdalena. 2004. "La constitucionalidad pendiente: La hora indígena en la Corte." In *El estado y los indígenas en los tiempos del PAN*, edited by Rosalva Aída Hernández Castillo, Sarela Paz, and María Teresa Sierra, 175–206. Mexico City: CIESAS.

Gómez Hernández, Antonio, and Mario Humberto Ruz. 1992. *Memoria baldía: Los tojolabales y las fincas: Testimonios*. Mexico City: UNAM.

Gómez Izquierdo, Jorge. 2000. "El discurso antirracista de un antropólogo indigenista: Juan Comas Camps." *Desacatos* (CIESAS) 4:80–102.

González, Pablo. 2011. "Autonomy Road: The Cultural Politics of Chicano/a Autonomous Organizing in Los Angeles, California." PhD diss., University of Texas at Austin.

González Casanova, Pablo. 2003. "Los caracoles zapatistas: Redes de resistencia y autonomía (Ensayo de interpretación)." *La Jornada*, September 26. http://www.jornada.unam.mx/2003/09/26/per-texto.html.

———. 2005. "Colonialismo interno (una redefinición)." In *Teoría Marxista hoy: Problemas y perspectivas*, edited by Atilio A. Boron, Javier Amadeo, and Sabrina González, 409–434. Buenos Aires: CLACSO.

González Stephan, Beatriz. 1995. "Modernización y disciplinamiento. La formación del ciudadano: Del espacio público y privado." In *Esplendores y miserias del siglo XIX: Cultura y sociedad en América Latina*, edited by Beatriz González Stephan, Javier Lasarte, Graciela Montaldo, and María Julia Daroqui, 431–456. Caracas: Monte Avila Editores.

Gordon, Edmund T. 1991. "Anthropology and Liberation." In *Decolonizing Anthropology: Moving Further toward an Anthropology for Liberation*, edited by Faye Harrison, 149–167. Washington, DC: AAA Association of Black Anthropologists.

Gotkowitz, Laura, ed. 2011. *Histories of Race and Racism: The Andes and Mesoamerica from Colonial Times to the Present*. Durham, NC: Duke University Press.

Grosfoguel, Ramón. 2007. "Descolonizando los universalismos occidentales: El pluriversalismo transmoderno decolonial desde Aimé Césaire hasta los zapatistas." In *El giro decolonial: Reflexiones para una diversidad epistémica más allá del capitalismo global*, edited by Santiago Castro-Gómez and Ramón Grosfoguel, 63–78. Bogotá: Siglo del Hombre.

Grosfoguel, Ramón, Nelson Maldonado-Torres, and Jose David Saldivar. 2005. *Latin@s in the World-System: Decolonization Struggles in the Twenty-First Century U.S. Empire*. Boulder, CO: Paradigm.

Gurdián, Galo, Charles Hale, and Edmund T. Gordon. 2004. "Derechos, recursos y memorias sociales de lucha: Reflexiones sobre un estudio acerca de los derechos territoriales de las comunidades indígenas y negras en la Costa Caribe de Nicaragua." In *Etnicidad, descentralización y gobernabilidad en América Latina*, edited by Salvador Martí-Puig and Joseph M Sanch_~ _____ ____ _ _.. Salamanca, Spain: Ediciones Universidad de Salamanca.

Gutiérrez Aguilar, Raquel, and Huascar Salazar. 2015. "Reproducción comunitaria de la vida: Pensando la trans-formación social en el presente." *El Apantle: Revista de estudios comunitarios* (October).

Hale, Charles R. 1996. "Mestizaje, Hybridity, and the Cultural Politics of Difference in Post-revolutionary Central America." *Journal of Latin American Anthropology* 2 (1): 34–61.

———. 2002. "Does Multiculturalism Menace? Governance, Cultural Rights, and the Politics of Identity in Guatemala." *Journal of Latin American Studies* 34 (August): 485–524.

———. 2006a. "Activist Research vs. Cultural Critique: Indigenous Land Rights and the Contradictions of Politically Engaged Anthropology." *Cultural Anthropology* 21 (1): 96–120.

———. 2006b. *Más Que un Indio (More than an Indian): Racial Ambivalence and the Paradox of Neoliberal Multiculturalism in Guatemala*. Santa Fe, NM: School for Advanced Research Press.

———. 2008. *Engaging Contradictions: Theory, Politics, and Methods of Activist Scholarship*. Berkeley: University of California Press.

Haraway, Donna J. 1991. "Situated Knowledges: The Science Question in Feminism and the Privilege of Partial Perspective." In *Simians, Cyborgs, and Women: The Reinvention of Nature*, by Donna Haraway, 183–202. New York: Routledge.

Hardt, Michael, and Antonio Negri. 2004. *Multitude: War and Democracy in the Age of Empire*. New York: Penguin.

Harlow, Barbara. 1992. *Barred: Women, Writing, and Political Detention*. Hanover, NH: Wesleyan University Press.

Hart, Gillian. 2002. *Disabling Globalization: Places of Power in Post-Apartheid South Africa*. Berkeley: University of California Press.

Harvey, David. 2004. "The 'New' Imperialism: Accumulation by Dispossession." *Socialist Register* 40:63–87.

Harvey, Neil. 2000. *La rebelión de Chiapas: La lucha por la tierra y la democracia*. Mexico City: ERA.

Hernández Castillo, Rosalva Aída, ed. 1998. *La otra palabra: Mujeres y violencia en Chiapas, antes y después de Acteal*. Mexico City: CIESAS/IWGIA.

———. 2001. "Entre el etnocentrismo feminista y el esencialismo étnico: Las mujeres indígenas y sus demandas de género." *Debate Feminista* 24:206–229.

———. 2002. "Zapatismo and the Emergence of Indigenous Feminism." *NACLA Report on the Americas* 35 (5): 39–59.

———. 2003. "Conocimiento para qué? La antropología crítica: Entre las resistencias locales y los poderes globales." Reunión Anual de LASA. Reconocimiento Martin Diskin Lectura, 1–15. Dallas: LASA.

———. 2006. "Socially Committed Anthropology from a Dialogical Feminist Perspective." Annual Meeting of the American Anthropological Association. Panel: "Critically Engaged Collaborative Research: Remaking Anthropological Practice."

———. 2015. "Hacia una antropología socialmente comprometida desde una perspectiva dialógica y feminista." In *Practicas otras de conocimiento(s): Entre crisis, entre guerras*, edited by Xochitl Leyva, 2:83–106. San Cristóbal de las Casas, Mexico: Cooperativa Editorial Retos.

Hernández Castillo, Rosalva Aída, and Adriana Terven Salinas. 2017. "Methodological Routes: Toward a Critical and Collaborative Legal Anthropology." In *Demanding Justice and Security: Inidgenous Women and Legal Pluralities in Latin America*, edited by Rachel Sieder, 263–288. New Brunswick, NJ: Rutgers University Press.

Hernández Navarro, Luís, and Ramón Vera. 1998. *Los acuerdos de San Andrés*. Mexico City: Ediciones Era.

Hidalgo, Onésino, and Carlo Calabró. 2006. *Tras los pasos de una guerra inconclusa: Doce años de militarización en Chiapas*. San Cristóbal de las Casas: CIEPAC, A.C.

Holt, Thomas C. 2000. *The Problem of Race in the 21st Century*. Cambridge: Cambridge University Press.

Hurtado, Aída. 1996. *The Color of Privilege: Three Blasphemies on Race and Feminism*. Ann Arbor: University of Michigan Press.

INEGI (Instituto Nacional de Estadística y Geografía). 2000. *Censo de población y vivienda (1990–2000)*. Mexico City: INEGI.

———. 2006. "Núcleos agrarios, tabulados básicos por municipio, Chiapas." Mexico City. PDF available at http://www3.inegi.org.mx/sistemas/tabuladosbasicos /default.aspx?s=geo&c=1972.

———. 2016. Información por entidad. INEGI. http://www.cuentame.inegi.org.mx /monografias/informacion/chis/poblacion/m_migratorios.aspx?tema=me&e=07.

Iribarren Pascal, Pablo. 1986. Gira pastoral por la Zona de Cardenás, Altamirano, Chiapas (unpublished notes). April 11–21. Archive of Santo Domingo, San Cristóbal de las Casas, Chiapas.

Ita, Ana de. 2005. "Land Concentration in Mexico after Procede." In *Promised Land: Competing Visions of Agrarian Reform*, edited by Michael Courville, Peter Rosset, and Raj Patel, 148–164. Oakland, CA: Food First Books.

Joseph, G., and Daniel Nugent. 1994. *Everyday Forms of State Formation: Revolution and the Negotiation of Rule in Modern Mexico*. Durham, NC: Duke University Press.

Kapur, Ratna. 2002. "The Tragedy of Victimization Rhetoric: Resurrecting the Native Subject in International/Postcolonial Feminist Legal Politics." *Harvard Human Rights Law Journal* 15 (1).

Kelley, Robin D. G. 2002. *Freedom Dreams: The Black Radical Imagination*. Boston: Beacon.

Klein, Hilary. 2015. *Compañeras: Zapatista Women's Stories*. New York: Seven Stories.

Kohler, Axel, and Xochitl Leyva. 2015. *Xchu'ulel jlumaltik: Compilación realizada por pueblos, colectivos, y redes de Chiapas*. Mexico City: Creative Commons.

Kumar, Corinne. 2005. "South Wind: Towards a New Political Imaginary." In *Dialogue and Difference: Feminisms Challenge Globalization*, edited by Marguerite Waller and Sylvia Marcos, 165–199. New York: Palgrave Macmillan.

Kyungwon Hong, Grace, and Roderick A. Ferguson. 2011. *Strange Affinities: The Gender and Sexual Politics of Comparative Racialization*. Durham, NC: Duke University Press.

Lau, Ana. 1987. *La nueva ola del feminismo en México*. Mexico City: Grupo Editorial Planeta.

Legorreta Díaz, María del Carmen. 1998. *Religión, política y guerrilla en las Cañadas de la Selva Lacandona*. Mexico City: Cal y Arena.

Lemus Jiménez, Alicia. 2013. "La transmisión de la historia a través de la oralidad por mujeres p´urhepecha de Cherán." In *Senti-pensar el género: Perspectivas desde los pueblos originarios*, edited by Georgina Méndez Torres, Juan López Intzín, Sylvia Marcos, and Carmen Osorio Hernández, 185–209. Guadalajara, Mexico: La Casa del Mago.

Lenkersdorf, Carlos. 2000. "Ergatividad o intersubjetividad en tojolabal." *Estudios y Cultura Maya* (Instituto de Investigaciones Filológicas, UNAM), no. 21: 231–247.

———. 2001. *El diario de un tojolabal*. Mexico City: Plaza y Valdéz.

Lewis, Stephen E. 2006. "The Nation, Education, and the 'Indian Problem' in Mexico,

1920–1940." In *The Eagle and the Virgin: Nation and Cultural Revolution in Mexico, 1920–1940*, edited by Mary Kay Vaughan and Stephen E. Lewis, 176–195. Durham, NC: Duke University Press.

Leyva, Xochitl. 2002. "Transformaciones regionales, comunales y organizativas en las Cañadas de la Selva Lacandona." In *Tierra, libertad y autonomía: Impactos regionales del zapatismo en México*, edited by Shannon Mattiace, Rosalva Aída Hernández, and Jan Rus, 57–82. Mexico City: CIESAS, IWGIA.

———, ed. 2015. *Prácticas otras de conocimiento(s): Entre crisis, entre guerras*. 3 vols. San Cristóbal de las Casas, Mexico: Cooperativa Editorial Retos.

Leyva, Xochitl, and Gabriel Ascencio. 1996. *Lacandonia al filo del agua*. Mexico City: CIESAS.

Leyva, Xochitl, and Araceli Burguete, eds. 2007. *La remunicipalización en Chiapas: La política y lo político en tiempos de contrainsurgencia*. Mexico City: CIESAS, Miguel Ángel Porrúa.

Leyva, Xochitl, Shannon Speed, and Araceli Burguete Cal y Mayor. 2008. *Gobernar (en) la diversidad: Experiencias indígenas desde América Latina. Hacia la investigación de co-labor*. Mexico City: FLACSO Ecuador, FLACSO Guatemala, CIESAS.

López Bárcenas, Francisco. 2011. "Pueblos indígenas y megaproyectos en México las nuevas rutas del despojo." In *Los derechos de los pueblos indígenas a los recursos naturales y al territorio: Conflictos y desafíos en América Latina*, edited by Marco Aparicio Wilhelmi, 181–202. Barcelona: Icarea Editorial.

López Estrada, Raúl Eduardo. 2011. "Políticas para la disminución de la pobreza en México: Consideraciones a partir del Programa Oportunidades." *CoFactor* 2 (3): 197–220.

López Intzín, Juan. 2013. "Ich'el ta muk': La trama en la construcción del Lekil kux-lejal (vida plena-digna-justa)." In *Senti-pensar el género: Perspectivas desde los pueblos originarios*, edited by Georgina Méndez Torres, Juan López Inztín, Sylvia Marcos, and Carmen Osorio Hernández, 73–106. Guadalajara, Mexico: La Casa del Mago.

Lozano Suárez, Leonor. 2017. "Participate, Make Visible, Propose: The Wager of Indigenous Women in the Organizational Process of the Regional Indigenous Council of Cauca (CRIC)." In *Demanding Justice and Security: Indigenous Women and Legal Pluralities in Latin America*, edited by Rachel Sieder, 173–194. New York: Rutgers University Press

Mackinlay, H. 1996. *La CNC y el "nuevo movimiento campesino" (1989–1994): Neoliberalismo y organización social en el campo mexicano*. Mexico City: UNAM, Plaza y Valdés.

Macleod, Morna. 2008a. "Luchas político culturales y auto-representación maya en Guatemala." PhD diss., Universidad Nacional Autonóma de México, Mexico City.

———. 2008b. "Voces diversas, opresiones y resistencias múltiples: Las luchas de mujeres mayas en Guatemala." In *Etnografías e historias de resistencia: Mujeres indígenas, procesos organizativos y nuevas identidades políticas*, edited by Rosalva Aída Hernández Castillo, 127–180. Mexico City: CIESAS, PUEG, UNAM.

Maldonado-Torres, Nelson. 2008. *Against War: Views from the Underside of Modernity*. Durham, NC: Duke University Press.

Marcos, Sylvia. 2011. *Mujeres, indígenas, rebeldes, zapatistas*. Mexico City: Ediciones y Gráficos Eón.

Martínez, Juan Carlos. 2013. "El derecho de los indígenas a conservar un sistema político propio y su brecha de implementación. El caso de santa maría peñoles." *Revista de Estudos e Pesquisas sobre as Américas* (Universidade de Brasília) 7 (2): 70–104.

Martínez-Torres, Maria Elena. 2006. *Organic Coffee: Sustainable Development by Mayan Farmers*. Athens: Ohio University Press.

Martínez Velasco, Germán. 2014. "Chiapas: Cambio social, migración y curso de vida." *Revista Mexicana de Sociología* 73 (July): 347–382.

Martoccia, Hugo. 2006. "Generan migrantes riesgo social en Cancún y Playa del Carmen." *La Jornada*, March 16. http://www.jornada.unam.mx/2006/03/17/index.php?section=estados&article=037n1est.

Mattiace, Shannon, Rosalva Aída Hernández, and Jan Rus, eds. 2002. *Tierra, libertad y autonomía: Impactos regionales del zapatismo en México*. Mexico City: CIESAS, IWGIA.

Mbembe, Achille. 2003. "Necropolitics." *Public Culture* 15 (1): 11–40.

McKittrick, Katherine, ed. 2015. *Sylvia Wynter: On Being Human as Praxis*. Durham, NC: Duke University Press.

Menchú, Rigoberta. 1985. *Me llamo Rigoberta Menchú y así me nació la conciencia*. Mexico City: Siglo XXI.

Millán, Márgara. 2014. *Des-ordenando el género/¿Des-centrando la nación? El zapatismo de las mujeres indígenas y sus consecuencias*. Mexico City: UNAM, Facultad de Ciencias Políticas y Sociales, Instituto de Investigaciones Antropológicas/Benemérita Universidad Autónoma de Puebla/Ediciones Del Lirio.

Mohanty, Chandra. 2003. *Feminism without Borders: Decolonizing Theory, Practicing Solidarity*. Durham, NC: Duke University Press.

Mohanty, Chandra, and M. Jacqui Alexander. 1997. *Feminist Genealogies, Colonial Legacies, Democratic Futures*. New York: Routledge.

Molyneux, Maxine. 2007. *Change and Continuity in Social Protection in Latin America: Mothers at the Service of the State?* Gender and Development Programme Paper Number 1, United Nations Research Institute for Social Development, UN.

Mora, Mariana. 2013. "La politización de la justicia zapatista frente a los efectos de la guerra de baja intensidad en Chiapas." In *Justicias indígenas y estado: Violencias contemporáneas*, edited by María Teresa Sierra, Rachel Sieder, and Rosalva Aída Hernández Castillo, 195–227. Mexico City: CIESAS, FLACSO.

———. 2014. "Repensando la política y la liberación en minúscula: Reflexiones sobre la praxis feminista desde el zapatismo." In *Más allá del feminismo, caminos para andar*, edited by Márgara Millán, 155–182. Mexico City: Red de Feminismos Descoloniales and Pez en el Árbol.

———. 2015. "The Politics of Justice: Zapatista Autonomy at the Margins of the Neoliberal Mexican State." *Latin American and Caribbean Ethnic Studies* 10 (1): 87–106.

Morales Bermúdez, Jesús. 2005. *Entre ásperos caminos llanos: Los Dióceses de San Cristóbal de las Casas, 1950–1995*. San Cristóbal de las Casas, Mexico: UNICACH.

Moreno Figueroa, Mónica. 2012. "Yo nunca he tenido la necesidad de nombrarme": Reconociendo el racismo y el mestizaje en México." In *Racismos y otras formas de intolerancia de Norte a Sur en América Latina*, ed. Alicia Castellanos and Gisela Landázuri, 15–48. Mexico City: UAM.

Morris, Courtney Desiree. 2015. "Where It Hurts: 2014 Year in Review." *American Anthropologist* 117 (3): 540–552.

Nahuelpan, Héctor. 2013. "Las zonas grises de las historias Mapuche, colonialism internalizado, marginalidad y políticas de la memoria." *Revista de Historia Social y de las Mentalidades, Historias Mapuche: Perspectivas para (Re)pensar la Auto-determinación* (Universidad de Santiago de Chile) 17 (1): 11–33.

———. 2016. "The Place of the 'Indio' in Social Science Research: Considerations from Mapuche History." *AlterNATIVE* 12 (1).

Naples, Nancy A. 2003. *Feminism and Method: Ethnography, Discourse Analysis, and Activist Research*. New York: Routledge.

Negri, Antonio. 1993. *La anomalía salvaje: Ensayo sobre poder y potencia en Baruch Spinoza*. Barcelona and Mexico City: Anthropos, UAM.

Newdick, Vivian. 2005. "The Indigenous Woman as Victim of Her Culture in Neoliberal Mexico." *Cultural Dynamics* 17 (1): 73–92.

Olivera Bustamante, Mercedes. 1970. "Alguno problemas de la investigación antropológica actual." In *De eso que llaman antropología mexicana*, edited by Arturo Warman, Margarita Nolasco, Guillermo Bonfil, Mercedes Olivera Bustamante, and Enrique Valencia, 66–94. Mexico City: Nuestro Tiempo.

———. 1998. "Acteal. Los efectos de la guerra de baja intensidad." In *La otra palabra: Mujeres y violencia en Chiapas, antes y después de Acteal*, edited by Rosalva Aída Hernández Castillo, 114–124. Mexico City: CIESAS/IWGIA.

———. 2015. "Investigar colectivamente para conocer y transformar." In *Prácticas otras de conocimiento(s): Entre crisis, entre guerras*, edited by Xochitl Leyva, 3:105–124. San Cristóbal de las Casas, Mexico: Cooperativa Editorial Retos.

Omi, Michael, and Howard Winant. 1994. *Racial Formation in the United States*. New York: Routledge.

Ornelas Delgado, Jaime. 2006. "La polìtica de combate a la pobreza en México, 1982–2005." In Papeles de Población, no. 47, UAEM, Toluca, Centro de Investigación y Estudios Avanzados de la Población.

Orozco, Mónica, and Cecilia Hubert. 2005. *La focalización en el programa de desarrollo humano Oportunidades de Mexico*. Series of Discussion Documents on Social Protection, no. 0531. Washington, DC: World Bank.

Otero, Gerardo. 1996. "Neoliberal Reforms and Politics in Mexico." In *Neoliberalism Revisited: Economic Restructuring and Mexico's Political Future*, edited by Gerardo Otero, 1–26. Boulder, CO: Westview.

Paolí, Antonio. 2001. "Lekil kuxlejal: Aproximaciones al ideal de vida entre los tseltales." *Chiapas*, no. 12. Mexico City: Ediciones Era, IIEc.

Pérez, Emma. 1999. *The Decolonial Imaginary: Writing Chicanas into History*. Bloomington: Indiana University Press.

Pérez Moreno, Patricia. 2012. "O'tan-o'tanil. Stalel tseltaletetik yu´un Bachajón, Chiapas, México. Una forma de ser-estar-hacer-sentir-pensar de los tseltaletik de Bachajón, Chiapas, México." Master's thesis, FLACSO Ecuador, Quito.

Pitarch, Pedro. 1996. *Ch'ulel: Una etnografía de las almas tzeltales*. Mexico City: Fondo de Cultura Económica.

Pozas, Ricardo. 1959. *Chamula: Un pueblo indio de los altos de Chiapas*. Mexico City: INI.

Presidencia de la República. 2007. Plan Nacional de Desarrollo 2007–2012. http://pnd
.calderon.presidencia.gob.mx/.

Price, David. 2000. "The AAA and the CIA?" *Anthropology News* 41 (8): 13–14.

Procuraduría Agraria. 2006. *Estadísticas agrarias*. Mexico City: PA.

Quijano, Aníbal. 2000. "Coloniality of Power, Ethnocentrism and Latin America."
Nepantla: Views from South 1 (3): 533–580.

Rabasa, Emilio. 1895. *Estado de Chiapas: Geografía y estadística*. Mexico City: Tipografía
del Cuerpo Espacial del Cuerpo Mayor.

———. 1921. "El problema del indio mexicano." *El Universal* (Mexico City), January 8.

———. 1987. *La evolución histórica de México: Las evoluciones violentas, la evolución pacífica, los problemas nacionales*. Mexico City: Porrúa.

Rabasa, Magalí. 2008. "Remembering Fanon: Zapatista Women and the Labor of Disalienation." Thinking Gender Papers. UCLA Center for the Study of Women. http://
repositories.cdlib.org/csw/thinkinggender/TG08_Rabasa.

Ramírez Cuevas, Jesús. 1998. "Estampas de la nueva guerra," *La Jornada*, March 29,
Masiosare (supplement).

RAN (Registro Agrario Nacional). 2007. "Dominio pleno desagregado." Registro
Agrario Nacional. http://www.ran.gob.mx/ran/pdf/registro/19_Dominio_Pleno
_Desagregado.pdf.

Rappaport, Joanne. 2005. *Intercultural Utopias: Public Intellectuals, Cultural Experimentation, and Ethnic Pluralism in Colombia*. Durham, NC: Duke University Press.

Reyes, Alvaro, and Mara Kaufman. 2011. "Zapatista Autonomy and the New Practices
of Decolonization." *South Atlantic Quarterly* 110 (2): 505–525.

Reyes Ramos, María Eugenia. 1992. *El reparto de tierras y la política agraria en Chiapas,
1914–1988*. Mexico City: UNAM.

———. 2008. "La oposición al PROCEDE en Chiapas: Un análisis regional." *El Cotidiano* (Universidad Autónoma Metropolitana Unidad Azcapotzalco) 23 (147): 5–19.

Rivera Cusicanqui, Silvia. 2010. *Ch'ixinakax utxiwa: Una reflexión sobre practicas y discursos descolonizadores*. Buenos Aires: Tinta Limón.

Roberts, Dorothy. 1998. *Killing the Black Body: Race, Reproduction, and the Meaning of
Liberty*. New York: Pantheon.

Robles Berlanga, Héctor. 2000. "Propiedad de la tierra y población indígena." *Estudios
Agrarios*, no. 14, 123–147.

Rojas, J. J. 1998. *Auge y decadencia del campo . . . . agrario en Mexico, 1934–1997*.
Mexico City: Universidad Autónoma de Chapingo.

Romano, Agustín. 2002. *Historia evaluativa el Centro Coordinador Indigenista Tseltal-
Tzotzil*. Vol. 1. Mexico City: Instituto Nacional Indigenista.

Rosas, Gilberto. 2012. *Barrio Libre: Criminalizing States and Delinquent Refusals of the
New Frontier*. Durham, NC: Duke University Press.

Rose, Nikolas. 1999. *Powers of Freedom: Reframing Political Thought*. Cambridge: Cambridge University Press.

Rousseau, Jean-Jacques. 1967. *The Social Contract*. New York: Washington Square Press.

Rovira, Guiomar. 2001. "Ahora es nuestra hora, la hora de las mujeres indígenas." *Debate Feminista* 24 (October): 191–205.

————. 2009. *Zapatistas sin fronteras: Las redes de solidaridad con Chiapas y el altermundismo*. Mexico City: ERA.

Rus, Jan. 1977. *¿El indigenismo contra el indígena? Balance de 50 años de antropología en Chiapas*. Apuntes de lectura, no. 3. San Cristóbal de las Casas, Mexico: INAREMAC.

————. 2012. *El ocaso de las fincas y las transformación de la sociedad indígenas de los Altos de Chiapas*. Tuxtla Gutiérrez: UNICACH, CESMECA.

Rus, Jan, Diane Rus, and Salvador Bakbolom. 2016. *El taller tzotzil, 1985–2002: Un proyecto colaborativo de investigación y publicación en los Altos de Chiapas*. Tuxtla Gutiérrez: UNACH.

Saldaña Portillo, Josefina. 2003. *The Revolutionary Imagination in the Americas and the Age of Development*. Durham, NC: Duke University Press.

Saldivar, Emiko. 2014. "'It's Not Race, It's Culture': Untangling Racial Politics in Mexico." *Latin American and Caribbean Ethnic Studies* 9 (1): 89–108.

Sánchez Vázquez, Adolfo. 1980. *Filosofía de la praxis*. Mexico City: Grijalbo.

Santana Echeagaray, María Eugenia, Edith F. Kauffer Michel, and Emma Zapata Martelo. 2006. "El empoderamiento de las mujeres desde una lectura feminista de la Biblia: El caso de la CODIMUJ en Chiapas Convergencia." *Revista de Ciencias Sociales* (Universidad Autónoma de México) 13 (January–April): 69–106.

Santiago, Cecilia. 2011. "Chiapas, años de guerra, años de resistencia. Mirada psicosocial en un contexto de guerra integral de desgaste." In *Luchas "muy otras": Zapatismo y autonomía en las comunidades indígenas de Chiapas*, edited by Bruno Baronnet, Mariana Mora Bayo, and Richard Stahler-Sholk, 341–370. Mexico City: UAM, CIESAS, UNACH.

Santos, Boaventura de Sousa. 1987. "Law: A Map of Misreading. Toward a Postmodern Conception of Law." *Journal of Law and Society* 14 (3): 279–302.

————. 2002. *Toward a New Legal Common Sense*. London: Butterworths, LexisNexis.

————. 2003. *Desigualdad/exclusión: La caída del Angelus Novus. Ensayo para una teoría social y una nueva práctica política*. Bogotá: Universidad Nacional de Colombia-ILSA.

————. 2005. *Reiventar la democracía, reiventar el estado*. Buenos Aires: CLACSO.

————. 2009a. *Una epistemología del Sur: La reinvención del conocimiento y la emancipación social*. Mexico City: CLACSO, Siglo XXI.

————. 2009b. *Sociología jurídica crítica: Para un nuevo sentido común del derecho*. Madrid: Editorial Trotta.

Santos, Boaventura de Sousa, and César Rodríguez Garavito, eds. *Law and Globalization from Below: Towards a Cosmopolitan Legality*. Cambridge and New York: Cambridge University Press.

Sartori, Giovanni. 2001. *La sociedad multiétnica, pluralismo, multiculturalismo y extranjeros*. Madrid: Editorial Taurus.

Schavelzon, Salvador. 2015. *Plurinacionalidad y vivir bien/buen vivir: Dos conceptos leídos desde Bolivia y Ecuador post-constituyentes*. Quito: Abya Yala/CLACSO.

Schild, Veronica. 2000. "Gender Equity without Social Justice: Women's Rights in the Neoliberal Era." *NACLA Report on the Americas* 34 (July): 25–28.

————. 2013. "Care and Punishment in Latin America: The Gendered Neoliberalization of the Chilean State." In *Neoliberalism, Interrupted: Social Change and Contested*

Governance in Contemporary Latin America, edited by Mark Goodale and Nancy Postero, 195–224. Stanford, CA: Stanford University Press.

Secretaría de la Reforma Agraria. 1998. *Informe de la situación agraria en Chiapas*. San Cristóbal de las Casas, Mexico: SRA.

Secretaría de Salud. 2015. "Estadísticas de cáncer de mama y cáncer cérvico uterino." Información Estadística. Gob.mx. September 8. http://www.gob.mx/salud/acciones-y-programas/informacion-estadistica.

SEDESOL (Secretaría de Desarrollo Social). 2007. "Acuerdo por el que se emiten las Reglas de Operación del Programa de Desarrollo Humano Oportunidades, para el ejercicio fiscal 2007." Diario Oficial. February 28. http://webcache.googleuser content.com/search?q=cache:mbscWBsaY8sJ:www.funcionpublica.gob.mx/scagp /dgorcs/reglas/2007/20%2520SEDESOL%252007/20-09%2520SEDESOL%252007 %2520P.%2520Des.%2520Hum.%2520Oportunidades%2520ROP%2520280207 .doc+&cd=2&hl=es&ct=clnk&gl=mx.

Segato, Rita Laura. 2011. "Género y colonialidad: En busca de claves de lectura y de un vocabulario estratégico descolonial." In *Feminismos y poscolonialidad: Descolonizando el feminismo desde y en América Latina*, edited by Karina Bidaseca and Vanesa Vázquez Laba, 11–40. Buenos Aires: Ediciones Godot.

Sieder, Rachel, ed. 2017. *Demanding Justice and Security: Indigenous Women and Legal Pluralities in Latin America*. New York: Rutgers University Press.

Sierra, María Teresa. 2013. "Desafíos al estado desde los márgenes: Justicia y seguridad en la experiencia de la policía comunitaria." In *Justicias indígenas y estado: Violencias contemporáneas*, edited by María Teresa Sierra, Rosalva Aída Hernández, and Rachel Sieder, 159–193. Mexico City: FLACSO, CIESAS.

Smith, Andrea. 2005. *Conquest: Sexual Violence and American Indian Genocide*. Cambridge, MA: Southend.

Smith, Dorothy. 1987. *The Everyday as Problematic: A Feminist Sociology*. Boston: Northeastern University Press.

Speed, Shannon. 2006. "At the Crossroads of Human Rights and Anthropology: Toward a Critically Engaged Activist Research." *American Anthropologist* 108 (March): 66–76.

———. 2008. *Rights in Rebellion: Indigenous Struggle and Human Rights in Chiapas*. Palo Alto, CA: Stanford University Press.

Speed, Shannon, and Álvaro Reyes. 2002. "In Our Own Defense, Rights and Resistence in Chiapas." *Political and Legal Anthropology Review* 25 (1): 69–79.

Staples, David E. 2006. *No Place like Home: Organizing Home-Based Labor in the Era of Structural Adjustment*. New York: Routledge.

Stavenhagen, Rodolfo. 1965. "Siete tesis equivocadas sobre América Latina." In *México como problema: Esbozo de una historia intelectual*, edited by Carlos Illades and Rodolfo Suárez, 327–342. Mexico City: Siglo XXI.

Stepan, Nancy Leys. 1996. *"The Hour of Eugenics": Race, Gender, and Nation in Latin America*. Ithaca, NY: Cornell University Press.

Stephen, Lynn. 2002. *Zapata Lives! Histories and Cultural Politics in Southern Mexico*. Berkeley: University of California Press.

———. 2013. *We Are the Face of Oaxaca: Testimony and Social Movements*. Durham, NC: Duke University Press.

Street, Susan. 1996. "La palabra verdadera del zapatismo chiapaneco (Un nuevo ideario emancipatorio para la democracia)." *Chiapas*, no. 2. Mexico City: Ediciones Era, IIEc.

Suárez Carrera, Mario Alberto. 2014. "¿Autogestión dentro de la autonomía? La experiencia de la cooperativa de cafeticultores indígenas zapatistas Yochin Tayel Kinal." *EntreDiversidades: Revista de Ciencias Sociales y Humanidades* (Universidad Autónoma de Chiapas), no. 3, 187–216.

Tamez, Margo. 2012. "Dáanzho ha'shi 'dał'k'ida,' 'áá'áná,' 'doo maanaashni': Welcoming 'Long Ago,' 'Way Back,' and 'Remember'—As an Ndé Decolonization and Land Recovery Process." *InTensions Journal* (York University), no. 6 (Fall/Winter): 1–23.

Tax, Sol. 1947. *Notes on Zinacantan, Chiapas*. Chicago: University of Chicago Libraries Microfilm Collection of Manuscripts on Middle American Cultural Anthropology, 20.

Tello Díaz, Carlos. 1995. *La rebelión de las cañadas*. Mexico City: Cal y Arena.

Tenorio-Trillo, Mauricio. 1996. *Mexico at the World's Fairs: Crafting a Modern Nation*. Berkeley: University of California Press.

Toledo, Sonia. 2002. *Fincas, poder y cultura en Simovojel, Chiapas*. Mexico City: UNAM.

Topouzis, Daphni. 1990. "The Feminization of Poverty." *Africa Report* 35 (3): 60–63.

Tuhiwai Smith, Linda. 1999. *Decolonizing Methodologies: Research and Indigenous Peoples*. Berkeley: Zed.

Van der Haar, Gemma. 2004. "Autonomía a ras de tierra: Algunas implicaciones y dilemas de la autonomía zapatista en la práctica." In *Tejiendo historias: Tierra, género y poder en Chiapas*, edited by Maya Lorena Pérez Ruiz, 119–142. Mexico City: Conaculta/INAH.

Vargas Costa, Joao H. 2008. *Never Meant to Survive: Genocide and Utopias in Black Diaspora Communities*. Lanham, MD: Rowman and Littlefield.

Velásquez Nimatuj, Irma Alicia. 2015. "Memory/Memoir, Challenges, and Anthropology." In *Indigenous Feminist Narratives: I/We: Wo(men) of an(Other) Way*, edited by Isabel Dulfano, 50–80. Basingstoke, UK: Palgrave Macmillan.

Villafuerte Solís, Daniel. 1999. *La tierra en Chiapas: Viejos problemas nuevos*. Mexico City: Plaza y Valdés, Universidad de Ciencias y Artes del Estado de Chiapas.

Villafuerte Solís, Daniel, and María del Carmen García Aguilar. 2006. "Crisis rural y migraciones en Chiapas." *Migración y desarrollo* (Universidad Autónoma de Zacatecas) (Tivot Simester): 102–130.

Viqueira, Juan Pedro. 2004. "Las comunidades indígenas de Chiapas." *Letras Libres*, no. 61 (January). http://www.letraslibres.com/mexico/las-comunidades-indigenas-chiapas.

Viqueira, Juan Pedro, and Mario Humberto Ruz. 2004. *Chiapas: Los rumbos de otra historia*. Mexico City: UNAM, CIESAS.

Visweswaran, Kamala. 1994. *Fictions of Feminist Ethnography*. Minneapolis: University of Minnesota Press.

Vogt, Evon Zartman. 1973. *Lo zinacantecos, un grupo maya en el siglo XX*. Mexico City: SEPSETENTAS.

Wade, Peter. 1998. "Music, Blackness, and National Identity: Three Moments in Colombian History." *Popular Music* 17 (1): 1–19.

————. 2008. "Race in Latin America." In *A Companion to Latin American Anthropology*, edited by Deborah Poole, 177–192. Malden, MA: Blackwell.

————. 2011. "Multiculturalismo y racismo." *Revista Colombiana de Antropología* 47 (July–December): 15–35.

Ward, Kathryn. 1990. *Women Workers and Global Restructuring*. Ithaca, NY: Cornell University Press/Industrial Labor Relations Press.

Weheliye, Alexander G. 2014. *Habeas Viscus: Racializing Assemblages, Biopolitics, and Black Feminist Theories of the Human*. Durham, NC: Duke University Press.

Williamson, John. 1990. *Latin American Adjustment: How Much Has Happened?* Washington, DC: Washington Institute for International Economics.

Winter, Sylvia. 2003. "Unsettling the Coloniality of Being/Power/Truth/Freedom: Toward the Human, after Man, Its Overrepresentation, an Argument." *New Centennial Review* 3 (3): 257–337.

World Bank. 2001. *Mexico Land Policy—A Decade after the Ejido Reform*. Report no. 22187-ME. Washington, DC: World Bank.

Yañez Muñoz, Fernando. 2003. "Los orígenes de la mística militante: EZLN." *Rebeldía*, no. 3: 62–70.

Index

makeup of, 39, 212–213; peasant organizations and, 105, 207

Aubry, Andrés, 46

autonomous council of Diecisiete de Noviembre: activities of, 222–223, 232; of autonomous government and, 3; internal dynamics of, 52; participation of, in research, 39–40, 53, 62, 63, 65, 218; political jurisdiction of, 50, 225; response of, to shifting priorities, 62

autonomous education, 3, 70, 72, 114, 209, 215–218, 234

autonomous governing bodies: and ceremony for transferring power to new representatives, 187–189; conflict resolution among, 138–139, 168; coordination among, 123, 138–139, 193–195, 211–212, 217; critique of PROCEDE and, 122; daily life and, 3; decision-making practices of, 55, 195; description of, 4, 33; gender relations in, 124; as grounded in community life, 194; intergenerational makeup of, 212, 234; mediation among peasant organizations and, 140, 226; as pedagogical, 192–193; prior to *juntas de buen gobierno*, 33; rebel army and, 34; regulation of natural resource use by, 138; response of, to research, 43, 52

autonomous government municipalities, jurisdictions of, 4

autonomy: as antiracist, 18, 58, 108, 233; communal lands and. 126. 147; as decolonial struggle, 132, 198, 203; as democracy, 72, 77; governing bodies in, 196; as *lekil kuxlejal*, 19; as life politics, 18, 150, 211; limits of, 146, 148, 169; meaning of, in Diecisiete de Noviembre, 6; meaning of traditions and, 162; Mexican state and, 6, 30–31, 34, 175; neoliberalism versus, 9, 51, 113; NGOs in, 204, 215; as pedagogy, 20, 157; as *"poder ser"* (power and ability to be), 151, 233; regulations of, 129; and relations between

mestizos, indigenous peoples, and Afro-Mexicans, 41; resource redistribution and, 127, 147; as struggle for *parejo* (complementarity), 164; territorial control and, 77; women's collectives in, 161

Ayotzinapa, 237–240

bastón de mando (staffs of authority), 39, 187, 189

Beverley, John, 68

biopolitical production, 22

biopower, 22

Blackwell, Maylei, 151, 163

Calderón, Felipe, 11, 237, 238

caracoles: as geographic regions, 1; variations among, 193

Caracol IV: assembly of, 208, 212–214, 218; description, 27; geographic region, 32; relationship of, to external actors, 41

cargo (as system of community responsibilities), 39, 204, 211

Central Independiente de Obreros Agrícolas y Campesinos (CIOAC [Independent Center for Agricultural and Peasant Workers]), 136

Centro de Derechos de la Mujer en Chiapas, 143

Césaire, Aimé, 18

Cherán, Michoacán, 195, 238

chisme (rumors) and gender, 166, 168

Cinco de Mayo (Zapatista community), ⸚ ⸗ ⸗⸗

closed corporate community, 46

CNC (National Peasant Confederation), 102

collective self-reflection, 20, 162, 164–165, 185, 214, 220

colonialism: as internalized, 220; postwar struggles against, 219–220; power-knowledge and, 10, 43, 61

color-blind neoliberalism, 10, 11, 108, 122, 141, 229, 240

Comandancia General (EZLN political military authorities), 2

Comandante Esther. *See* Esther, Comandante

Comité Clandestino Revolucionario Indígena (Clandestine Indigenous Revolutionary Committee), 2, 29

command-obedience, 192

Commission for Peace and Reconciliation (COCOPA), 36, 37

commission of elders (Diecisiete de Noviembre), 193

Congreso Nacional Indígena (CNI), 240

consciousness-raising, critique of, 64

continuum of violences, 185

Coordinación Diocesana de Mujeres (CODIMUJ [Diocesan Women's Group]): history of, 97–99; participatory methodology of, 156, 170

Coordinadora Regional de Autoridades Comunitarias (Regional Coordinator of Community Authorities), 157, 195, 238

counterinsurgency: and containment strategies in *ejidos* after 1994, 85; control of natural resources and, 137, 222; control of women's reproduction and, 181; displacement camps and, 35; family production base dismantled by, 182; as military threats, 3, 215; military surveillance and, 29; social programs and, 185; Zapatista women's response to, 63

critical anthropology, Mexican, 45, 46

Cumes, Aura, 9

Das, Veena, 78

decolonization, 23, 37, 61, 67, 96, 155, 161, 186, 220, 240–241

decolonizing feminist framework, 42, 47, 55

decolonizing research: community contributions to method of, 59, 61, 69; community involvement in, 8–9, 25, 42; as dialogic, 7, 42; as fieldwork, 5, 41, 43, 49, 61; limits of, 62; role of *testimonio*, 67; struggle for self-determination and, 22

development ideology, 45

De Vos, Jan, 200

Díaz Gordillo, Martha Cecilia, 119, 137

Diecisiete de Noviembre: administrative center, description of, 27; agrarian disputes in, 118, 222; autonomous regulations of, 142–143; decision making in, 192, 209–211; disputes in, 138; food security in, 145–146; gender relations in, 209; intercommunity relations of, 194, 199; land reform and, 31; local state and, 223–225; and Mexican army, incursions by, 35; neoliberal policies and, 144; organizational makeup of, 193; paramilitary presence in, 136; participation of, in research, 49; subsistence agriculture in, 134

dispossession of indigenous territories: extractivist economies and, 124–125; in Tzaconejá River valley, 81, 144

domestic violence in Zapatista communities, 160, 163, 164

Dussel, Enrique, 197

education system, Mexican, 71, 215

ejidos: as antidemocratic, 121, 126; assembly and, 119–121, 132–134, 206–207; communal work in, 205; corporatist state and, 120, 126; critique of, Zapatista, 122, 124–125, 134; daily subsistence in, 87; defense of, 126; land struggle in, 71, 103–104; life in, 56, 95, 132–133; as political struggle, 78, 96; privatization of, 5, 6, 117; as satellite villages, 126; the state and, 87, soliciting antcorrections of 78. See also *ejidos* in Tzaconejá River valley

ejidos in Tzaconejá River valley: Lázaro Cárdenas, 5, 73, 85, 87–88, 96, 104, 202, 216; list of, 83–84; Morelia, 27–28, 35, 84, 88, 96, 97, 104, 110, 131–134, 180, 194, 212, 222, 230

electoral politics: critique of electoral system, 71, 75, 101; federal level, 228; local level, 188

embodied knowledge, 78, 192, 215, 217

enganchadero economy (forced recruited labor), 82

biological and social reproduction targeted by, 152, 160, 181–182; in Zapatista communities, 30, 135, 161, 225
modernity as civilizing project, 61
Mohanty, Chandra, 219–221
Moises, Subcomandante Insurgente, 239, 244n11
Montes Azules, 119, 122
mozo/mozos (peon/peons): in Chiapas legislation, 84; impact of *ejidos* on, 88; as institution of servitude, 9; racialized cultural project and, 73, 88–94; as social niche, 7, 16, 71, 76, 113, 203; working conditions for, on estates, 89
multiculturalism: as juridical reform, 6, 7, 11; limits of, 9, 175, 239; neoliberal, 7

NAFTA, 9, 71, 116
Naples, Nancy, 8
national liberation struggles, 18, 219–220, 238
Negri, Antonio, 22
neoliberal reforms: agricultural sector and, 112, 116–117; coffee production and, 5; first wave of, 5; gender and, 175–176; indigenous communities and, 113, 122, 146; NGOs, Zapatista autonomy, and, 29; as racialized gendered division of labor, 113; second wave of, 6, 118, 152, 158; social programs and, 6, 151
núcleos agrarios (communal agrarian lands), impact of PROCEDE on, 117
Nueva Revolución (Zapatista community), 70, 87, 90, 164, 183–184, 202–203, 214, 216

Ocho de Marzo (Zapatista community), 55–56, 59, 60, 76, 91, 93, 182
Olivera Bustamante, Mercedes, 44, 46, 47, 246n1
Oportunidades (Opportunities social program): in Altamirano region, 180–181; as constructivist miscegenation, 17, 177; description of program, 11;

racialized and gendered aspects of, 16, 151; social-reproduction activities regulated by, 24, 152, 171–177, 179
Organización para la Defensa de los Derechos Indígenas y Campesinos (OPDDIC [Organization for the Defense of Indigenous and Peasant Rights]), 135–136
orthodox research methods, 60–61

Pancho Villa (Zapatista community), 127, 133, 197
paramilitary groups, 34, 115, 135–136
parejo (complementarity), 163–164
participatory action research, 21, 42–43, 46
peasant organizations in Chiapas, demands of, 105
Pérez Moreno, Patricia, 99
political formation. *See* feminist political formation; women's political formation; Zapatista political formation
political genealogies in Diecisiete de Noviembre, 107
political parties, Diecisiete de Noviembre and, 34
political subjectivity, indigenous. *See* indigenous political subjectivity
politics as daily life, 3
politics of research: autonomy's role in, 40; as co-labor, 43; community participation and, 8, 21, 24, 25, 39, 40, 43, 49–55, 58–59, 62, 64, 68, 195, 218; contradictions engaged in, 48; as coproduction of knowledge, 7, 120; as dialogic, 47, 48, 122–123, 198; racialized and gendered alliances and, 8; researchers' role in, 59–60, 68; solidarity's role in, 47; Third World feminism's contributions to, 41, 48
politics of translation, 51, 56, 61
population education: methods used in, 58; Paolo Freire's influence on, 18, 21, 43, 46, 157; solidarity methodologies and, 4; in Zapatista autonomous municipalities, status of, 166–167
positivist research, 7, 41, 54

poverty: culture of, 179; feminization of, 175

principales (elder authorities), 187–189, 193, 204, 212, 221

privilege, racialized, 10, 82, 84

production collectives, women's. *See* women's production collectives

Programa de Certificación de Derechos Ejidales y Titulación de Solares Urbanos (PROCEDE [Program for the Certification of Ejido and Land Ownership Titles]): implementation of, 116–121; state governance and, 11, 113, 147; state resource redistribution eliminated by, 134, 141; Zapatista critique of, 123–124

progress as whitening, 16

Rabasa, Emilio, 82–83

racialization: civilizing projects and, 82, 200, 233; culturally marked, 13; and division of labor, 68–69, 94, 113, 116, 147; on estates, 9, 88, 108; global tendencies in, 11; juridical frameworks and, 83–84; Latin American debates on, 14; neoliberal reforms and, 17, 18; Oportunidades and, 177–179

racialized effects: of counterinsurgency tactics, 185; as explained by Zapatista community members, 14–15; of neoliberal policies, 9, 11, 121, 123

racialized geographies, 17, 85

racialized tropes: "born to obey," 9, 75, 190, 201, 228; "born to work," 16, 90, 91, 94, 147; cultural degeneracy, 185, 201; estate economy as producing, 79, 203; infantilization, 16, 203

racialized violence, 57–58

racism: critical anthropology's response to, 13; as dehumanization, 14–15, 92, 94, 96, 184, 202, 239; in education, 216; elimination of category race, 12; on estates, 15, 201; eugenics as source of, 93–94; by government officials, 37, 120, 188, 227; internalized, 202–203, 205, 216; knowledge production and, 15; *mozo* as figure reproducing, 73;

Zapatista community's use of term, 14; Zapatista critique of, 244n11

regions of refuge, 46

research. *See* politics of research; socially committed research

rights and culture, indigenous. *See* indigenous rights and culture

Riviera Maya: day laborers' working conditions in, 110–111; racialized segregation of, 111, 113

Roberts, Dorothy, 179

Rodríguez-Garavito, César, 196

Ruiz, Samuel, 18, 46, 65, 66, 79, 94, 246n1

Rus, Jan, 45, 46

Sabines, Juan, 11

Salazar, Pablo, 11, 140, 224, 226

Saldaña Portillo, Josefina, 2

Salinas de Gortari, Carlos, 5, 243n5

San Andrés peace talks: dialogues during, 243n4; political context of, 4, 30, 31, 128; San Andrés Accords, 4, 36, 158, 196, 250n3

San Carlos Nacaxlan, 80, 144

Sánchez Vázquez, Adolfo, 165

San Pedro Guerrero (Zapatista community), 15, 18, 21, 35, 89, 204, 216

Santos, Boaventura de Sousa, 44, 196, 203

Schild, Verónica, 175, 176, 177

scientific racism, 12

securitization of social reproduction activities, 152, 180, 184, 185

Segato, Rita Laura, 161

self-determination, 1, 30, 37, 147, 158, 161, 174, 195–196, 238

sexual violence: cases of, in Zapatista territory, 183; on estates, 71, 73, 92; militarization and, 183; as racialized domination, 76, 87. See also under *mestijaze*; *testimonio*

Siete de Enero (Zapatista community), 32, 50–51, 53, 55, 153–154, 159, 163, 187, 194, 212

silence as political, 2

Smith, Andrea, 183

socially committed research, 8, 42

war against organized crime, 238
"welfare queens," 179
women's commission, in Diecisiete de Noviembre, 193
women's participation: in Catholic Church, 97; decolonization and, 151; feminist trajectories as related to, 152, 155; in leadership roles and cargos, 159, 163, 166, 169–170, 227; against Mexican army, 63; research methods and, 56; in Zapatista autonomy, 4, 33, 35, 36
women's political formation: beginnings of, 149; catechist boarding school's role in, 131; CODIMUJ's influence on, 98–101, 153, 170; collectives' role in, 155; politicization of household tasks and, 157–158
women's production collectives: activities in, 153, 159, 167; AMMAC's and CODIMUJ's role in, 97–101, 158; in *caracol* center, 149; "collective eye-opening" as praxis in, 166, 170; eugenics tropes and, 108; *kuxlejal* politics and, 20, 24, 151; neoliberal governance destabilized by, 172; political formation and, 100–101, 153–155, 167–168, 210; as politicization of everyday life, 152, 155, 161
women's rights, role of NGOs in, 143
World Bank, report on *ejido*, 116, 119
World's Fair (Paris, 1889 [Exposition Universelle]), promotion of Chiapas commodities at, 82

Zapata (Zapatista community), 14, 30, 66, 68, 89, 102, 104, 106–107, 141–142, 149, 159, 162, 198, 222
Zapatismo: as decolonization, 4; as global network, 3; as movement, 2, 3; as politics of refusal, 3
Zapatista agrarian reform. *See* agrarian reform, Zapatista
Zapatista communities: abandoning struggle, reasons for, 131; agricultural production in, 112, 145, 154; daily life

in, 110, 112, 129, 132, 141–142; decolonizing research methods benefiting from, 61; Diecisiete de Noviembre and, 114; domestic disputes in, 138; external actors and, 64, 230; founding of, 31–32, 128; gender relations in, 66, 97, 142, 150, 154, 159, 162, 164–166, 168, 222–223; intercommunity relations and, 142, 166, 226; intergenerational dynamics in, 59, 66, 110, 112–113, 133–134, 147, 150, 212–214, 219; regulations in, 142–143; relevance of cornfields to, 127, 131; *testimonio* used in, 68; Tojolabal–Tseltal relations in, 14
Zapatista justice system. *See* justice system, Zapatista
Zapatista political formation: AMMAC's role in, 99–101, 157; analysis of oppression and, 76; Catholic Church's role in, 66; CODIMUJ's role in, 100–101; collective self-reflection's role in, 165; external actors and, 64, 65; history and, 54, 58, 59, 206, 218–219; intergenerational, 56; liberation theology and, 71, 77, 78, 94; narratives of life on estates and, 15, 52, 58, 69, 78; peasant organizations and, 77, 102, 104–107; production collectives and, 166, 210; reflections on experiences of racism and, 111; social reproduction activities and, 101; of support bases, 9; of women, 66, 79
Zapatista public events: Caracol anniversary celebration, 230–232; December 12, 2012, 1; Encuentro Intercontinental por la Humanidad y contra el Neoliberalismo (Intercontinental Meeting for Humanity and against Neoliberalism), 27, 28, 153, 231; Festival of World Resistance and Rebellion against Capitalism, 239; in CIDECI, 44; March the Color of the Earth, 36; National Democratic Convention, 37; national referendum of 1999, 36
Zedillo, Ernesto, 4, 29, 36, 159, 224